ROUTLEDGE LIBRARY EDITIONS: MANAGEMENT

Volume 17

MANAGERIAL DECISION MAKING

MANAGERIAL DECISION MAKING

J. BRIDGE AND J. C. DODDS

LONDON AND NEW YORK

First published in 1975 by Croom Helm Ltd

This edition first published in 2018
by Routledge
2 Park Square, Milton Park, Abingdon, Oxon OX14 4RN

and by Routledge
711 Third Avenue, New York, NY 10017

Routledge is an imprint of the Taylor & Francis Group, an informa business

© 1975 J. Bridge and J. C. Dodds

All rights reserved. No part of this book may be reprinted or reproduced or utilised in any form or by any electronic, mechanical, or other means, now known or hereafter invented, including photocopying and recording, or in any information storage or retrieval system, without permission in writing from the publishers.

Trademark notice: Product or corporate names may be trademarks or registered trademarks, and are used only for identification and explanation without intent to infringe.

British Library Cataloguing in Publication Data
A catalogue record for this book is available from the British Library

ISBN: 978-1-138-55938-7 (Set)
ISBN: 978-1-351-05538-3 (Set) (ebk)
ISBN: 978-0-8153-6932-5 (Volume 17) (hbk)
ISBN: 978-1-351-20047-9 (Volume 17) (ebk)

Publisher's Note
The publisher has gone to great lengths to ensure the quality of this reprint but points out that some imperfections in the original copies may be apparent.

Disclaimer
The publisher has made every effort to trace copyright holders and would welcome correspondence from those they have been unable to trace.

MANAGERIAL DECISION MAKING

J. BRIDGE AND J. C. DODDS

CROOM HELM LONDON

© 1975 J. Bridge and J. C. Dodds

Croom Helm Ltd, 2-10 St John's Road
London SW 11

ISBN: 0-85664-103-0 (hardback)
0-85664-118-9 (paperback)

Printed and bound in Great Britain by
Redwood Burn Limited
Trowbridge & Esher

CONTENTS

Acknowledgements

Preface

1.	The Firm and Managerial Decisions	1
2.	Imperfections in Knowledge	24
3.	Production Functions and Linear Programming	54
4.	Cost Analysis	91
5.	Demand Analysis	133
6.	Market Structure	175
7.	The Pricing Decision	216
8.	The Investment Decision	241

Bibliography 294

Index 303

ACKNOWLEDGEMENTS

This book has emerged from our own courses of lectures, mostly from 1969 onwards. Parts of it have been in manuscript form since early 1973 although the bulk of the writing and revision took place during the latter half of 1974. The people to whom we owe most gratitude are our own teachers, and in this regard Dr Martin Howe requires the most credit and no doubt he can see the impression he has made on us throughout the whole text. We are also extremely grateful to the various people who have read earlier drafts and commented upon the material. A. J. Buxton read Chapters 1, 5 and 6 and C. W. Neale the whole manuscript. Both have made a valuable contribution in their incisive comments which have materially improved the style and content of the book. At times, however, our opinions did diverge and for this reason, as well as the usual rider, we alone are responsible for the material in this book.

J. Bridge is appreciative of the encouragement given by Professor G. F. Thomason in the development of a course with an emphasis on decision making. His help and advice over the years have proved invaluable. J. C. Dodds is grateful to the Esmée Fairbairn Charitable Trust for continuing financial assistance and although this book is a by-product of teaching undertaken before his present appointment, the completion of the book had occurred whilst being financed by the Trust.

Table 1.1 from *Corporate Strategy* by H. I. Ansoff (Editor), 1965, McGraw Hill, is used with the permission of the McGraw-Hill Book Company and Table 2.1 from *Insurance Company Investment, Principles and Policy* by G. Clayton and W. T. Osborn, 1965, Allen and Unwin, is used with permission of George Allen and Unwin Ltd.

PREFACE

To write another book in the general subject area of managerial economics requires some justification and we have been conscious of two objectives which we hope this book will fulfil. In the first place we have attempted to bridge the gap between economic theory and decision making in business, mindful of J. W. McGuire's* quip that 'Business is a practice in search of a theory' and secondly to provide a text which can be used for courses in Business Studies at Postgraduate Diploma level and for management oriented undergraduate courses at both Universities and Polytechnics.

'Managerial economics' means so many things to so many people that in the choice of our material we could, like others, be criticised for our selection but throughout this book we have adopted a unifying theme of 'decision making' with an emphasis on the normative approach — i.e. how managers can improve their decisions. In places we have felt it necessary to cover some of the theoretical underpinnings which the traditional/neo-classical theory of the firm can offer and while such references to positive economies might be questioned in a book of this nature, we feel that we have gone some way towards providing a 'blend' which we feel from our own teaching experience is necessary in business studies courses which include economics. Inevitably in a book of this length a lot of material has been omitted and some other issues have, or may appear to have been glossed over but we have, where we felt appropriate, provided references which the reader can consult in order to develop a deeper understanding of the subject matter. A complete list of these can be found at the end of the book, including the collections of readings by G. C. Archibald [7], B. V. Carsberg and H. C. Edey [23], L. Wagner and H. Baltazzis [151] and D. S. Watson [152] in which many of the articles can be found.

A first year undergraduate course in economics is desirable but not essential before reading this book and although macroeconomics is not treated explicitly here, the reader should have an understanding of the fundamentals of this subject. To this end, M. Stewart's book *Keynes and After* [137] is a useful addition to the other books we have recommended. Of all the articles we have referred to, probably the most useful as preliminary reading, is that by D. C. Hague [48], "The Economist in a Business School'. Taken together with Chapter 1 of our book this provides a firm foundation for what follows.

---

* J. W. McGuire, *Theories of Business Behaviour*, Prentice Hall, 1964.

1 THE FIRM AND MANAGERIAL DECISIONS

1-1 The Business Enterprise and the Nature of Management

When one reads of the business enterprise one normally thinks of a large company in which decisions are made by managers. The type of business unit usually discussed in management textbooks is the Joint Stock Company, possessing limited liability and financed by shareholders.

Large scale production has accompanied technological change and the raising of the necessary capital has been facilitated by the issuing of shares to the public at large. Sole traders, partnerships and family concerns are increasingly rare in the world of big business. The increasing presence of large companies during this century has probably contributed to the improvement in our living standards with the frequent innovations that are characteristic of our industrial system. J. K. Galbraith [43], however, while accepting the ability of the industrial system to create a large volume of output, feels that many of the so-called innovations are wasteful product modifications designed to boost sales and that the increased demand is *created* through advertising. Industrial growth may also be accompanied by pollution and the depletion of resources, but government economic policy is still in part directed towards growth in output as a means of increasing the welfare of the nation.

Whatever one's views may be about the merits or drawbacks of business enterprise as we know it, it is apparent that the management of large firms is a complex matter. In recent years the talents of economists, accountants, psychologists, sociologists, mathematicians and statisticians have been brought together in such areas as operational research, organisation theory, managerial economics, management science, management accounting and so on, with 'General Systems Theory' as the ultimate in terms of the multidisciplinary approach. These subjects serve two aims: to improve our understanding of management and to teach managers methods of analysis which will make them more effective in their work.

Before we develop this further we must be more explicit about what a manager's work consists of. J. L. Massie [88] describes the functions of management as: decision making and policy formulation, planning and controlling, organising and staffing, communicating and directing. Decision making is singled out for special attention since it pervades most managerial activity. Indeed all the other functions that Massie describes involve decision at some stage or another. Decision is the act of consciously choosing from among alternative courses of action and while one must always relate any decision to the action that ensues, conceptually the two can be separated for purposes of analysis. It is our view that any analysis of managerial decision making, in particular the kind of analysis designed to *improve* decisions, can benefit enormously from the subject matter of economics. This is the theme which runs through this book.

1-2 General Systems Theory

Our understanding of organisations and their behaviour has been promoted through general systems theory as described by K. E. Boulding [20]. A system is any entity which consists of inter-related, interacting or interdependent parts. In engineering we encounter mechanical systems and in the natural sciences we encounter physical and biological systems. In the social sciences we are concerned with more complex systems like social organisations and national economies in which the relationships between the parts or subsystems are often numerous and difficult to identify.

In a subject like industrial management which is concerned not just with the disciplines of social science but also technical processes, it is important to understand how all the facets of the managerial function inter-relate. We look here briefly at general systems theory because it attempts to blend the ideas of the many disciplines which are relevant in a study of management.

The most important contribution, in our view, that general systems theory has to offer the subject of management is the emphasis on the *total* system. The reason for stressing this is that in a large organisation, managers often become obsessed with the subsystems for which they are responsible. The production manager makes decisions about the manufacturing part of a business's operations, the sales manager is concerned with sales, the personnel manager with acquiring and developing human resources and so on. There is a great danger in this kind of organisation of losing sight of the business as a total entity — how the decisions made in one part of the system interact with those made elsewhere and how these influence the direction in which the whole firm will move. To emphasise the sales function in its own right, for example, may result in a level of advertising expenditure and a price structure incompatible with the profitability of the enterprise.*

---

*   See for example, W. J. Baumol's [14] Sales Revenue Maximisation Hypothesis, considered further in Chapter 6.

The growing complexity of military and space missile systems has been very significant for the study of all types of system. In military and space programmes it is vital to ensure that individual components or subsystems within a missile are reliable, particularly in their relationships with other components. All elements must function as an operating, integrated whole. Systems analysis* in its strict sense involves breaking the system with which one is concerned down into increasingly smaller subsystems until one arrives at the basic components.

Figure 1.1   The basic parts of a system

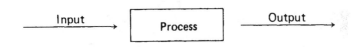

Systems are usually represented by flow charts in which the input, the process and the output are represented (Figure 1.1). For example, a firm can be described as a system in which inputs of financial, human and physical resources are converted via a process (in fact a complex of managerial and technical processes) into outputs of goods and services, in order to achieve various objectives, e.g. profit.

In order to understand just how a firm achieves this conversion, systems analysis is necessary in which the components of the firm and their relationships are identified. However, quite a lot can be learned about a system by treating it as a 'black box', i.e. without probing into the process, or attempting to break the system down into its components. Instead of trying to discover how it works we can simply attempt to relate the input entering the black box to the output which leaves it. This type of approach, which relies on observation over time, helps one to make predictions about the probable behaviour of the system, even if we remain unsure of how it works.

Suppose for instance, we were to study the operation of a particular factory. Over time, the inputs of materials, labour and other resources would vary and the outputs of goods produced in that factory would respond to these variations. Although it would be impossible to deduce a precise relationship from these observations, it should at least be

---

*   The term 'systems analysis' is nowadays used in a rather wider sense, so as to include the measurement of effectiveness of alternative systems or subsystems, *vis-à-vis* their cost, so as to identify the preferred alternatives.

possible to predict in probabilistic terms, the output that would result from a given input.* The production manager can up to a point regulate output by controlling input. It may therefore be that good management is not so much a question of understanding every little intracacy inside the 'black box', but good judgement of the timing and degree of corrective action. We shall return to the question of judgement later in the present chapter.

Figure 1.2   Input, output and management process

It is now time to look at the nature of management in systems terms. Decision making pervades all functions of management. Taking this a step further, it is reasonable to regard the management of an organisation as a problem solving apparatus, which produces decisions and subsequent action in response to the organisation's needs as represented in Figure 1.2. Systems analysis would reveal the management subsystems within the complex, such as sales management, production management and financial management, etc. Each of the latter being concerned with the solution of sales problems, production problems or financial problems by making appropriate decisions. How are organisational problems recognised? The prime source of information for management in recognising problems is feedback data. These are the data which arise from the measurement of the organisation's output in terms of profit, sales and other appropriate characteristics. Accounting statements, sales records and other documents are ways of communicating feedback data. The firm has a multitude of objectives expressed in terms of profit, sales, production, etc. (see Section 1-5) and comparison of actual performance as measured against the objectives or desired performance reveals organisational problems. For example, a sales revenue target of £50,000 for the year 197X might be set at the beginning of the year. At the end of nine months perhaps only £20,000 sales would have been realised with a forecast of a further £10,000 for the remaining three months. This gap between desired and actual (plus

---

*   This is related to the concept of a production function. See Chapter 3.

forecast) reveals a problem for management to tackle. Systems analysis might reveal that the sales manager is typically called upon to provide solutions to sales problems by making appropriate decisions. A systems analyst however would always look at the sales part of the organisation in relation to the firm as a whole and recognise that solutions might be found in some related subsystem within the organisation. Perhaps the shortfall in sales in this example was caused by poor quality control in production, rather than any deficiency in the pricing and advertising activities of the sales department.

When solutions to a problem have been found they are implemented by acting on the input of the firm, and here it must be borne in mind that management can only partially control the firm's output, not only because of the complexity of inter-relationships within the system, but also on account of the multitude of external or environmental factors which influence the results that a firm produces. This means that when decisions are made, their outcomes are not known precisely (see Chapter 2).

Figure 1.3   Control loop

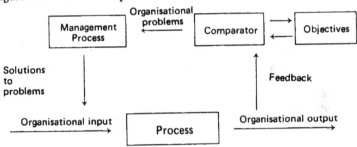

We can show the sequence of organisational output, feedback, comparison, problem recognition, problem solving and acting on organisational input in a flow diagram drawn as a control loop (Figure 1.3). We use the expression 'control loop' because the control or regulation of the organisation within desired limits is achieved by the sequence of activities which form this loop. Readers acquainted with simple mechanical systems such as the thermostat will find Figure 1.3 very familiar. The principle difference is that simple mechanical systems have a closed control loop with no management process necessary for regulation. In the case of the thermostat, measurement of the actual temperature and comparison with the desired, if different, automatically adjusts input (the fuel supply) to control output (temperature).

Before probing into the black boxes of the firm and its management

5

so as to appreciate the nature and structure of decision making, it is time to return to the claim we made at the end of the first section, namely that economics has a substantial contribution to make in the context of managerial decision making. This may not be readily apparent, for as we are about to explain, economics has traditionally failed to treat the firm other than as a black box.

1-3 The Theory of the Firm

Economics is customarily divided into macroeconomics and microeconomics and the 'firm' is decisively involved in both aspects. Macroeconomics is concerned with the functioning of the economy in broad aggregate levels, with the factors that determine the level of national income, inflation, employment, economic growth, foreign trade balance and so on, and in doing so recognises that the 'firm' plays an important part in determining these key variables. In economics the firm is seen as a unit which employs productive resources and transforms these into goods and services. An appreciation of macroeconomics is important to the business student not only because it allows him to see the part the firm plays in the economy but because it shows him the environment within which decision making takes place. It is beyond the scope of this book to cover macroeconomics in any detail and we shall take as our starting point microeconomics which has as its focal concern the working of the market system. Attention is concentrated on the two principal economic institutions; firms and households (consumers). But it is important to note that the economist regards these institutions only as essential actors or elements as part of a larger system. The basic functions performed by them may be carried out under a variety of economic systems. At one end of the continuum lies the pure market system where the functioning of the price mechanism shapes the pattern of resource allocation, and at the other the pure command economy where decisions on resource allocation and the prices of goods and services produced in the economy are centralised under a planning authority. Between these two extremes are mixed economies which incorporate features of both, as in the advanced economies of the western world.

Microeconomics starts with an examination of resource allocation within a market or price system where a multitude of individual decisions shape the ultimate pattern. Both groups of institutions are presumed to behave in a purposeful fashion which is motivated by self-interest. For instance profit maximisation is alleged to be the entrepreneur's motivating force as he transforms the productive resources (given a technologically determined production function*) into goods

---

* The exact technical transformation of inputs into outputs is usually expressed in equation form known as a *production function*. See Chapter 3.

and services. The consumer is assumed to be rational and pursues an objective of utility maximisation where utility in this sense refers to the total benefit, satisfaction and pleasure that a consumer enjoys from his purchases. It is the price system which harmonises and coordinates these separate decisions.

The economist's theory of the firm is in fact a collection of theories examining the behaviour of firms in the context of the market economy. It is not about *a* particular firm, say ICI or Unilever, but the concept employed may help us to draw conclusions about the chemical industry, for example, within the total market system. However, the theory of the firm sheds little light on decision making within the firm *per se*. In other words whilst the firm is recognised as an institution which influences resource allocation, it is more of a black box in economic theory with little attempt to study its internal structure, thus restricting the subject matter of economics. This firm has no balance sheet and no organisational structure and therefore is not to be confused with the firm in practice. The economist's firm is concerned with price and output decisions which determine resource allocation in the economy. It is this confusion over the purpose of the theory of the firm which led F. Machlup to state that:

> '... The model of the firm in that theory is not, as so many writers believe, designed to serve to explain and predict the behaviour of real firms; instead, it is designed to explain and predict changes in observed prices ... as effects of particular changes in conditions (wage rates, interest rates, import duties, excise taxes, technology, etc.). In this causal connection the firm is only a theoretical link, a mental construct helping to explain how one gets from the cause to the effect.' ([83] p. 9)

Economic forces cannot be described, explained and/or predicted by mere observation and the number of variables which can influence a particular event is large so that without the possibility of controlled experiments* economists construct theoretical models, where we are defining a model in this context to be '... a set of assumptions from which a conclusion or a set of conclusions is logically deduced'. (K. J. Cohen and R. M. Cyert, [28] p. 18.) One of the critical methodological problems is the reality of the assumptions. We are not in a position here to discuss this at length but suffice it to say that these need not be exact representations but rather abstractions from reality. The economist will select those crucial variables which in his judgement will enable him to achieve predictions through deductive logic. These predictions can then be tested against the available evidence and accepted or refuted. In other words, 'Economists believe that they can success-

---

* There have been attempts at controlled experiments to test the relationship between price and consumer demand. See Chapter 5.

fully predict market actions of firms without knowing how the firm makes decisions'. (D. Bodenhorn, [19] p. 168.) Models of this type are general, applying to all firms in the economy but whilst they lead to prediction they may do so without any explanatory power (see R. M. Cyert and E. Grunberg [31]). Moreover they are not designed to be able to answer the different set of questions which may be posed about resource allocation *within* the firm.

There are four elements or parts to the economist's theory of the firm. We described firms and households earlier as being purposive institutions and we ascribed profit maximisation to be the motivating force behind the firm. The objective of the firm is the first of these four elements. The second element concerns the production transformation process; transformation because inputs are changed into outputs. But this process can only take place with given information flows (third element) not only on the technology of production but on the availability of factors of production and the market demand curve for the product(s) produced by the firm. It is assumed that perfect knowledge is possessed by management. The fourth element transcends the first three parts since it is concerned with the decision making process within the firm. We have stressed that decision making is the most important function of management and if there is one single feature that can distinguish managers within a hierarchy it would be the degree of autonomy they possess in their decision making and also the type of decisions they take; whether for instance they are taking decisions which can mould the future of the firm or day to day operating decisions. It must of course be re-stated that because the focus of interest of the traditional theory is outward looking the decision making element is simplified almost to an automatic stimulus — response. Because of the assumptions made of rationality and perfect foresight the entrepreneur has a clear cut course of action and will behave in a predictable fashion.

Traditional theory, however, consists of not just one model but a collection of models where the main distinguishing feature between each of these is the structure of the market within which the firm operates. Indeed if one views the theory in terms of a continuum there are competitive markets at one end and monopoly at the other (see Chapter 6, Section 6-3). The competitive market model is normally referred to in the textbooks as perfect competition. This is a situation where there are large numbers of firms selling homogenous products to large numbers of buyers with perfect information on prices of finished goods and factors of production prices as well as perfect foresight as to the courses open to the firm. Monopoly is the other extreme where the firm controls the supply of the product (and its substitutes). The 1930s was a period of advance in the theory of the firm when a number of attempts were made to chart the area between these two extremes* — an area often referred to as imperfect competition. These models which dealt, for instance, with fewness of sellers or the differentiation of products, were still cast in the traditional framework with profit maximisation being retained as the motivational force. But the 1930s also witnessed parallel developments which have led to the redefinition of the four elements of the traditional theory. The starting point can be said to have occurred with the attempt by economists to place their theories under empirical scrutiny with a view to examining how decisions were taken — particularly on price — compared with how economists hypothesised they were taken. This is best illustrated by the famous Oxford Study in 1939** which revealed that in practice the pricing decision was not based on the analysis found in textbooks covering the theory of the firm. This seeking of empirical validity amounts to a departure from the black box approach, and coupled with the widening of the traditional theory of the firm to include imperfections in the markets for goods and factors led economists to a redefinition of their concept of the firm. The small firm *without* influence in the market was replaced by the large Joint Stock Company or Corporation. These large companies were also shown to have market power. Admittedly not the power of the absolute monopolist but power that could be wielded to influence not only the pattern of resource allocation but that of the distribution of income in the community. In addition, the separation of ownership and management in these companies was recognised, and the possible conflict in objectives that might result from this (see especially A. A. Berle and G. C. Means pioneering work [16]).

The changing emphasis in economic theory, in particular the concern with its empirical foundations brought the following comment from Professor E. A. G. Robinson writing in 1950:

> 'But we shall not, I believe, make useful progress by writing down a series of alternative generalizations. What we need most is comparative detailed study of the processes in particular industries with particular frameworks of cost and demand.' ([118] p. 780)

---

* Monopoly in traditional theory was normally reserved for certain special situations but the pioneering work of E. Chamberlin [25] and J. Robinson [119] recognised that imperfections and monopolistic elements were commonplace in markets not only for goods and services but also for factors of production, e.g. labour.

** In this study by R. L. Hall and C. J. Hitch [52], evidence from thirty-eight entrepreneurs' interviewed on their price/output decisions appeared to show that most did not aim at the maximisation of profit, but followed business conventions or rules of thumb, developed by firms compelled to make decisions in the absence of complete information. The most commonly observed pricing rule was 'full cost' plus a percentage markup to allow for profit. See Chapter 7.

In addition to discovering how decisions are actually made for positive purposes, the business economist is very much concerned with how they might be improved. In fact the emphasis of the business economist is normative in that he attempts to analyze how a system ought to behave and present the conditions necessary to bring this about. This is his part in business education* but he must temper his advice with the recognition that the firm is a complex organisation without possession of full information. The models that he constructs will often be inductive, starting with observed phenomena and then devising a model to explain them. Studies of the firm, whether normative or positive, necessarily involve an interdisciplinary approach, but before we can fully appreciate the economist's contribution, it is necessary to look rather more closely at the nature of decision making.

1-4 Three Types of Decision

A useful starting point we can employ in the classification of business decisions is the tripartite one suggested by H. I. Ansoff [6]. He argues that firms, when they are involved in the transformation of productive resources into the output of goods and services, feature strategic, administrative and operating decisions. These he sees as both interdependent and complementary. To illustrate the nature of decisions within those broad classes we have reproduced his chart as Table 1.1.

Strategic decisions, as the name suggests, are concerned with the overall place of the firm within its environment — in other words the product it makes, the markets it operates in and its ability to meet future changes. Decisions about product mix and marketing dictate the firm's long run possibilities and hence the type of decisions it can make in the future. Consequently the firm must have an adequate flow of information to permit strategic decisions to be made. But the strategic decisions which are taken depend upon the objectives of the firm and the large firm may have discretion in the objective(s) it wishes to pursue. Unlike the unequivocal assumption of profit maximisation allegedly pursued by the firm in traditional theory a real firm will not be in a position to adopt such a simple objective. This is because management does not have perfect information and cannot therefore be sure which course of action will yield the maximum. Even if it did have this perfect knowledge, profit might only enter as a constraint on the pursuit of other objectives, in order to ensure long run survival. Furthermore, strategic decisions cannot be taken in isolation from what other firms in the industry might do in response to a major change in strategy. In the cases of perfect competition and monopoly referred to earlier, the

---

*   For a further discussion of the normative nature of business economics see D. C. Hague [48].

Table 1.1 Principal decision classes in the firm

	Strategic	Administrative	Operating
Problem	To select product-market mix which optimises firm's ROI* potential	To structure firm's resources for optimum performance	To optimise realisation of ROI potential
Nature of problem	Allocation of total resources among product-market opportunities	Organisation, acquisition and development of resources	Budgeting of resources among principal functional areas Scheduling resource application and conversion. Supervision and contact
Key decisions	Objectives and goals Diversification strategy Expansion strategy Administrative strategy Finance strategy Growth method Timing of growth	Organisation: structure of information, authority, and responsibility flows Structure of resource-conversion: work flows, distribution system, facilities location Resource acquisition and development: financing, facilities and equipment, personnel, raw materials	Operating objectives and goals Pricing and output levels Operating levels: production schedules, inventory levels, warehousing, etc. Marketing policies and strategy R & D policies and strategy Control
Key characteristics	Decisions centralised Partial ignorance Decisions non-repetitive Decisions not self-regenerative	Conflict between strategy and operations Conflict between individual and institutional objectives Strong coupling between economic and social variables Decisions triggered by strategic and/or operating problems	Decentralised decisions Risk and uncertainty Repetitive decisions Large volume of decisions Suboptimisation forced by complexity Decisions self-regenerative

Source: H. I. Ansoff [6].

* ROI stands for 'return on investment'.

individual firm need not take account of its competitors' reactions because in the case of perfect competition each firm is deemed to be such a small part of the market its individual actions can have no effect on market price and in the case of monopoly there are no competitors. As soon as we depart from these two extremes and consider the kind of enterprise which has market power and also a few rivals (what economists refer to as oligopoly) then the interdependence of decisions — particularly strategic decisions — becomes important. Information is therefore required on the anticipated behaviour of rivals to a given policy change and some conjecture may have to be made as to how they will behave in the face of such a change. We shall discuss this feature of decision making in Chapter 6 where we explicitly deal with the behaviour of firms under oligopoly and examine some of the approaches open to decision makers.

In the absence of a single objective for the firm various alternatives have been suggested and we shall cover these in more detail later in this chapter. For our present purposes we can jump ahead of our story a little and argue that a firm may for instance have a target rate of return on its capital investment and this target becomes an objective of the firm or at the very least, a constraint. Decisions can then be made on the product mix, for instance, in line with this objective. Alternatively, it may have an objective of increasing or maintaining its market share but at the same time making positive profits.

Strategic decisions then are very much bound up with both time and knowledge. So far as the consideration of time is concerned we must stress that the firm's objective in pursuing profits is subservient to the ultimate goal of survival as a long run entity. Knowledge leads us to the question of information flow and the uncertain world outside the firm and to the fact that the firm is making crucial and often non-repetitive decisions on which little information is available. These decisions which can have a profound effect on the firm's future position and in the management structure, are the concern of top management.

Operating decisions are concerned with internal resource allocation and they translate the overall objectives into effective action. They tend to be short run decisions, concerned essentially with day to day or current operations. As Ansoff argues, 'operating decisions usually absorb the bulk of the firm's energy and attention',* and of course operating decisions of one sort or another will be spread downwards in the managerial structure. Some of these decisions may be routine, in which case it is possible to have standardised procedures. Others will be unique and require judgement in particular with reference to the firm's environment. We illustrate in Chapter 7 that pricing decisions feature

---

*   *op. cit.*, p. 18.

a combination of internal and external factors in that it is inadequate simply to relate price to the firm's costs. Pricing must also take account of the market structure of which the firm is a part and the nature of demand. Operating decisions in their entirety can be termed the bread and butter of management.

The third class of decisions, administrative, are principally organisational. They are concerned with the structuring of the organisation so as to maximise the performance of the firm. Ansoff recognises two types of administrative decisions. On the one hand are those that are concerned with the organisational structure *per se*, the authority and responsibility patterns through which the information flows and work loads are determined. On the other are those that are vital to both operating and strategic decisions. The organisation has to ensure the supply of resources (raw materials, manpower, finance and information) both for the present and future operations of the firm.

The business economist *cannot* be expected to make an equal contribution to all three types of decision. If we break down the decisions process into separate elements we can distinguish where the economist has a part to play.

1-5 The Decision Making Process

As we indicated in Section 1-1, to emphasise decision making as a function of management is not to deny the importance of the action that decisions give rise to, it merely acknowledges that conceptually decision and action can be separated. Organisations must be designed to ensure effective action as well as decision making but the economist's contribution is restricted to the latter.

Four main stages in the decision making process can be identified:

(1) Recognising and Defining the Need

Decisions are only necessary if there is a gap between what is desired or required, and what is actually going to be achieved. Reverting to Figure 1.3 we observe that comparison between objectives and performance as revealed by feedback, indicates where organisational problems exist and the need for decision. Feedback is not the only source of data for the decision process but perhaps the most important one. Desired performance may be expressed as a target rate of return on capital employed, although this is only one possible organisational objective, as we shall see shortly. The need for a decision would be expressed in terms of the short-fall in performance. There may be some kind of trigger mechanism which warns management that the reality is different from the desired state of affairs, or managerial judgement may be involved. Sir G. Vickers [149] calls the latter 'reality judgement'.

Inventory control involves the setting of minimum stock levels which act as an automatic warning device for inventory management. Re-ordering is more or less an automatic process, akin to regulation in a thermostat. Managerial judgement is not necessary. Automatic devices like this form closed loops so that comparing actual with desired, if different, generates an 'error signal' which triggers off decision and action. The organisation is often able to respond appropriately by using standard procedures for routine decisions, in response to the feedback or signal. Higher level, or strategic decisions, however, involve forecasting and managerial judgement before the need for decision is recognised. Having recognised this need, search is then instigated.

(2) The Search for Alternative Solutions

The complexity of search therefore depends upon the class of problem. For operating decisions like stock control search is only initiated if standard procedure fails whereas strategic decisions can rarely be reduced to set methods of solution. Generating the alternatives may require research, fact finding or discussion. In strategic decisions it may be necessary to consider alternatives outside the confines of the firm's existing activities. Finding courses of action which are feasible and likely to be successful may involve managerial judgement (Vickers talks about 'action judgement' in this context). Ideally the firm should consider all solutions, but in practice it will normally base its decisions on relatively few alternatives for which it is possible to ascribe 'payoffs'. It will not in practice seek complete or perfect information, but consider alternatives which are feasible in that they can be subsequently implemented. These alternatives will consist of manipulations of factors which are within the control of management. In decision theory (Chapter 2) they are called 'strategies'. R. M. Cyert and J. G. March [32] point out that search tends to be localised initially, managers perceiving conspicuous alternatives, and that activity only becomes more widespread if a feasible alternative does not emerge in the early stages. Certainly the idea of search behaviour taking place as a consequence of a need or problem arising is very much a part of Cyert and March's 'Behavioural Theory' and something not immediately apparent to the economist whose study of the firm has revolved around a 'mental construct' or black box with an unknown internal structure.

(3) Evaluation of Alternatives

The decision maker must then identify and where possible quantify the consequences of the alternatives. Somehow alternatives which are to be preferred must be isolated from the rest. Ideally, a strict ranking should be obtained before the decision is made. The term 'systems analysis' encompasses formal analytical studies designed to help a decision maker identify preferred courses of action, especially in military decisions. Unfortunately it is one of those terms which means all things to all men (see Section 1-2 above). Whatever the nature of the systems, subsystems, or alternative courses of action put forward, analysis is necessary both in terms of the resources used and the effectiveness of each alternative in attaining a specified objective. For this purpose models are required, showing for each alternative what resources will be used and the extent to which objectives can be attained, the latter involving a 'pay-off' measure. Such models may be abstractions of the real world with or without empirical validity or mathematical equations, the important feature being their ability to relate cause and effect, input to output, usage and cost to effectiveness (see Figure 1.4).

Figure 1.4   The structure of analysis

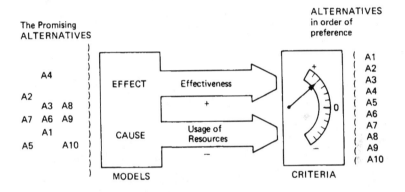

Criteria are then applied in order to rank the alternatives. Some measure of profitability will obviously be involved as it is a means of comparing outgoings of the enterprise with incoming revenues. Return on investment is the principal measure of cost-effectiveness* of the

---

*   Cost-effectiveness is the term used by systems analysts in their assessment of efficiency. The latter must take account of the input cost as well as the magnitude of output in a world where resources are scarce and costly.

business organisation. Unequivocal criteria, however, are hard to come by and rankings are moreover confounded by risk and uncertainty which preclude any unique figure being placed on an outcome. Vickers again points to the role of judgement, in this instance 'value judgement' which may be exercised by the decision maker in evaluating alternatives. There may be conflict situations with the biases and the aspirations of the various subunits of the organisation precluding an unequivocal choice. It is thus vital that criteria should be established wherever possible if the evaluation procedure is to be straightforward.

(4) Decision – The Act of Choosing

A decision is a conscious choice from among alternatives. What has been emphasised so far is that decision making is directed towards definite objectives, that several alternatives may be possible, and that each of these may consume different amounts of resources and result in varying degrees of effectiveness in meeting the objectives. If the criterion (or criteria) adopted gives a definite ranking, then the best alternative should be chosen by the decision maker. In this book we shall be discussing a number of optimisation techniques: for example in Chapter 3, linear programming will be advocated as a powerful technique for optimal decision making in such diverse areas as planning the product mix, blending and transportation, and in Chapter 8 we shall show how preferred investments can be identified using discounted cash flow techniques.

When uncertainty, the lack of a suitable criterion or managerial inability to judge precludes an optimal choice, choosing an alternative which is satisfactory may prove a less demanding task. Indeed it is argued by H. A. Simon [132] that 'satisficing' behaviour is all we can strive for in organisations and it is for this reason that the profit goal is most likely to be expressed as a *target* rate of return rather than the maximum possible.

Furthermore, once a satisfactory alternative has been discovered, Cyert and March have shown that decision often follows immediately; so that the first satisfactory alternative is chosen and implemented. This implies that search and evaluation and even choice may take place more or less simultaneously. This is particularly true of repetitive operating decisions which often involve standard procedures. Such decisions may become programmed, i.e. a set response follows the recognition of a specific problem. So although decisions can be regarded as involving these four steps, in practice a simplified procedure may be possible.

Having decided on the course of action, managers must ensure that the decision is implemented. As stated earlier, this in itself is an important function of management but the book's main emphasis is on the decision rather than the action which follows. After implementation comes measurement — the control function of management. The control mechanism provides a means of perceiving the need for decision, in comparing actual with anticipated. A continuous cycle of decision-action-control-decision-action-control then results.

1-6 The Role of the Economist

The economist will find that his understanding of the business environment enables him to play a vital part in anticipating the firm's short and long term needs. Moreover he may have an important part to play in the discovery of feasible courses of action.

However, managerial economics is primarily concerned with the evaluation of alternatives. The reason that economic analysis is suitable for this purpose is that whatever its shortcomings may be in describing and explaining the behaviour of real firms, the principles that are employed are logically consistent. In evaluation, each alternative must be appraised in terms of cost and returns if resources are to be allocated efficiently. Economics shows how costs should be measured in terms of displaced opportunities and emphasises the distinction between fixed and variable costs (see Chapter 4). It provides a framework for demand analysis within which sales revenue can be estimated (see Chapter 5). Probably the two most valuable concepts used in evaluation are those of marginal analysis and opportunity cost. The logic behind marginal or incremental analysis is beyond dispute. Quite simply if a manager wishes to commit resources to a particular course of action he should first estimate the additional costs the firm will incur and the additional revenue it will receive.* The difference between these two is called the 'contribution'. However, an alternative showing a positive contribution (incremental revenue exceeds incremental cost) offers no guarantee that the firm's financial position will be improved on its adoption. The reasons for this is that the course of action may require productive facilities that the firm already owns. The cost of using these facilities would not be included under incremental cost since the latter only includes *additional* outlays. The economist argues that the use of any resource can only be justified if it brings a return at least as great as the best alternative use for that resource. Opportunity cost measures the return foregone by rejecting the best alternative use.

This is perhaps best seen in a numerical example. Suppose a manufacturing concern is producing 5,000 units of product X per month

---

*   Marginal analysis is often used in a more restricted sense. Marginal cost to an economist is the change in cost brought about by a *unit* change in output. Similarly for marginal revenue. When dealing with proposals which refer to other than unit changes in output, the term 'incremental' is normally preferred to 'marginal'.

which sell at £3 per unit and add £2 per unit to the firm's production costs for the labour and raw material resources used. A proposal for product Y is then considered. Each unit of the latter would sell for £4 and add £2.50 to production costs, again for labour and material inputs. Three thousand units of Y could be sold each month but the output of X would have to be halved to a monthly figure of 2,500 units in order to release the necessary machine time for Y's production.

In order to analyse this proposal, it is first necessary to apply marginal or incremental analysis. Marginal cost of Y is £2.50 and marginal revenue is £4.00. We are assuming these figures remain constant for all output levels in this example, so that for 3,000 units of Y,

incremental revenue	=	£12,000
incremental cost	=	£7,500
contribution	=	£4,500

The second step is to measure the cost of using the firm's productive capacity in terms of displaced opportunities. If product X is the only competitor for machine time, we can measure the opportunity cost of that resource as the contribution foregone by displacing 2,500 units of X. This amounts to 2,500(£3 − £2) = £2,500.

The firm would therefore benefit from the production of Y but not by the £4,500 per month revealed by the first step in the analysis. After allowing for the opportunity cost of machine time (step 2) the true profit obtainable from the manufacture of Y would be £4,500 − £2,500 = £2,000 per month. Taking this further, it can be seen that if Y could only be sold for £3 per unit, the total contribution from 3,000 units would only be (£9,000 − £7,500) = £1,500. This would be insufficient to compensate for the return foregone of £2,500 per month.

An interesting case is the one where existing productive capacity is standing idle. The opportunity cost of using it is zero, since no alternatives are being displaced. The decision to use this capacity then rests solely on the first step, i.e. marginal or incremental analysis. These two stages (marginal analysis and opportunity costing) in evaluation will be referred to repeatedly in the chapters which follow. Together they amount to the 'golden rule' of economic appraisal. The criteria used in assessing the alternatives are consistent with this kind of analysis. This is true of all levels of decision, including investment which is a higher level decision. In investment appraisal, the criteria of net present value and internal rate of return provide the basis of testing for acceptability and for ranking projects (see Chapter 8).

One of the major issues in the decision process is allowing for risk and uncertainty. Unfortunately economic analysis has no ready solution to this. Consequently a text such as this has to consider the contributions of decision theory and game theory in handling imperfections of knowledge. Decision theory is dealt with in Chapter 2 and game theory follows later in Chapter 6.

1-7 Objectives

Before any analysis can be developed to help managers improve their decisions, the objectives of the firm must be stated. Obviously different advice would be appropriate for a firm which sought the achievement of short-run profit maximisation from that given for an objective of market share maximisation. The latter might involve lower prices and higher advertising expenditure than is compatible with profit maximisation.

Economic theory has normally assumed profit maximisation with some justification because a private firm has to make some profit in order ro survive. In looking for an objective which is characteristic of all firms, profit is undoubtedly of widest applicability. The idea of maximisation should not be taken too literally. It is easy to see that if knowledge is less than perfect the alternative which is capable of yielding the maximum profit possible may not be known. And even if all alternatives were available for evaluation it is generally impossible to estimate precisely what outcome or pay-offs will result (see Chapter 2). The reason why maximisation is retained in economic theory is that definite predictions are more readily available with it than without it. Moreover it is surely a reasonable belief that the interests of firms will be better served by a bigger profit than a smaller profit so that maximisation is at least a useful approximation.

Of course, when the theory of the firm is only a means to an end as has been suggested and not a study of the firm *per se*, the use of such approximations is defensible. Profit maximisation comes under attack in the analysis of large firms with substantial discretion in decision making and which are significant entities in their own right to warrant special study. W. J. Baumol [14] argues that large firms operating in markets where the forces of competition are weak don't have to maximise profits in order to survive. So long as sufficient profit is being made to keep shareholders happy and to provide adequate internal finance, managers can pursue other objectives which reflect their own interests. Unless management has substantial holdings of shares, Baumol argues that sales revenue is likely to be a key managerial goal in the short run, and growth of sales in the long run. These views are also held by J. K. Galbraith [43] and R. Marris [87] though their emphasis is mainly on long term growth rather than the short run. Williamson [157, 158] believes that managerial utility depends partially upon profit but he also includes expenditure on managerial perquisites and staffing in his objective function.

At this juncture it is appropriate to say a few words about managerial utility. Williamson uses the concept of utility in much the same sense that it is used when referring to a consumer's utility from his purchases. In the same way that certain patterns of consumption will offer a higher level of satisfaction to the consumer than others, certain combinations of profit, managerial 'perks' and staffing expenditures will be preferred by management to other allocations of resources.

A further use of the word utility is encountered in the next chapter (Section 2-8). This is the usage of J. Von Neumann and O. Morgenstern [105] and it refers to an individual's preferences when confronted with risky choices. The latter have a psychological impact on the individual and this varies with the probability of gain viewed against the probability of loss. Certain options will offer a higher sense of well-being to an individual than others and the degree of such preferences is also referred to as utility.

R. M. Cyert and J. G. March [32] in their 'Behavioural Theory of the Firm' recognised, like Baumol, that when competitive pressures are weak, the organisation can survive with satisfactory profits which are less than the maximum possible. Thus 'organisational slack' which includes excessive costs or unprofitable sales, can build up, without the company's livelihood being endangered. A similar concept to organisational slack is Leibenstein's [78] 'X-inefficiency'. This refers to inefficiency in internal resource allocation which can reduce the welfare of the community in the same way that allocative inefficiency in product markets is alleged to do. Cyert and March observed that the targets of organisations changed over time as aspirations changed, with success stimulating aspiration and failure inducing search and the dampening of aspiration. Instead of restricting their discussion to *managerial* goals, Cyert and March point out that the firm is normally departmentalised and that each sub-unit will work towards one or more of the following five goals: profit, sales, market share, production and inventory, target levels for each goal being set as a result of a bargaining process. Sales and marketing personnel would normally work towards a sales or market share goal. Employees in production departments would generally strive towards production targets, etc. Even here profit retains some importance as it is the only goal which all parties are involved in regardless of which department they work in or their seniority in the hierarchy.

None of the authors mentioned are arguing that managers should be encouraged to pursue these non-profit maximising objectives, they are trying to improve our understanding of resource allocation in situations where large firms are predominant and where market constraints no longer determine a firm's behaviour. Cyert and March in particular are concerned with resource allocations within the firm and actual decision processes. They have gone the furthest in making their firm more like a real firm, but at the expense of tractability and the provision of general predictions about prices and outputs in markets. If we were to use the objectives described in these managerial and behavioural theories for normative purposes we could be wrong on two counts. First of all they pertain to business as it currently exists. The purpose of this book is to provide a framework of analysis within which management can improve decision making and we must state what the aims of a business should be rather than what they are in practice. Secondly, there is the danger of using objectives which reflect the needs of departments or subsystems within the firm or individual interest groups. Our concern is with the enterprise as a whole, a view consistent with systems thinking as depicted by R. A. Johnson, F. E. Kast and J. E. Rosenzweig, who say,

> 'Managers are needed to convert disorganised resources of men, machines, and money into a useful effective enterprise. Essentially, management is the process whereby these unrelated resources are integrated into a total system for objective accomplishment.' ([65] p. 301*)

This however still begs the question of what constitutes 'a useful effective enterprise', and what yardstick measures effectiveness.

Short run profit maximisation, abandoned by managerial and behavioural theorists as inadequate for their positive theories has also been regarded as unsuitable for normative purposes. P. F. Drucker [36] points out that the firm's ultimate long-term aim is survival. Referring to short run profit maximisation, he says: 'To emphasize only profit, for instance, misdirects managers to the point where they may endanger the survival of the business.' (p. 82).

In particular he points to the neglect of research, promotion and postponable investments which can result from this objective. Drucker, however, does include profitability as one of the key objectives a business should aim for. Profitability differs from profit in that it is expressed as a rate of return on capital and is ideally calculated over the total life of an investment,** or at least over a long time period if one is measuring the performance of a whole company rather than a single project. Profitability also satisfies the shareholders' requirements

---

*   The page number refers to that in B. V. Carsberg and H. C. Edey [23] where the article is reprinted.
**   We shall discuss the problems of measuring profit in Chapter 4, when we examine the differences between economic and accounting concepts of cost. See also Chapter 8 where 'internal rate of return' is used as a measure of profitability.

because this is the source of their dividends and capital gains. Shareholders after all, are the legal owners of the company and quite obviously managers must at all times look after their interests. At the same time it is generally accepted that the responsibilities of management do not stop at the shareholder. Employees and the public at large must also be considered and this may impose constraints on the quest for profitability. Such considerations mean that high profits do not guarantee an effective enterprise. Though the measures of profitability show whether or not the firm is earning sufficient revenue to cover outgoings and provide a return on capital, they are imperfect measures of efficiency in terms of output to input. Perhaps they are the best guides available, but large surpluses can be enjoyed by companies, not only by satisfying consumer demands and utilising resources efficiently, but by virtue of their market power.

Exploiting market power enables companies to charge higher prices and receive higher profits than if perfect competition were the order of the day.* Galbraith [43] believes that consumer demands can be created by persuasive selling techniques so that producing outputs to satisfy these contrived demands has no virtue, despite the profits that are enjoyed by companies. A further point is that high profitability can be achieved by paying inadequate wages and avoiding costs by neglecting responsibilities to employees generally. However, this latter argument is unlikely to have much relevance where employees are unionised and are able to wield their own market power. Moreover paying higher wages and improving working conditions may increase worker productivity and ultimately profitability.

A rather different drawback to the usual profitability measures is that only private costs and returns are included. Costs which society has to bear, such as pollution of the atmosphere and rivers are not included in a company's calculations. Neither for that matter are any social benefits which the company may provide either directly or indirectly. Social *costs* are the more controversial since they are generally believed to exceed the social benefits. A firm which is profitable in terms of private costs and returns can hardly be regarded as efficient if it is only profitable at a high cost borne by society in the form of environmental damage.

From this brief discussion it is apparent that profitability, while satisfying shareholder needs, is not necessarily consistent with the other responsibilities of management. But despite the reservations we have made, it is unlikely that any other goal is so widely applicable. As far as possible the analysis developed in this book will be sufficiently general so as to facilitate decision making for the achievement of other

---

*   Although it is often difficult to use 'profit' as an indicator of monopoly. See C. K. Rowley [121].

goals which may arise in practice, but because of the universality of the profit goal this will be the prime one referred to from now on. Basically the emphasis will be on long run profitability, though some of the models will be short run in nature, to show how existing resources might be used more efficiently. Occasional reference will be made to other objectives, for example sales revenue as an aim for marketing, or possibly a short run objective for the whole company (see Baumol, *op. cit.*, [14]), but it is assumed that any such departmental or short run considerations are consistent with the overall long term aims of the enterprise.

Finally, we accept that *maximum* profitability is an ideal which cannot be realised in practice. Nevertheless, we hope that in the following chapters, the reader will learn how to improve profitability, not through neglecting employee and customer interests, but through the efficient use of scarce productive resources.

2 IMPERFECTIONS IN KNOWLEDGE

2-1 Informational Requirements in Decision Making

Economists advocate marginal analysis and opportunity costing in the evaluation of decision alternatives. This necessitates information about costs, revenue and alternative uses for productive facilities, but in the real world this information is imperfect. In fact informational deficiencies become apparent even before the evaluation stage is reached in the decision process, because the possible courses of action themselves may not be fully known. In practice decision alternatives are generated by a search process and the latter being constrained by time (and cost!) will seldom if ever reveal all possible ways of achieving objectives or solving a particular problem. Consequently the alternatives which are considered are only a subset. Then, when the decision maker does reach the evaluation stage of the process, he will not have the precise information he ideally requires. Economics being a social science can never state exactly what the costs and effectiveness of a particular pattern of resource allocation will be. While, for example, an economist would be able to indicate whether or not a decision to increase price would improve sales revenue from a particular product, details of the precise change will in general not be available.

In order to improve the analysis of decision making, given imperfect knowledge, decision theory has evolved. Decision theorists have tended to concentrate on the lack of certainty surrounding outcomes rather than the problem of discovering all alternative solutions to a particular problem. What decision theory attempts to achieve is an improvement in the selection procedure — the *choice* among alternatives, given that each course of action can result in a number of possible outcomes.

2-2 Strategies, Pay-Offs and States of Nature

Decision theory has a terminology of its own. The decision alternatives are called 'strategies' and are denoted by the symbol S. The outcome of each strategy, often given monetary values, are referred to as 'pay-offs', to which are given the symbol P. There is no reason why this classification cannot be used for the analysis of decisions under certainty. For example a problem may consist of choosing from four options, each having a known pay-off. The problem could be drawn up as in Table

2.1, where the options are presented by S_1, S_2, S_3, and S_4 and the pay-offs associated with each by P_1, P_2, P_3, and P_4 respectively. In game theory, which we cover in Chapter 6, a similar terminology and notation is adopted, but since games have two or more players it is necessary to identify the player when listing the strategies. However here we are concerned with only one decision maker, or decision making unit.

Table 2.1 is an example of a pay-off matrix, in this case a very simple matrix, consisting only of four strategies, each having a unique pay-off. When dealing with perfect knowledge, we can evaluate decision problems with as many strategies as we care to consider, but we will always have one pay-off, and only one, associated with each strategy. The solution to such a problem is only a matter of selecting the strategy which yields the highest pay-off with regard to the objective sought.

Table 2.1   Simple Pay-Off Matrix

Strategies	Pay-offs
S_1	P_1
S_2	P_2
S_3	P_3
S_4	P_4

If a manager were asked to present a decision situation in pay-off matrix form, he would probably feel capable of listing the relevant strategies. Admittedly many possibilities would have been omitted, but those having a prime bearing on the problem in question would have been isolated. He would have much more difficulty in assigning pay-off values to each strategy once isolated, explaining that the outcome of any action taken is subject to a multitude of factors outside his control. The manager would prefer to quote a range of outcomes, to allow for different events or contingencies, rather than a single figure.

Thus, in making a decision, the manager realises that he has limited control over the firm's destiny. Alternative strategies can be devised by appropriate manipulation of resources at his disposal, but the pay-off from any decision will also depend upon numerous factors outside the decision maker's control. These uncontrollable factors are called 'states of nature' in decision theory.

Once we recognise the part played by external factors, it is apparent that the decision maker's problem is not simply a matter of choosing a strategy which maximises his profit, sales or any other goal he may wish to achieve, but to make a choice from among alternatives, each of which offers him the possibility of various levels of profits, sales, or satisfaction. We represent such a decision situation using a pay-off matrix with as many rows as there are strategies and as many columns as there are possible states of nature. Associated with each strategy/ state of nature pair will be a pay-off. Thus in Table 2.2 we have represented a decision problem consisting of four strategies, two states of nature, and eight pay-offs. We label the pay-off P_{ij}, for strategy i and state of nature j. Thus P_{32} is the pay-off from strategy 3 when state of nature 2 occurs. These pay-offs are said to be conditional values, which means that for a given strategy, the pay-off attained is conditional upon the state of nature which happens to result.

Table 2.2   Pay-Off Matrix with Alternative Outcomes

	States of Nature	
	N_1	N_2
S_1	P_{11}	P_{12}
S_2	P_{21}	P_{22}
S_3	P_{31}	P_{32}
S_4	P_{41}	P_{42}
Strategies	Pay-offs	

To be of practical use our matrix must, of course, be expressed in units of an appropriate scale. If our objective is profit, each pay-off should be so expressed in monetary units. An objective of furthering one's utility or satisfaction would require a matrix built up from pay-offs measured in utility units.* Having ensured that the matrix is complete and that the conditional values are measured in appropriate units, the issue which confronts us is how to analyse the information we have accumulated, how much attention should be paid to each element in the matrix before choosing a strategy. This in fact will depend upon how imperfect our knowledge is. In general we distinguish between two shades of imperfection: risk and uncertainty.

2-3   Decision Theory and Risk

It is common for the terms 'risk' and 'uncertainty' to be used indiscriminately, particularly in the business sector of the community, yet economists and decision theorists normally distinguish between the two according to F. H. Knight's [70] classification. Risk refers to the

---

* The concept of utility is considered in Section 1-7 above, and the implications of this concept are discussed further in Section 2-8 below.

situation in which the outcome of each strategy is not certain, but where the probabilities of the alternative outcomes can be determined. Uncertainty on the other hand is characterised by total ignorance both as regards which outcome will occur and its likelihood of occurrence. To illustrate the issues involved let us consider the following problem.

The marketing department of a company has been allocated a budget for promotion over the current financial year, but has autonomy over the use to which this budget is put. The marketing manager feels that the four best possibilities are:

(1) A new advertising campaign on television.
(2) A new advertising campaign in the national daily press.
(3) The modification of the presentation and packaging of the company's major product.
(4) A campaign involving gifts and coupons.

All of these are concerned with manipulating variables within the control of the business organisation and are hence strategies which we will designate S_1, S_2, S_3 and S_4 respectively. The marketing department is confident that if the government continues with its present monetary and fiscal policies, the results of these campaigns in terms of sales revenue would be as presented in Table 2.3.

Table 2.3   Sales Revenue under Present Conditions

Strategies	Pay-offs (£ million)
S_1	4
S_2	2
S_3	5
S_4	3

If we assume that each campaign fully utilises the promotions budget, a marketing department confronted with the task of achieving as high a sales level as possible, would undoubtedly opt for S_3. This would however be contingent upon the government continuing with its existing policies. Perhaps tighter monetary control would yield an entirely different set of figures. Suppose the measures the authorities are likely to introduce would modify the pattern of sales revenue as suggested in Table 2.4. In practice the pattern would not be so disrupted as this, but for the purposes of exposition let us assume that this is a realistic picture of the situation. We can call the event of tighter monetary policy state of nature two (N_2), and that of continuing policies state of nature one (N_1). Table 2.5 shows the resultant four by two pay-off matrix.

Table 2.4 Sales Revenue if Conditions Change

Strategies	Pay-offs (£ million)
S_1	1
S_2	4
S_3	2
S_4	3

Table 2.5 Combined Pay-Off Matrix for Sales

	States of Nature	
	N_1	N_2
S_1	4	1
S_2	2	4
S_3	5	2
S_4	3	3

Strategies — Pay-offs (£ million)

S_3 is no longer an obvious choice since we no longer know whether N_1 or N_2 will be in operation. Given the pay-off matrix as it stands the only definite conclusion we can draw is that S_1 is inferior to S_3 whatever event occurs and this means that we can eliminate S_1 from our consideration in this case. What we have done here is to establish 'dominance', S_3 dominates S_1 because whatever state of nature occurs, S_3 gives as good as, or better pay-off than S_1, namely five or two units as compared to four or one. This is sometimes called, 'the sure thing principle'. The problem of choosing between the other strategies, i.e. those which have not been dominated, still remains. Our task would be facilitated if we knew the relative likelihood of N_1 and N_2 occurring. If this information were available the situation would be classified as risk rather than uncertainty.

The simplest types of situation in which probability computations are involved include coin tossing and dice throwing games. For example heads and tails would be assumed equally likely outcomes from tossing a normally balanced coin. We might express this assumption by saying that we have a 50/50 chance of obtaining heads or tails on any given throw. Entirely equivalent to this is the statement that the probability of heads is 0.5 and the probability of tails is also 0.5 on every trial. Similarly if one throws a normal die, each face is equally likely to appear, which means that each number has a one in six chance of appearing on any one throw. In other words the probability of turning up a one is 1/6th, this being true for each of the other five faces of the die.

Suppose now that in our hypothetical business problem represented in Table 2.5, N_1 and N_2 are equally probable. In Table 2.6, the probabilities of N_1 and N_2 have been entered as $P(N_1) = 0.5$, $P(N_2) = 0.5$. In addition to the basic pay-off matrix we have a new column headed 'expected pay-off'. Expectations are formed in the mathematical sense by taking each conditional value and weighting it by the appropriate probability. An 'expected' value is thus very similar to the concept of arithmetic mean. Taking strategy two by way of example, we have pay-offs of two and four units depending on whether N_1 or N_2 happens to occur. On average this strategy yields a pay-off of three units. This is a fair summary statistic of the situation given that N_1 and N_2 are equiprobable as we are suggesting here and we could compute average pay-offs for S_3 and S_4 in the same manner. But if N_1 and N_2 were not equally likely events, we would wish to compute a weighted average, i.e. a statistic which is more heavily influenced by the more probable outcome. This is precisely what happens when we take expected values. To derive the expected pay-off from a risky choice, each conditional value is multiplied by its probability of occurrence and the sum of all such products taken. Represented algebraically, if a variable X can take any one of n values: $X_1, X_2, X_3, \ldots X_n$, and the probability of X_1 occurring is $P(X_1)$, the probability of X_2 occurring is $P(X_2)$, etc. — then the expected value of X, written E(X) is given by

$$E(X) = X_1 \cdot P(X_1) + X_2 \cdot P(X_2) + X_3 \cdot P(X_3) + \ldots + X_n \cdot P(X_n)$$

or

$$E(X) = \sum_{i=1}^{i=n} X_i \cdot P(X_i).$$

Table 2.6 Expected Sales

	N_1	N_2	Expected Pay-off
S_1	4	1	2.0 + 0.5 = 2.50
S_2	2	4	1.0 + 2.0 = 3.00
S_3	5	2	2.5 + 1.0 = 3.50
S_4	3	3	1.5 + 1.5 = 3.00
	$P(N_1) = 0.5$	$P(N_2) = 0.5$	

Thus strategy three above can yield pay-offs of either five or two units with probabilities of 0.5. The expected pay-off from that strategy is therefore: $5(0.5) + 2(0.5) = 3.5$ units, the same figure as the simple average in this case where both outcomes are equally likely.

The expected pay-offs for this decision problem are as set out in Table 2.6. The best choice appears to be S_3 on this basis and it does seem reasonable that in choosing among risky options, the expected pay-off will be a very important factor. An important point to bear in mind at this stage is that expected value is only a summary statistic. It is quite feasible that some other attribute of the figures from which it is derived may still have some significance to the decision maker. In particular the spread of the conditional pay-offs about their expected value may have some special relevance, a consideration to which we will return to in Section 2-8 below.

Continuing with the same pay-off matrix (Table 2.5), let us now evaluate the decision problem in which N_1 and N_2 are no longer equally likely to occur but where N_1 has a 1/6th probability of occurrence while N_2 is five times as likely, having a probability of 5/6ths. Now that the probabilities have changed, the conditional values in our matrix will be re-weighted accordingly and this means of course that we will arrive at a new set of expected pay-offs, shown in Table 2.7.

Table 2.7 Expected Sales with Changed Probabilities

	N_1	N_2	Expected Pay-off
S_1	4	1	$\frac{4}{6} + \frac{5}{6} = 1\frac{1}{2}$
S_2	2	4	$\frac{2}{6} + \frac{20}{6} = 3\frac{2}{3}$
S_3	5	2	$\frac{5}{6} + \frac{10}{6} = 2\frac{1}{2}$
S_4	3	3	$\frac{3}{6} + \frac{15}{6} = 3$

$$P(N_1) = \frac{1}{6} \quad P(N_2) = \frac{5}{6}$$

Strictly speaking it is unnecessary to consider S_1 on every occasion because we have already established dominance given that S_3 always yields a superior result. Moreover S_4 always results in a pay-off of three units so there is no need to compute expected value here, actual and expected will always agree. Analysis with the new probabilities indicates S_2 as the best choice since it possesses the highest expected pay-off.

We can see intuitively why the decision advocated has switched from S_3 to S_2. This is because now that N_2 is considered five times as likely as N_1, we tend to pay five times as much attention to the figures in that column as to those in the first. Though S_3 admittedly gives us the chance of attaining five units, the result is much more likely to be two units. When we weight these two pay-offs in our expected value calculation, the result is now much closer to two units than to five, instead of being exactly midway as was the case when N_1 and N_2 were equiprobable. With regard to S_2, our expected result is now much closer to four units than before.

2-4 A Priori and A Posteriori Probabilities

Coin tossing, die throwing and card drawing situations and games of chance in general all have the property of being solvable on an *a priori* basis. The nature of the game speaks for itself: we don't have to toss a coin under experimental conditions to appreciate that there is a fifty per cent chance of it falling heads. Similarly with a six sided die no empirical evidence is necessary to inform us as to our chances of rolling a particular figure.

If decision theory were solely concerned with *a priori* probabilities, it would be very limited in its scope, and certainly business decision problems would be intractable. Fortunately the boundaries of the subject are not confined to games of chance and the like, but once we depart from this type of problem, the probabilities we require have to be derived by means other than direct inspection. We cannot tell, for example, by studying the characteristics of a product what chances there are of it achieving £5 million sales in a year. We may be able to make a fairly accurate estimate of the likely sales figure but probabilities cannot be imputed on an *a priori* basis and it would clearly be impossible to study actual performance by a long series of repetitions of the operation. Some alternative means of assessment has to be found. Direct market experimentation or other market research techniques may give some information, and coupled with the historical evidence of sales records the firm may be able to assess some likelihood of success. Probabilities so derived are termed *a posteriori*.

Example: The Litron Publishing Company schedules production of diaries in October so that they can be distributed to retail outlets before the end of November. Litron are anxious to schedule the right number because over-production means writing the surplus off at a loss, while under-production means lost sales and it is impracticable to set up a further production run if the first one is too small. In previous years Litron have always over-produced and there has been no upward or downward trend in sales for some time and no change is foreseen for the coming year.* There have however been small variations in sales from year to year as Table 2.8a shows. By observing the frequency of each sales level, we can deduce *a posteriori* probabilities on the assumption that past events are representative of current prospects. Probabilities are then shown in Table 2.8b.

Table 2.8a. Number of Diaries Sold over the Last Ten Years

Year	Number Sold
1	11,000
2	9,000
3	12,000
4	10,000
5	11,000
6	10,000
7	12,000
8	10,000
9	11,000
10	9,000

Table 2.8b. Frequency of Sales Level in Ten Years

Number Sold	Frequency	Probability
9,000	2	0.2
10,000	3	0.3
11,000	3	0.3
12,000	2	0.2

If production can be varied in blocks of 1,000 diaries, Litron have a choice of four strategies, *viz.* production of 9,000, 10,000, 11,000 or 12,000 diaries. There are also four states of nature which correspond to the possible sales levels and the final piece of information Litron requires to make an optimal output decision is variable production cost, which is 30p, and the selling price to the trade which is 50p. (N.B. Overhead costs such as depreciation will be common to all levels of production and do not influence this decision.)

---

* Sales forecasting is explained in Chapter 5.

Table 2.9 Sales Revenue Pay-Off Matrix (£s)

		Number Sold			
		9,000	10,000	11,000	12,000
Production Level		$N_1(0.2)$	$N_2(0.3)$	$N_3(0.3)$	$N_4(0.2)$
9,000	S_1	4,500	4,500	4,500	4,500
10,000	S_2	4,500	5,000	5,000	5,000
11,000	S_3	4,500	5,000	5,500	5,500
12,000	S_4	4,500	5,000	5,500	6,000

The solution utilises a pay-off matrix, Table 2.9, which shows the sales revenue, price times quantity, obtainable from each strategy/state of nature pairing. Thus S_3/N_2 (where 11,000 are scheduled to meet a demand which only amounts to 10,000) yields 10,000 × 50p = £5,000. Probabilities for each state of nature (derived from Table 2.8b) are shown in parentheses. Expected sales revenue can now be calculated for each strategy and total variable production costs (at 30p per diary) can easily be determined to give Table 2.10. The difference between the expected sales revenue and the variable costs gives the expected contribution.

Table 2.10 Expected Sales Revenue, Costs and Contribution

	Expected Sales Revenue (£s)	Variable Costs (£s)	Expected Contribution (£s)
S_1	4,500	2,700	1,800
S_2	4,900	3,000	1,900
S_3	5,150	3,300	1,850
S_4	5,250	3,600	1,650

In conclusion Litron can maximise its expected contribution to profit by scheduling 10,000 diaries (S_2). Higher production levels would obviously give the *possibility* of higher sales revenue but this is more than offset by the *certainty* of higher production costs.*

---

*   Opportunity costs were not brought into the calculations but in practice other profitable opportunities could be displaced if Litron were to increase its output of diaries.

2-5 Insurable and Non-Insurable Risks

'The essence of insurance lies in the elimination of the risk of loss for the individual through the combination of a large number of similarly exposed individuals who each contribute to a common fund premium payments sufficient to value good the loss caused to any one of them.' (G. Clayton and W. T. Osborn [26] p. 11)

Insurance illustrates that what for an individual is a unique experience akin to a non-divisible experiment can become for an insurance company part of a divisible situation. Risks can be pooled through insurance. In principle any contingencies which can be assessed in probabilistic terms can be insured and if events are non-insurable then the situation is normally one of uncertainty. The main forms of insurance are listed in Table 2.11.

Table 2.11   A Classification of Insurance

A.   *Personal Insurance*: Loss of income or increased expenditure through:

DEATH	SURVIVAL	ILL HEALTH	UNEMPLOYMENT
Life	Juvenile	Sickness	Unemployment
Burial	Old Age	Invalid	
	(Pensions)	Accidental Injury	
		Maternity	

B.   *Property Insurance*: Loss resulting from damage to, or destruction of property:

TANGIBLE PROPERTY	INTANGIBLE PROPERTY
Fire	Credit (Bad Debts)
Flood and Storm	Title and Mortgage
Marine	Corporate Bonding
Motor Vehicles	Business Interruption
Crop and Livestock	Market Loss
Aircraft	Loss of Profits
Property Depreciation	Strikes
Embezzlement	Compensation
Forgery	Public Liability
Burglary	Employers Liability
Theft	Re-insurance
Plate Glass	
Radiation	

Source: G. Clayton and W. T. Osborn [26] p. 12.

They do cover a vast area but as risks are not identical they must be assessed before the contract is made to ensure that the premiums are a true reflection of the right of each individual (or company) to benefit from the fund. For instance in the case of 'Fire Insurance' the actuary can consult past records of fire incidence and determine the proportion of various categories of building which catch fire in any one year. For each category of building, the actuary can assess within reason the likelihood of fire damage and also the likely extent of the claim should this occur. The expected outlay for fire claims can then be calculated, which then becomes the basis for offering quotations. Varying circumstances which increase or decrease the risk can be taken into account. For example, the storage of inflammable material would naturally increase the risk, and the existence of a full time fire officer and crew could lessen the risk. For life assurance ('assurance' rather than insurance given the inevitability of death), the actuary has life tables which have been derived from mortality statistics. The tables divide the population into age and sex groupings and show the expectations of life for each group. If a large enough sample of the population is taken the total number of years eventually lived will closely conform to that anticipated in the life tables. Any event which the insurance company feels will increase the risk — smoking, being overweight, a family history of coronary trouble — can be taken account of by increasing the basic premium.

Acts of God

This expression refers to highly unpredictable events such as earthquakes, floods and hurricanes. Because of their highly unstable nature, it would be very difficult and in some cases impossible to calculate insurance premiums on an actuarial basis. We should logically exclude this type of contingency from insurable risks and regard acts of God as more properly belonging to the realms of uncertainty. Indeed with many types of insurance policy this is borne out in practice. For example in obtaining personal insurance for foreign travel, a clause is frequently inserted exempting occurrences of this nature from the coverage of the policy. On the other hand if one takes out a general household insurance policy, the insurance company may well underwrite such contingencies within its scope, even though assessment is not feasible on a purely actuarial basis. Clearly the insurance company is introducing some form of subjective probability or hunch into its computations, namely that such events are unlikely (at least in the United Kingdom) and should be covered by a small increase in the premium.

Economic and Business Risks

Some of the risks inherent in running a business are insurable. Premises will be insured against fire and theft, and vehicles will be insured in the normal way. From Table 2.11 it can be seen that many other business risks can be insured against, even loss in profits through interruption of business following a fire or other disaster. However, falls in profit brought about by deteriorating conditions in product markets and in the economy as a whole as distinct from losses resulting from damaged property are clearly not insurable. This remains within the province of entrepreneurship where profits are in part the result of the successful bearing of risk and uncertainty. The firm, we noted in Chapter 1, has to make profits in order to survive. The value of the firm's shares will depend upon its ability to make profit and the risks that it has to bear.

Major companies can forecast their annual profits and sales performance with a fair degree of accuracy. Movements in business performance are, however, often cyclical, and so far as insurability is concerned it is not so much that a firm's profits are random and unpredictable, but rather than they tend to follow the overall pattern of economic activity and business profits in general. Consequently there is no scope for pooling such risk.

In conclusion, the availability of probabilistic information is usually but not always the sole requirement for insurability. The insurance company must also be confident that the contingency insured against is random in its incidence and experienced independently by policy holders.

2-6 Uncertainty

When no probabilities can be derived on either an *a priori* or an *a posteriori* basis we may try to use judgement or at least guesswork to assess the relative likelihoods of the possible outcomes. The treatment of business decisions under uncertainty relies heavily on the use of such subjective probabilities so that we set out our decision as if risk were present and use subjective probabilities to form expected values. However, this approach, usually presented as the Bayes or Laplace criterion, is not the only criterion which decision theorists have proposed for making choices when uncertainty is present. The reason for this is that once we recognise this added degree of ignorance, we can no longer retain our motivational assumptions with any degree of confidence. In particular, business managers may take prevention of catastrophe as their basic goal rather than the pursuit of gain if they regard their environment as not just uncertain but somewhat hostile and threatening, as the Wald criterion suggests below. This ties in with the concept of diminishing marginal utility of wealth considered in 2-8 below.

Bayes-Laplace Criterion

The Bayes-Laplace model considers a situation in which the decision maker is faced with complete *a priori* ignorance at least in so far as probabilities are concerned. The 'Principle of Insufficient Reason' states that when a decision maker is faced with an exhaustive set of events (i.e. all possible states of nature have been determined), these events being mutually exclusive, (i.e. one and only one will occur), the only way to assign probabilities under uncertainty is to consider each possible event equiprobable. Thus when faced with two possible states of nature, each will have an *a priori* probability of ½, with four states of nature each will take an *a priori* probability of ¼, and in general n states of nature would yield *a priori* probabilities of 1/n.

Table 2.12a   Criteria for Uncertainty — The Pay-Off Matrix

	N_1	N_2	N_3	N_4
S_1	110	20	80	40
S_2	40	60	120	8

Table 2.12a is a pay-off matrix which we now use to illustrate the Bayes-Laplace criterion. Four states of nature are possible, these are exhaustive and mutually exclusive. If no probabilistic information is available, we would tend to assign prior probabilities of ¼ to each state of nature. On this basis, the expected pay-offs from the two strategies are:

S_1:   27.5 + 5 + 20 + 10 = 62.5

S_2:   10 + 15 + 30 + 2   = 57.0

The Bayes-Laplace solution is the first strategy since it possesses the higher expected pay-off.

So far we have only considered the crude version of the model. The refined model accepts that in many cases the individual has initial hunches which render the equiprobability assumption inappropriate. In the above example initial guesswork may suggest probabilities of 1/8, 1/8, 1/2, 1/4 respectively, the expected value calculation being modified accordingly:

S_1:   13.75 + 2.5 + 40 + 10 = 66.25

S_2:   5 + 7.5 + 60 + 2   = 74.50

S_2 would then be the better strategy given these subjective probabilities. Having started with prior probabilities determined in ignorance or derived on the basis of hunches, the decision maker can revise these in the light of experience.

The uncertainty surrounding a decision may be lessened over time. When information feeds back to the decision maker, uncertainty is transformed into risk because experience enables him to make some judgement about probabilities. Many decisions are sequential in nature, i.e. rather than being once and for all, they can be broken down into a sequence of decisons which may be modified in the light of experience, as J. Margolis [86] suggests. Information available for later decisions is likely to be contingent on the nature and consequences of earlier decisions. Low level pricing decisions are of this type, where the pricing executive initially has very little idea concerning likely sales at a given price. Ultimately experience accumulated in the form of sales records can guide the pricing function, the situation gradually becoming one of risk. Margolis also discusses minor product modifications in the context of sequential decision making.

Major strategic (or higher order) decisions, however, cannot be regarded in the same light. For instance, in planning a new plant, the decision is unique in the sense that it relates to a specific organisation at a particular point in time, with a pattern of assets of available factors of production, a given technology and market opportunities which are most unlikely to be duplicated elsewhere in the economic system, in the past, now or in the future.

Having committed the resources of the company, the critical step has been taken because all future developments will be influenced by it and the firm cannot go back and repeat the experiment. So strategic decisions are unique and crucial and non-divisible (into a sequence of similar decisions). There is thus no sense in which we can transform our initial decision made under uncertainty, into a decision made under risk. The decision will rely entirely on the initial subjective probabilities if the Bayes-Laplace criterion is adopted.

Professor G. L. S. Shackle [125, 126] has rejected the extension of probability analysis to decision making where the decision is both non-divisible and crucial. In the first place he argues that'. . . the decision maker can make no use of objective actuarial probability. He is reduced to using subjective probability, which has no claims to be knowledge . . .'. Secondly he points out that 'When the experiment is a non-divisible one, the hypotheses regarding its outcome are cut-throat rivals, denying and excluding each other'. 'What then', he asks 'is the sense of averaging them?' ([125] p. 60).

Shackle then abandons the Bayesian approach to decision making under uncertainty and proposes the concept of 'potential surprise' as a decision criterion ([125] p. 4).

Potential Surprise

Unlike the Bayes-Laplace criterion, it is not easy to illustrate potential surprise in a numerical example. In any case Shackle's work is intended to provide new methods of analysis for positive economics rather than a technique which managers should adopt to improve their decisions.

While Bayes-Laplace reduces the outcome distribution of each strategy to a single (average) value, Shackle argues that there is a pair of possible results to which attention is directed. Shackle here contends that in an outcome distribution, some outcomes can be excluded as impossible. With other outcomes we may be surprised if they were to occur, some of these being good and some bad outcomes. This leaves an inner range of outcomes whose occurrence would not surprise us at all. In Shackle's terminology each of these outcomes, in the inner range, carries zero potential surprise. While the upper and lower limits of this inner range are important characteristics for the decision maker's consideration, some of the outcomes carrying a degree of surprise will outbid for his attention even the best and the worst of the inner range. Shackle summarises:

> '... we suggest that an enterpriser who is deciding whether to invest or not will place himself in imagination in the position of having actually laid out a cash sum on ... equipment, and will then weigh against each other the two elements of the immediate mental experience which this position would afford him: the enjoyment by anticipation of the greatest gain whose attractiveness is not undermined by association with too high a degree of potential surprise, and the suffering, by anticipation, of the greatest loss whose unpleasantness is not weakened by being associated with too high a degree of potential surprise. It is these two extremes which will focus the enterpriser's attention.' ([125], p. 5)

Shackle's conclusion is that an individual's valuation of an investment or strategy depends upon the hope of gain and the fear of loss. As such, each situation should be analysed in terms of these two dimensions instead of a single mean value. Unfortunately there is no unique method of evaluating available strategies when each is represented by a pair of focus elements. For this reason we shall not develop the notion of potential surprise into an operational criterion for management. However, the idea of focusing attention on the extreme values of an outcome distribution is emphasised in the criteria subsequently discussed in this section, and in Section 2-9 below techniques suitable for handling uncertainty in major projects are considered.

The Maximin Criterion

In introducing the subject of uncertainty, it was suggested that in some circumstances the prevention of disaster may be a better approximation to managerial motivation than the customary pursuit of gain. Since Profit *maximisation* is seldom a prerequisite for survival, which is the ultimate aim of an organisation, this view is certainly plausible. This is the reasoning behind the 'maximim' criterion proposed by A. Wald [152]. Originally this was devised for analysing games against opponents rather than games against nature and its application to the latter has always been in question.* In particular we cannot rely on nature to do anything systematic whereas when playing against a human opponent it is indeed a reasonable assumption that our every move will be thwarted, at least in situations where our loss is our opponent's gain and vice versa.** Clearly this reasoning cannot be applied to decision theory where we are concerned with alternative states of nature rather than competitive strategies. We can only accept Wald's criterion for our present purposes through reinterpretation, this being that when operating in a world with all the terrors of uncertainty, we are justified in being pessimistic. Decisions should therefore be made with the intention of avoiding failure and enjoying a security value.

If a pay-off matrix is drawn up in the normal way to represent the decision situation, pessimistic decision makers will focus their attention on the worst possible pay-off associated with each strategy. Using the matrix shown in Table 2.12a, S_1 yields a minimum pay-off of twenty units, while S_2 can lead to a pay-off as small as eight units. Confining our attention to these minima, the preferred strategy is S_1. The maximin choice is then that strategy which gives the maximum from among all the minimum pay-offs, in this case S_1. Having chosen in this way, the manager can rest assured that disaster has been averted.

The Maximax Criterion

This criterion would be adopted by a decision maker whose outlook were vastly different from the user of maximin. Far from trying to prevent a crisis, our manager in this situation is trying to gain the highest return possible. If an individual is thus motivated, the only way in which his aim can be realised is by the selection of that strategy yielding the maximum possible pay-off. Referring to the matrix in Table 2.12a, S_2 would be chosen since it is capable of giving a pay-off of 120 units.

Our maximax decision maker is content to ignore most of the values

---

* Game Theory is developed further in Chapter 6.
** We are referring here to the two-person zero sum game, an example of which would be a pair of duopolists competing for market shares. See Chapter 6, Section 6-7.

in the pay-off matrix and to this extent he resembles the maximin decision maker. The only pay-offs of relevance for maximax purposes are the best possible from each strategy, the one giving the maximum of these maxima being selected.

The Hurwicz α Criterion

Maximin and maximax satisfy widely differing attitudes to uncertainty. On the one hand we have the conservative, perhaps cowardly, approach displayed in maximin behaviour. Maximax on the other hand depicts the somewhat reckless type of behaviour more appropriate to the inveterate gambler than the business executive. L. Hurwicz's argument [63] is that the majority of individuals fall between these two extremes and in view of this he suggested that a criterion should be established which recognised varying degrees of optimism.

The criterion he proposed involves a coefficient of optimism α, which can take values on a scale from zero to unity, zero reflecting the depths of pessimism and unity the heights of optimism. Setting α equal to zero gives the maximin answer, and to unity gives the maximax result. Let us see how this works out in relation to the pay-off matrix we have been using (Table 2.12a).

The coefficient is entirely subjective and would have to be determined by introspection. However, suppose a manager set α at 0.75, indicating a relatively optimistic outlook. For each strategy we take the best and worst pay-offs and attach weights of $\alpha = 0.75$ and $(1 - \alpha) = 0.25$ respectively. $(1 - \alpha)$ is in effect the coefficient of pessimism. The sum of these weighted pay-offs for each strategy then becomes the basis for decision:

S_1: (0.75 × 110) + (0.25 × 20) = 87.5
S_2: (0.75 × 120) + (0.25 × 8) = 92.0

Hence S_2 is the preferred strategy.

If the decision maker were rather less optimistic, say $\alpha = 0.5$,

S_1: (0.5 × 110) + (0.5 × 20) = 65.0
S_2: (0.5 × 120) + (0.5 × 8) = 64.0

S_1 would now be slightly preferable.

The Minimax Regret Criterion

This is perhaps the most fascinating of all the criteria which have evolved. L. J. Savage [123], its originator, suggested that individuals when faced with uncertain outcomes were motivated by a desire to avoid regret. Regret would be experienced when the outcome actually realised fell short of what could have been attained had another decision been made. The measure of regret in this sense is the difference between the actual pay-off achieved under a given state of nature and the best pay-off attainable under that state of nature. With reference to Table 2.12a, should N_1 occur, the decision maker will only be fully content if S_1 had been selected, giving him a pay-off of 110 units, the best possible in this event. Given hindsight S_2 would be seen to be inferior, an individual having thus chosen would experience 70 units of regret, i.e. (110 – 40) units. We can then construct a second matrix derived from our basic table, showing regret figures for each strategy/state of nature pairing as in Table 2.13a. Column one has been derived already. The reader should check the computation of the other figures noting that the regret matrix is constructed by consideration of the implications of a given state of nature occurring.

Table 2.12b

	N_1	N_2	N_3	N_4
S_1	0	40	40	0
S_2	70	0	0	32

In the same way that the maximin decision maker tries to avoid catastrophic pay-offs, the individual as depicted by Savage also wishes to avoid disaster, this to the latter individual being excessive feelings of regret. In protecting himself against such adversity, his prime concern in looking at each strategy in turn is the maximum regret. His choice is that course of action which yields the minimum of these maximum regret values: hence 'minimax regret'. S_1 would be the choice according to these principles, for at the worst the individual only ever has to tolerate 40 units of regret. Choosing S_2 would leave him vulnerable to possible regret of magnitude 70 units.

The regret matrix is really expressed in terms of opportunity cost. The costs involved are those of making an incorrect decision (given hindsight of course). In practice when a businessman is faced with two distinct alternatives, he does often try to protect himself against choosing wrongly by hedging. Thus to guard against currency realignments, speculators will opt for partial conversion of their holdings. Professional punters may back two horses in the same race. Managers may pursue mixed strategies, i.e. instead of playing S_1 or S_2 as in Table 2.12a, it may be possible to opt for half and half, the mixed strategy S_3 yielding intermediate pay-offs (Table 2.12b). This could represent adopting a combination of two promotional campaigns instead of going all out for one or the other. We can see from the regret matrix (Table 2.13b) that S_3, hedging, is the minimax regret choice and in many other examples the same result will follow.

Table 2.13a   Regret Matrix

		N_1	N_2	N_3	N_4
	S_1	110	20	80	40
	S_2	40	60	120	8
($\frac{1}{2}S_1 + \frac{1}{2}S_2$)	S_3	75	40	100	24

Table 2.13b

	N_1	N_2	N_3	N_4
S_1	0	40	40	0
S_2	70	0	0	32
S_3	35	20	20	16

2-7   Evaluation of Criteria Used in Decision Theory

We have seen that the objectives and attitudes of the individual when faced with imperfect knowledge shape the choices he makes and there is thus no universal criterion. Advocates of financial prudence would stress the advantages of maximin while the adventurous amongst us would belittle any approach other than maximax. So whatever conclusion is reached is going to be subjective.

We feel that all information having a bearing on the outcome of a decision, if available, should be used. Moreover, if one has knowledge of the relative likelihood of various outcomes occurring this too should be brought into the calculation. Under conditions of risk we have seen how expected value satisfies these requirements, but under uncertainty, only the Bayes-Laplace criterion seems to meet these demands. It is the only criterion in which the choice is based on a figure built up from all possible pay-offs from a given strategy, appropriately weighted. Maximin, maximax, and the Hurwicz α criterion all advocate decisions influenced by the extreme magnitudes in the pay-off matrix. The intermediate values of the matrix are ignored, this also being true of the regret criterion once the regret matrix has been derived. If paucity of information is a managerial hazard as we are led to believe, it hardly seems rational to ignore most of the information which has been acquired, no doubt at great expense. In weighing up these criteria individually, one feels that maximax can be dismissed without further thought. Although business decisions involve the pursuit of gain, one could only visualise the maximax choice being appropriate if the alternative pay-offs associated with that choice, and not just the absolute maximum, were also favourable. Clearly the adoption of this criterion depends upon the psychological make-up of the individual decision maker as well as the financial backing. Maximax may be an adequate representation of gambling situations but it is of restricted use in the business world.

The Hurwicz α is perhaps better than maximax in that rather more information is taken into consideration, but one can hardly imagine professional managers assessing their coefficient of optimism before making a decision. It is in doubt whether this criterion was ever meant to be taken seriously — it could be regarded as a satirical comment on the state of decision theory at the time of its conception.

In some circumstances the other two criteria may appear viable. A firm with a poor liquidity position may have as its first priority the prevention of further loss, rather than the pursuit of high profits. As such the worst outcome of any strategy will have special significance for the firm in question and the reasoning behind the decision may well conform to maximin principles. The business would therefore have ample justification for fearing the worst, but in better circumstances, when collapse is not imminent, one would expect a rather more positive attitude.

In many companies managers are salaried employees and have little at stake in the ownership of the firm, so that the penalties for incorrect decision making may appear to the manager to be far greater than the rewards for being successful. The safety first approach to decisions, attempting to avoid mistakes or regret, will have undoubted appeal to managers in this position. Minimax regret would then come into its own.

We can see that conflict may exist between shareholder and managerial objectives. H. A. Simon [132] in observing cautious behaviour by 'administrative man' says that he is 'satisficing' (see Section 2-10 below). However minimax regret and maximin are rather different in that there is some function which is being optimised. As we have seen, managers may find it to their advantage to adopt a cautious approach to decisions, but is this what they are being paid to do? As managerial economists attempting to provide advice to managers for the improvement of resource allocation, we can scarcely condone such approaches unless the firm is in a critical position, in which case, maximin may be appropriate.

In conclusion, the Bayes-Laplace seems to have most merit, or at least fewest drawbacks. Moreover it enables us to use a single method for both risk and uncertainty, namely expected value. If circumstances are truly uncertain, equal probabilities can be assigned to possible events, these being modified by personal judgement and experience as more information is revealed.

2-8 Diminishing Marginal Utility

While expected value may offer guidance to the decision maker, one substantial drawback to relying solely on this statistic is that it normally represents monetary value. Thus managers may calculate expected profits or sales in terms of money. The reason why this is contentious is that money is not a perfect measure of 'utility', i.e. the psychic gains and losses of an individual.

It is apparent that each extra £1 of income or wealth brings less satisfaction to the individual than previous increments to his financial position. While an old age pensioner benefits from his Christmas bonus of £10 a millionaire would hardly notice it, being already in possession of all the necessities and most of the luxuries of life. An individual's utility function would probably approximate to the curve shown in Figure 2.1. The slope of the function is a measure of marginal utility and this can be seen to be decreasing as wealth increases.

Figure 2.1 Diminishing Marginal Utility

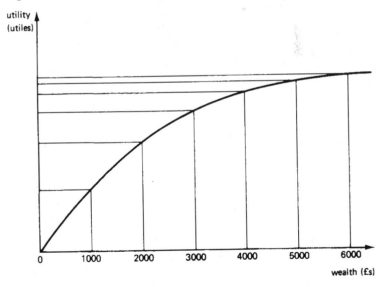

It follows that one's attitude to gaining or losing money and hence one's attitude to risk is governed at least partially by financial circumstances. There is nothing new about this hypothesis; D. Bernoulli [17] explained the rejection of apparently fair bets in terms of diminishing marginal utility. So far as the business decision maker is concerned, his principal requirement is for an understanding of how the company's interests can be safeguarded given the effects that risk may have on the utility from each individual's share in the company's income.

J. Von Neumann and O. Morgenstern [105] have explained how a utility function can be derived for a particular subject, questioned and observed under controlled conditions. While this has led to many interesting developments at a theoretical level, it is impossible to derive a utility function representing the collective interest of shareholders or any other participants in the company. Consequently its practical usefulness is limited at least for our purposes. Fortunately, allowance for utility can be made without recourse to an empirically derived utility function. To illustrate this, imagine that a utility scale measured in 'utiles' is available for the outcomes facing a decision maker. The worst possible monetary outcome is set at zero on the scale, and the best at 100 (Table 2.14).

Table 2.14   Outcomes and Utility

Monetary Outcome (£s)	Utility Value (Utiles)
50,000	0
100,000	40
150,000	65
200,000	85
250,000	95
300,000	100

These figures exhibit diminishing marginal utility. An expected monetary value of £200,000 can be derived in a number of ways, each giving different (expected) utility:

(a)   50/50 chance of gaining £100,000 or £300,000 :   70 utiles.
(b)   50/50 chance of gaining £150,000 or £250,000 :   80 utiles.
(c)   A certain gain of £200,000   :   85 utiles.

This shows that the bigger the dispersion of outcomes about the expected (monetary) value, the more important is diminishing marginal utility. A measure of dispersion such as variance or standard deviation can be used as a measure of the risk involved. This means that the certain gain of £200,000 could be shown to be preferable to either of the other options (which have standard deviations of £100,000 for (a) and £50,000 for (b)) without prior knowledge of the utility function.

One problem we encounter is that the size of the returns in relation to their risk may not be accurately represented by the conventional measures of dispersion. For example:

(b) 50/50 chance of gaining £150,000 or £250,000:
expected value £200,000.

and (d) 50/50 chance of gaining £50,000 or £150,000:
expected value £100,000.

Both have the same standard deviations of £50,000 yet for option (d) the risk is much greater than for (b) when related to the size of the returns. 'The Coefficient of Variation' helps us to solve this problem because it consists of the standard deviation divided by the expected monetary value. Thus for (b)

the coefficient of variation is $\frac{£50,000}{£200,000} = 0.25$

and for (d) the coefficient of variation is $\frac{£50,000}{£100,000} = 0.50$

which reflects the greater proportionate risk in (d).

The standard deviation is however adequate in its own right as a measure of risk when percentage rates of return are considered, since the latter are already expressed as a proportion of the size of the project.

When considering the profit in £s rather than percentages we would tend to use the coefficient of variation in the following way, to take account of risk aversion:

(i) When alternatives have the same degree of risk (coefficient of variation) choose the one offering the greatest expected monetary value.
(ii) When alternatives have the same expected monetary values, choose the one with the smallest coefficient of variation.

This procedure will enable us to eliminate a number of unsuitable alternatives from a decision situation without recourse to a utility index, thus simplifying our problem of choice.

Thus, in Table 2.15:

S_5 dominates S_3 in the usual manner (see Section 2-3 above)
S_4 dominates S_1 in the usual manner
S_2 is inferior to S_5 on the grounds of risk and expected profits.

This leaves S_4 and S_5 for final selection. Which is the better of these two is not completely obvious; this will depend upon the individual's attitude to risk. Nevertheless the choice from among five alternatives has been reduced to a more simple decision problem where only two strategies have to be assessed. Even though we have failed to give a definite answer, the figures in the example are highly suggestive of the optimal decision. It should be noted that the consideration of variation coefficients is an alternative to the use of a utility index. It is not appropriate to calculate expected *utility* and then make allowance for coefficient of variation, because we would then be adjusting for risk aversion twice over.

Table 2.15 The Coefficient of Variation (Pay-Offs in £s Profit)

	N_1	N_2	Expected Profit	Standard Deviation	Coefficient of Variation
S_1	250	50	150	100	0.667
S_2	250	150	200	50	0.250
S_3	150	150	150	0	0.000
S_4	400	100	250	150	0.600
S_5	200	250	225	25	0.111
	$P(N_1) = 0.5$		$P(N_2) = 0.5$		

For practical purposes it is almost impossible to derive a utility function for business decisions. So the advice we offer to management for decision making in a risky or uncertain world is twofold:

(1) All possible outcomes and their probabilities of occurrence (if available) should be considered. Expected value should be used under risk, the Bayes-Laplace criterion being advocated for uncertainty.
(2) Individuals normally experience diminishing marginal utility of wealth. This applies to shareholders and all other interest groups in the organisation. Managers should accommodate this factor into their computations by using the coefficient of variation in conjunction with expected monetary values.

2-9 Alternative Approaches to Uncertainty

For major decisions which involve entirely new experiences and which are non-repetitive, there will be no probability distribution available, nor will one emerge relevant for future decisions. Managers may try to avoid making such decisions or perhaps pursue diversification strategies which prevent any one project from being too crucial. Managers do prefer options which are flexible and capable of modification if necessary. Nevertheless some strategic decisions will approximate to Shackle's unique, crucial and non-divisible category (Section 2-6). Objective probabilities may be unattainable and while the Bayes-Laplace criterion can be operated with subjective probabilities, Shackle's antipathy to this approach is understandable. Another drawback to the probability approach is that the expected or average outcomes may never be experienced in practice and for some decisions the manager would prefer figures which represent outcomes which are actually attainable to guide his choices. This is true of short run optimisation problems (including those discussed in Chapter 3) as well as the selection of major projects.

The alternative approach to statistical decision theory is to treat the decision as if perfect knowledge were available, so that for each strategy a unique outcome is assessed. These outcomes will not be averages or expectations in the mathematical sense, but outcomes which will actually be attained given the assumptions made about the environment or responses of competitors. On the basis of this initial assessment a tentative choice can be made.

Allowance for uncertainty is made by changing the assumptions and examining the effects that these changes have on the pay-off from the strategy. This approach can best be described using the terminology of systems analysis as employed by E. S. Quade [115].

Sensitivity Analysis

We have suggested that individuals are risk averse and that consequently options with a wide dispersion of possible outcomes will be regarded as inferior to options with a narrow range of outcomes, other things remaining equal. Another way of looking at this problem is to think in terms of sensitivity. If there are two decision alternatives offering similar outcomes but one of these is highly sensitive to parameter changes while the other is relatively insensitive, then the latter would be preferred.

Suppose in choosing a car you had narrowed your choice down to two models which under present circumstances would offer you similar performance at similar cost. As yet however you have not explored the uncertainties surrounding the key variables. Allowing for risk or uncertainty through sensitivity analysis means asking the question 'What if?' For example: what if the local dealer stops servicing the model under consideration? Are there adequate servicing facilities provided elsewhere? What if it becomes necessary to use the car for business? Is the car capable of carrying extra goods? (e.g. with a folding rear seat).

The car capable of withstanding such eventualities would be the preferred choice. So too with business decisions. Take for example the choice of a piece of equipment. It is inadequate to assess the alternatives in terms of what will happen in one set of circumstances. Management must explore the consequences of breakdown, maintenance, capacity to meet market expansion, flexibility in accommodating changed product characteristics, etc. We shall look at numerical examples where sensitivity analysis is employed in the context of investment decisions (Chapter 8) and in production decisions (Chapter 3). Its application in production decisions is facilitated when linear programming is being employed.

Contingency Analysis

This is similar to sensitivity analysis but response to a more radical change in the environment is tested for. Thus while sensitivity analysis might test the alternatives for variations in the projected growth rate of demand, contingency analysis might test for the impact of a sudden curtailment of energy supplies which has a drastic effect on some types of production, rather less on others.

A Fortiori Analysis

Through sensitivity and contingency analysis, a preferred alternative may well emerge. As a really acid test *a fortiori* analysis may make the claims for such an alternative even more convincing if the test is passed. What happens here is that we do our best to make assumptions which are detrimental to the preferred alternative but which will enhance the prospects of the other alternatives. If after all this, the handicapped alternative still emerges as the best, we can make recommendations 'with stronger reason' (*a fortiori*).

A variant of this approach is to set parameter values such that all possible alternatives are equally preferred. If an alternative still breaks even with rival possibilities and the assumptions about the former are highly pessimistic while those about the latter are highly optimistic* then once again this gives us a basis for establishing preferability.

Risk and uncertainty are vital considerations in any analysis for the improvement of managerial decisions. The economist has gradually come to terms with the problem of imperfections in knowledge, but the credit for many of the developments must go to statisticians or systems analysts rather than economists. But despite these developments we are

---

* This appears to be related to the Hurwicz α, coefficient of optimism approach outlined in Section 2-6. However the analysis under consideration here does not require a precise valuation of a coefficient and is therefore an operational technique unlike Hurwicz α.

still a long way from the state of sophistication where we can relegate the issue of imperfect knowledge to the class of matters that can be resolved through mechanical methods.

2-10 The Implications of Organisation Theory

H. A. Simon [132] warns economists that the advances in management techniques brought about through the blending of economics, statistics, systems analysis, can easily be overestimated. He explains that attempts to optimise may be futile and that 'satisficing' (the search for a solution that works, or gives a satisfactory result) is a more realistic aim than maximising or optimising.

This concept of satisficing has been widely adopted in organisation theory and while it is easy enough to understand and explain, its implications for management science* are often misunderstood. First let us consider the reasons for satisficing rather than optimising behaviour.

(1) Uncertainty is rather more than a lack of knowledge concerning which state of nature will occur. The approaches we have considered in this chapter assume that complete pay-off matrices can be derived, yet in practice a matrix only consists of a subset of the possible strategies (see Section 2-1) and it is is never possible to contemplate every conceivable eventuality or state of nature. In short the pay-off matrix is incomplete. Even where strategies and states of nature have been enumerated it is not always possible to state precisely what pay-off would occur when a particular strategy met with a particular state of nature. So there are gaps in the pay-off matrix and there is no way in which one can be confident of making an optimal choice.

(2) Search is problem oriented, so that alternatives and information about them are discovered when performance falls short of what is described. But what is the desired performance? Is it maximum profit or a target level of profit? If business organisations behave like other groups of human beings or individuals they will aspire to certain levels of performance such that once desired performance is achieved action ceases. The evidence we have about organisational goals (Chapter 1) especially in the context of pricing (Chapter 7) is suggestive of target levels changing in the light of experience rather than a single minded pursuit of the absolute best.

(3) We have also seen that goals are multiple but not always consistent with one another. For example each department, or sub-unit within the firm has its own goal. We cannot assume that achieving the maximum performance for each sub-unit goal will result in success for

---
* In its widest sense to include operations research, managerial economics, systems analysis, etc.

the firm as a whole. This is a fundamental lesson of general systems theory. Rather than suboptimise (by pursuing each goal to the maximum extent possible) it is normally preferable to seek satisfactory performances for each goal which are consistent with success for the firm as a whole, this also being assessed in satisficing terms.

(4) Decisions are often sequential in nature as J. Margolis [86] has suggested. The information which comes to light as a result of experience helps the decision maker in later decisions. It would be unwise therefore to try to find an optimal course of action at the outset when information is hard to come by. It is perhaps more realistic to think in terms of 'trying it on for size' initially, trying to achieve results which are satisfactory and capable of improvement over time as aspirations rise.

When a decision cannot be broken down into a sequence but by necessity has to be taken on a once and for all basis, it is all the more important to get it right first time. Yet it is in precisely these circumstances that lack of knowledge confounds the decision maker most. So that even though he intends to be rational, he may be able to do no better than satisfice. The intended rationality limited by human, organisational and informational constraints is termed 'bounded rationality' by Simon.

(5) The human constraints refer to the individual's inability to digest and coordinate all the information that might be relevant in a particular instance; also his perception of the world about him where he looks for immediate cause and effect rather than complex and intricate chains of causes and consequences.

This is the great paradox of uncertainty. There is on the one hand insufficient information for (omniscient) rationality, yet on the other too much information for the decision maker to assimilate. Simon [132] summarises by saying 'Administrative man satisfices because he has not the wits to maximise' (p. xxiv).

(6) The time factor is also an important consideration. Even if 'administrative man' did want to trace all the complex inter-relationships at work and gather all relevant information, he would not have unlimited time to do so. Many decisions have to be made very quickly relative to the time needed for adequate search. Moreover information gathering is costly as well as time consuming. The end product in terms of improved decisions must justify the expenditure on search. Search may be subject to diminishing marginal returns in which case there would come a point when additional expenditure on it would not be economic. It is perhaps therefore simply not cost-effective to make decisions which are optimal and based on complete information.

Does the recognition of the constraints on decision making, resulting in satisficing behaviour radically change the aims of this chapter and indeed the whole book? It is our view that this need not be the case. The issue revolves around the distinction between normative and positive analysis. What Simon has done is to explain what *does* happen in practice. R. M. Cyert and J. G. March [32] have built their behavioural theory of the firm around satisficing behaviour and have been successful in predicting some of the decisions made by organisations they have studied.

But description, explanation and prediction are all part of positive analysis, while this book is normative in nature. Thus while we recognise that the difficulties which managers face in the real world are substantial, we feel that there is scope for improving this state of affairs. Just because satisficing is understandable does not mean that it is acceptable. Given that resources are scarce, it is important to use them efficiently.

3 PRODUCTION FUNCTIONS AND LINEAR PROGRAMMING

3-1 The Firm as an Input-Output System

The firm can be viewed as an input-output system which converts human, physical and financial resources into goods and services in order to achieve its objectives (see R. A. Johnson, *et al* [65] and Chapter 1). In this 'systems' representation of the firm there is a process of feedback which permits learning and improvement (see Figure 1.3, Chapter 1), a feature which is absent from the economist's model because of the usual assumptions about rationality — i.e. profit maximisation under perfect knowledge and foresight. The economist uses the concept of a production function which is a mathematical expression showing the maximum output possible from a particular input usage with a given technology. Despite its simplicity, it does provide a convenient framework within which the conversion of inputs into outputs can be understood and it also forms the basis for cost analysis which follows in Chapter 4.

For some production situations the over-riding problem may be to find the best uses of fairly inflexible available inputs. If these inputs can be converted into several different outputs, the firm has to decide which outputs and in particular which combination of outputs best achieves the firm's objectives. In contrast, another firm may have little choice over final outputs but may have a choice of production methods utilising different combinations of inputs. In general, every enterprise has to make a decision about input usage or the mix of final outputs, or both, and the two decisions must be consistent with one another if maximum profit or any other relevant objective is to be achieved.

In the case of the production decision, an objective of maximising profit and of achieving optimum resource allocation within the firm lead to the same answer. A profit maximising firm will try to obtain the maximum output from a given level of inputs by using the best production techniques possible given current knowledge. If the firm wished to make fewer goods or services than this, it could save money and scarce resources by using fewer inputs.

3-2 The Production Function

The production function is written:

$$Q = f(a, b, c, \ldots n)$$

Restricting our discussion to single-product firms for the moment, Q shows the maximum quantity of output that can be produced from *a* units of input A, *b* units of input B, etc. ..., or the maximum *flow* of output that can be produced from the corresponding set of input *usage rates*.* By adjusting the combination of factor inputs different output levels can therefore be achieved. The production function is a technological relationship and its direct estimation in any instance would rely on engineering data relating outputs to inputs. Economists however can test hypotheses concerning production functions, indirectly, by studying cost data (see Chapter 4).

An example of a *production* function is

$$Q = \sqrt{k \cdot l}$$

where Q is the maximum output that can be produced from *k* units of input K and *l* units of input L. If inputs are infinitely divisible and can be substituted for each other without restriction, then a particular level of output can be produced by an infinite number of input combinations. For example, given the production function $Q = \sqrt{(k \cdot l)}$, 1,000 units of output can be produced from:

½ unit of input K and 2,000,000 units of L
or 1,000 units of input K and 1,000 units of L
or 4,000 units of input K and 250 units of L

or indeed any other combination of inputs where $\sqrt{(k \cdot l)} = 1,000$. The *best* combination for a particular output will depend on the relative prices of the factor inputs. All input combinations yielding a particular output Q are said to be on a particular production 'isoquant' as illustrated in Figure 3.1a, which involves two factor inputs, K and L.

This representation follows the neo-classical** approach and possesses two principal features:

(1) Moving NE from the origin, successive isoquants represent increasing levels of production, such that a higher production level is represented by an isoquant which is entirely above that for a lower

---

* The distinction between rate and volume of production is emphasised by A. Alchian [2]. In particular he warns against analysis in terms of rate of output alone, when total contemplated volume of output and programmed time schedule of production are characteristics which also influence factor usage and cost.

** Neo-classical production theory is adequately treated in most modern economic textbooks, see Chapter 7 of K. J. Cohen and R. M. Cyert [28].

Figure 3.1a Isoquants for the Production Function $Q = \sqrt{(k \cdot l)}$

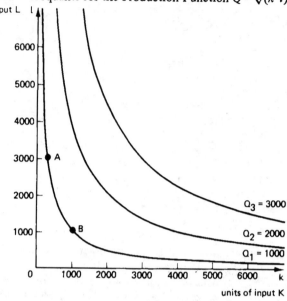

Figure 3.1b Isoquants and Ridge Lines

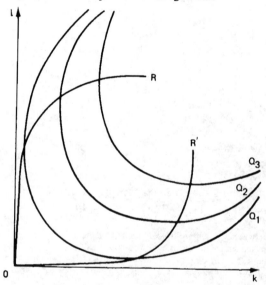

production level. This means that isoquants cannot cross each other.

(2) While factor inputs are alleged to be continuously substitutable, the rate of substitution changes as the factor proportions themselves change. So that if we look along a particular isoquant, e.g. from point A to point B in Figure 3.1a, the input of L is being gradually reduced and output $Q_1 = 1000$ is maintained by substituting input K. However, each successive unit reduction of L requires an increasing amount of K to keep output at 1000. The convexity towards the origin of isoquants thus represents increasing rates of factor substitution. Why should this be so? The neo-classical assumption that a particular level of output can be achieved by an infinite number of input combinations is perhaps rather optimistic. As we shall see later in discussing the programming approach to production, some types of manufacture have fairly rigid input requirements and it simply wouldn't be possible to maintain output by substituting, say, capital for labour. Nevertheless in other types of manufacture some substitution may well be possible, but it is unlikely that this would be on a 'straight line' basis. The neo-classical assumption is that substitution is possible, but only if one is willing to accept that more and more of the substitute factor will be needed eventually in order to keep up output. The relative cost of factors will determine precisely what combination of inputs is desirable given the profit goal.

If isoquants were to bend backwards as in Figure 3.1b this would imply that additional units of factor $\binom{K}{L}$, when employed with a given amount of factor $\binom{L}{K}$, could reduce total output. Such additional units would never be employed by a rational manager. He would only use factor combinations bound by the two 'ridge lines' OR and OR' which exclude the extreme portions of the isoquants.

If the prices of inputs are given and insensitive to the quantities which the firm purchases, which would be the case in competitive factor markets, then we can write:

$$C = a\text{PA} + b\text{PB} + c\text{PC} + \ldots + n\text{PN}$$

where C is the cost of employing a units of factor A purchased at a unit price of PA, with b units of factor B, etc.

Returning to the two factor case with inputs K and L, if the unit prices of K and L are known, then ISOCOST lines can be drawn as in Figure 3.2. As their name suggests these lines show the combination of the two inputs which will result in a given cost. For example, if each unit of K cost the firm £5 and each unit of L cost £3.20, then isocost C = £16,000 could re reached by employing 3,200 units of K or 5,000 units of L or any combination of K and L on the (straight) isocost line connecting these intercepts. The equation of this isocost line is

$5k + 3.2l = 16,000$. Moving NE from the origin, successive isocost lines represent increasing levels of cost. The equation of isocost line $C = £24,000$ is $5k + 3.2l = 24,000$ having intercepts at $k = 4,800$ and $l = 7,500$. The slope of these isocost lines is the same and depends upon the relative prices of the inputs.

Figure 3.2   Isocost Lines

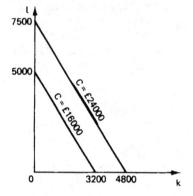

Figure 3.3   The Isocost Line and Isoquants Together

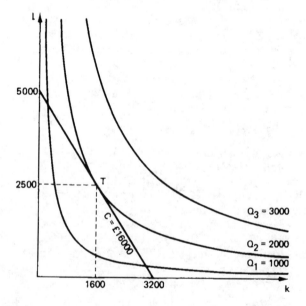

For a given cost level, the maximum output the firm can attain can be seen in the two input case by drawing the relevant isocost line in the isoquant diagram as in Figure 3.3. Suppose we take isocost C = £16,000. All points lying on this line by definition represent combinations of factor inputs which add up to £16,000 cost to the firm. The maximum output available for £16,000 total cost can be determined by finding the highest isoquant lying on, or within that isocost line. In Figure 3.3, the isoquant Q_2 = 2,000 is just attainable by using the combination of k and l at the point of tangency T. This gives values of 1,600 for k and 2,500 for l.

So the maximum output available from a given outlay on inputs can in theory be identified from the isocost line and isoquants, where as point of tangency will occur at some input-output level. At this point of tangency, the slope of the isocost line (tangent) is equal to the slope of the isoquant. The latter shows the additional amount of input L which would have to be introduced into production to maintain a given level of output when one unit of K is withdrawn from the process. This is called the 'marginal rate of substitution' of factor L for factor K and is more strictly given by the *negative* of the slope of the isoquant.*

3-3 The Short and the Long Run

The manager of a manufacturing company would think of the short run as being a period which is of insufficient duration for new productive facilities (capital equipment) to be acquired. If however major projects involving an increased capital input could be contemplated as a means of expanding output then this would be viewed as a long run situation. The time scale will vary between different industries depending on the complexity of technology and the sophistication of planning. So it is impossible here to define precisely in terms of months or years, the short run and the long run or any intermediate period. However, the distinction between the short and the long run is a useful one for the analysis of decision making.

---

* In the present example, the maximum output is reached where the isocost line $5k + 3.2l = 16,000$ is tangential to an isoquant of the production function $Q = \sqrt{(k \cdot l)}$. This is found to be Q = 2,000 from the diagram. The marginal rate of substitution of factor L for factor K is $-dl/dk$ which, for isoquant Q = 2,000, is equal to $4,000,000/k^2$.

dl/dk must equal the slope of the isocost line for tangency to occur.

$$\therefore \frac{-4,000,000}{k^2} = \frac{-50}{32}$$

$$\therefore k^2 = \frac{32 \times 4,000,000}{50}$$

$$\therefore k = 1,600$$

and the corresponding value of l is 2,500.

In economics, the short run applies to a period in which some factor inputs are not variable. The long run applies to a period sufficiently long for most if not all factor inputs to be considered variable. This means in theoretical terms that the isoquant/isocost analysis discussed in the previous section must take account of the length of the decision making period — whether all or few inputs can be varied. Returning to our two factor input case, we can think of the long run as permitting any combination of K and L which may be necessary to achieve the company's objectives. The short run however would limit management's options by keeping one factor, say K, fixed at a given level k'. Because of this restriction in the short run it is rather easier to understand long run production theory and this is the direction we now take.

Production in the Long Run

Here we examine the consequences of allowing all inputs to increase together. Suppose the firm is initially producing at point T (on Figure 3.4), i.e. 2,000 units of output with 2,500 units of input L and 1,600 units if input K which costs £16,000. If the inputs were to double to $l = 5,000$ and $k = 3,200$ this would be represented on the diagram by a movement from T to U. It can be seen that the doubling of inputs is represented by a doubling of the distances from the axes and also from the origin. If K refers to capital input and L to labour input it can be seen that the whole *scale* of operation is being increased; factory size, plant and machinery, etc., as well as the work force.

Figure 3.4   Changes in Scale

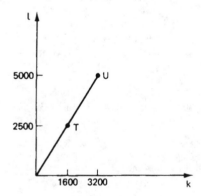

The outputs achieved in response to this change of scale may be constant, increasing, or decreasing.* If production exhibits constant returns to scale, the doubling of inputs will lead to a doubling of outputs, in this particular case to 4,000 units of output. If increasing returns to scale are experienced, more than double the output will be achieved, i.e. more than 4,000 units and conversely for decreasing returns. The production function we have used for illustrative purposes, $Q = \sqrt{(k \cdot l)}$ exhibits constant returns to scale, since a doubling of k and l will result in a doubling of Q and similarly for any other proportionate increase.

Increasing returns may reflect the indivisibility of machinery. At reduced output levels it may not be possible to reduce capital input because machines cannot be broken down into smaller units. If output is then increased, it is not necessary to purchase new machines until capacity is reached. Increasing returns may occur in some circumstances as a result of geometric relationships between surface area and volume. For example, if one wishes to double the capacity of a containing vessel used in production, it is not necessary to double the materials used in constructing that vessel. Capacity depends on the volume enclosed whereas the amount of material forming the enclosure is approximately proportional to the surface area of the vessel. Pipes too involve geometric considerations. A bigger flow results from an increased cross-sectional area which varies with the square of the radius but the material used in constructing the pipe varies with the circumference and hence directly with the radius.

Human inputs too may bring about increasing returns. A doubling of output may be possible with little or no change in supervisory labour, particularly if the original output level was very small and the task well within the scope of one man. This is another example of indivisibility of inputs. Another is the increasing returns arising from specialisation or division of labour. At low outputs, specialisation is not possible unless labour is employed part time, but when output rises labour can be used more effectively by dividing the work force into specialist tasks. The principle of division of labour is attributed to Adam Smith, but its universal applicability is now doubted given the monotonous routine which is the consequence for the worker. This is particularly true of the car industry where division of labour is practised extensively. Work on the assembly line is typically repetitive, so much so that the frequent disruptions to production are often attributed to that cause. Experiments in this industry include job rotation and teamwork which are attempts to reduce monotony, but even if they bring a reduction in the number of stoppages the benefits enjoyed must be set against those

---

* We shall not be discussing *external* returns to scale here, which reflect expansion of a whole industry rather than the firm itself.

foregone by departing from specialisation of tasks.

Empirical evidence suggests that increasing returns to scale arising from these and other causes occur in many industries (see Chapter 4). However constant and even decreasing returns may be experienced by some firms. So far as decreasing returns are concerned, these are supposed to occur after the enjoyment of increasing returns according to traditional theory so that if firms were to increase the scale of operation beyond a certain point, peculiar to the technology employed, decreasing returns to scale would set in (see for example G. L. Bach [8] p. 289). This belief is based on the idea of managerial control loss, which is supposed to result from inability to coordinate the diverse specialised activities of the big business enterprise. The organisation becomes heavily reliant on standard rules in its attempt to maintain control, but this only adds to the difficulties, retarding effective decision making through bureaucratic 'red tape'. Channels of communication between worker and manager become more complex, not only restricting information flow, but also creating human relations problems.

Some firms may be in a transition stage where they have fully exploited the opportunities for increasing returns but have not yet reached the stage where decreasing returns are supposed to set in.

Figure 3.5   Constant Returns to Scale

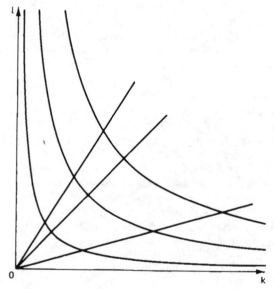

Or quite simply perhaps the organisation is sufficiently versatile to prevent decreasing returns from arising, through the application of modern principles of business organisation. Indeed while empirical evidence is suggestive of increasing returns to scale in many industries, the case for decreasing returns is not proven. Either way there is a strong possibility that over some range of long run output, constant returns to scale will be experienced.

In the isoquant diagram, increasing returns are shown by drawing successively higher isoquants more closely packed when viewed along any ray from the origin, decreasing returns by spacing successive isoquants further apart and constant returns by even spacing for each increment in output. This is illustrated in Figure 3.5. We shall return to the question of returns to scale in the context of cost (Chapter 4) where we discuss economies and diseconomies of scale.

Production in the Short Run

In economics textbooks, short run production revolves around the law of diminishing returns which may be stated as follows:

> 'An increase in some inputs relative to other fixed inputs will, in a given state of technology cause total output to increase; but after a point the extra output resulting from the same additions of extra inputs is likely to become less and less. This falling off of extra returns is a consequence of the fact that new "doses" of the varying resources have less and less of the fixed resources to work with.'
> (P. A. Samuelson [122] p. 26)

It is important to note that this has nothing to do with the phenomenon of decreasing returns to scale which may be experienced in the long run as a result of managerial control loss. Diminishing returns are a result of varying factor proportions brought about by the planning period being too short to permit appropriate adjustment of all inputs to the desired level of output. Indeed the law is sometimes called the law of variable proportions. Even if production is characterised by constant returns *to scale*, the short run phenomenon of diminishing returns can still arise *when some of the inputs are held fixed*. This is shown in Figure 3.6 where input K cannot be varied in the short run. It is held fixed at k'.

Even though the isoquants show constant returns to scale, we can see that the law of diminishing returns is operative. As one moves up the vertical drawn at k' ($k = 2,000$) higher output levels can be achieved by adding inputs of L. Starting at zero input of factor L employed in combination with the 2,000 units of factor K, output will be zero.*

---

* In many short run situations, there will be capital factor inputs which are present even if output is negligible or even nil. These give rise to unavoidable cost commitments in the short run (see Chapter 4).

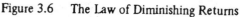

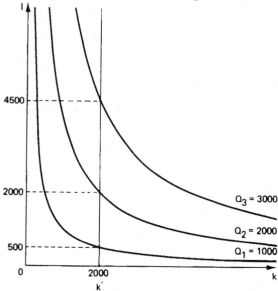

Figure 3.6 The Law of Diminishing Returns

The first 500 units of factor L take output to $Q_1 = 1,000$ but $Q_2 = 2,000$ requires a further 1,500 units of L and $Q_3 = 3,000$ requires another 2,500 units of L on top of that. We get diminishing returns to factor L eventually because when L becomes excessive in the production process, large increments of that factor are required in order to change output by just a small amount. This is because of the convexity of the isoquants which display increasing rates of factor substitution as explained above.

The most important thing to remember in this distinction between the short and long run is that *diminishing* returns are as result of variable factor proportions while *decreasing returns to scale* are a result of the firm becoming too large for effective management. If increasing returns to scale are present because of indivisibilities which only enable a factor to be used fully when output is increased, it is possible that this will make an impact on the short run situation as well. This effect would delay the arrival of diminishing returns, but the latter are normally assumed in economic theory to be experienced eventually in the short run.

3-4 An Alternative View on the Nature of Production

The law of diminishing returns is a central concept in economic theory. As we shall see in Chapter 4, the economist's short run cost curves are deduced from this law. However, the universal applicability of this law is doubted largely because of the nature of modern production processes which are in many instances relatively inflexible in terms of input requirements. The alternative view is that used in linear programming, perhaps best represented in the writings of R. Dorfman [34] who argues that the complete factor substitutability assumed in neo-classical production theory is completely unrealistic in practice.

If modern machinery is inflexible in that it cannot tolerate wide variations in production rates and the mix of materials, labour, power and other inputs, then the choice of inputs is limited and determined by the nature of the process.* There are of course choices as to which type of production process is used in most instances, but this is a far cry from the infinite variation in inputs suggested by neo-classical production theory. Let us now examine the linear programming approach in more detail.

If production of a particular product or service cannot be achieved by a multiplicity of means but has inflexible input requirements, then we say that the technological coefficients are fixed. A situation characterised by fixed technological coefficients is a process where the

Figure 3.7   Isoquant for a Production Function with Fixed Technological Coefficients

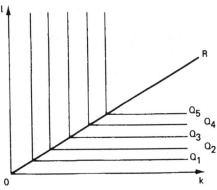

---

* Henceforth the term 'process' will refer to a particular set of input requirements for the production of a unit of output. Processes will then be distinguished by their idiosyncratic input-output relationships.

factors are most efficiently combined in specific proportions irrespective of their relative costs. In the two-factor case each isoquant consists of a horizontal and vertical segment, parallel to the axes, meeting at a point representing optimal factor proportions for the level of output under consideration (Figure 3.7). The two ridge lines would be coincident shown as OR passing through all such optimal points.

As well as this assumption of fixed technological coefficients, the linear programming approach normally assumes constant returns to scale, in other words the technological coefficients remain fixed even if the scale of production changes. In mathematical terms, linear programming assumes that the production function is linear and homogeneous. Perhaps these assumptions are an oversimplification but they may be preferable to those in neo-classical production theory because of the nature of modern production processes, especially where elaborate machinery is involved.

With modern machinery, efficient operation is often possible only over a restricted range of speeds, labour and material input rates, etc. If input proportions are to be varied, this normally requires a switch to a different kind of machine involving another process and there are only a finite number of such processes available for each type of production. Nevertheless, even in highly automated operations, on an assembly line for example, it is not completely true that factors like labour and capital equipment are non-substitutable. One worker equipped with power tools may be able to replace two or three only having hand tools at their disposal. Clearly there are some instances where the programming assumptions just do not fit the facts, either over constant returns to scale, of fixed technological coefficients, but many authors including W. J. Baumol [12] now believe that as a general rule, they are closer to the truth than the neo-classical assumption of complete factor substitutability and the accompanying hypothesis about eventual decreasing returns to scale.

The programming assumptions also preclude diminishing returns from arising in the short run. This is because with fixed technological coefficients, factors are always combined in the same proportions in a particular process. Programming becomes operative when constraints are present which limit the pursuit of the firm's objectives. This may suggest that it is capable of handling only short run production situations, since in the long run all constraints are in principle removable. This conclusion is not strictly true because as part of the analysis it is possible to determine profitability of removing one or more constraints for instance by installing extra capacity. Nevertheless, for the moment let us stay with the short run situation. Typically the inability to increase the stock of capital equipment acts as a constraint, but there are many other limiting factors such as availability of materials and components, the number of trained personnel, warehousing and distribution capacity and so on.

When the firm can use its limited facilities for a variety of final outputs, its problem is to choose the optimum quantity of each output per period of time in terms of profit or whatever objectives are being pursued. The technique known as linear programming can often be used to solve this kind of problem. The following characteristics must be possessed by the problem if the technique is to be applicable:

(i) There is a clearly defined objective function. This is normally profit ot cost which is to be maximised or minimised respectively.*

(ii) There are constraints which limit the attainment of this objective. Thus profit is maximised or cost is minimised subject to these constraints.

(iii) The resources available have alternative uses. In production applications of the technique, various inputs can be converted into a number of outputs.

(iv) The value of the objective function changes when the parameter values change, e.g. profit will normally change in response to variations in input or output mix.

(v) The problem should be capable of numerical expression in linear relationships. (Other programming techniques are possible when relationships are not linear, but we shall be concentrating on those that are.)

In fact many industrial problems have those characteristics and not just production problems. Later in this chapter we shall be looking at applications in transportation. For the moment, though, let us stay with production and in particular the product-mix problem.

3-5 Product-Mix Decisions

The simplest situation in which decisions about product-mix have to be made are where each of the alternative products is made by a single process, but where the constraints are non-specialised. In plainer language this means that though there is only one way in which each product is made, in terms of input usage per unit of final output, some of the productive facilities which are used in one type of manufacture are also used in other types of production. Several products may share productive facilities, being made under the same roof so that if the output of one product is expanded, the others will have to be reduced if the

---

* Programming is consistent with the total systems approach (see Chapter 1, Section 1-2). It involves looking at the whole problem and maximising profit overall or minimising cost overall. Programming cannot start until there is a clear cut aim stated for the system concerned.

plant is working at full capacity. The problem then is to find which combination of these outputs will yield the most profit.

The first step in the solution of such a problem is to determine the net revenue from each product. Each process is defined in terms of a set of input usage rates and if the unit costs it incurs in purchasing inputs are constant, then the variable factor requirements (i.e. variable with output) involve constant unit cost. Thus for a given product type, there is a constant variable production cost. Some of the factors are fixed, perhaps a great many in a short run situation, but the total usage of raw materials, power and labour will at least in part vary according to output rates.

If the selling price of each product can be taken as given and insensitive to changes in the quantity supplied by one manufacturer,* then the difference between the selling price and unit variable production cost will also be constant. This is called the 'contribution' or 'net revenue' of each product and its characteristic is that it makes no allowance for the costs of fixed factors which are very difficult to apportion between different products when facilities are shared. We shall return to this point in the next chapter.

In order to maximise profit, or minimise loss, the firm must try to maximise total net revenue from its outputs as this will provide the biggest possible fund out of which fixed costs and profits will be financed. Let the unit variable costs for each product 1, 2, ... n, be
$$\nu_1, \nu_2, \ldots \nu_n$$
the selling prices of each product be
$$s_1, s_2, \ldots s_n.$$
If $x_1, x_2, \ldots x_n$ units of each output are sold, then the total net revenue is given by:

$$\text{TNR} = x_1(s_1 - \nu_1) + x_2(s_2 - \nu_2) + \ldots + x_n(s_n - \nu_n).$$

Let each product use $i_1, i_2, \ldots i_n$ units of non-specialised factor I per unit of output produced where the total availability of that factor per period is F_i. Similarly for any other scarce factor inputs J, K, etc.

The problem is to choose a set of values for $x_1, x_2, \ldots x_n$ so as to maximise total net revenue given the constraints.

i.e. Maximise $\text{TNR} = x_1(s_1 - \nu_1) + x_2(s_2 - \nu_2) + x_n(s_n - \nu_n)$
   Subject to $x_1 i_1 + x_2 i_2 + \ldots + x_n i_n \leqslant F_i$
   $x_1 j_1 + x_2 j_2 + \ldots + x_n j_n \leqslant F_j$
   etc.

---

*   The assumptions about constant factor (input) prices and constant selling (output) prices are satisfied if both factor and product markets are perfect. This may also be a reasonable assumption in other market types. See Chapter 6.

The non-negativity constraints for output quantities would be written as:

$$x_1 \geqslant 0$$
$$x_2 \geqslant 0$$
$$\cdot$$
$$\cdot$$
$$\cdot$$
$$x_n \geqslant 0$$

Example: A firm manufactures two products X and Y using two non-specialised limited inputs, machine *a* and machine *b*. Machine *a* is available for 240 hours in each production period while machine *b* is only available for 120 hours in the same period. Each unit of X produced uses two hours of machine *a*'s time and each unit of Y uses three hours of machine *a*'s time. X and Y use two and one hours of machine *b*'s time, respectively, per unit produced. A single process is used for each product so that usage rates of other inputs are given. Both factor and selling prices are also given and the net revenue from each product is therefore constant and is calculated to be £50 per unit of X and £40 per unit of Y.

The problem is to choose the best combination of outputs X and Y per period, so as to maximise total net revenue and therefore profit. If we let these outputs be x and y respectively, the problem may be expressed as follows:

Maximise   TNR = 50x + 40y
Subject to 2x + 3y ≤ 240   (machine *a*)
            2x + y ≤ 120   (machine *b*)
            x, y both positive.

Note that this satisfies all five requirements of linear programming listed above. The solution to the problem can be found using either the graphical or simplex methods of linear programming.

The Graphical Method

This method is limited to the most straightforward product-mix problems, like the present one where only two outputs X and Y are involved. The axes of the graph (Figure 3.8) denote the quantities of X and Y produced per period, i.e. *outputs* are now marked on the axes. The first constraint means that x and y can never take values given by points above the line AA'. The line drawn is in fact the equality 2x + 3y = 240 with intercepts at x = 120 and y = 80. The second constraint means that the solution cannot lie above the line BB', which represents the equality 2x + y = 120 with intercepts at x = 60 and y = 120. Furthermore, the conditions $x \geqslant 0$, $y \geqslant 0$ require that the solution lies in the positive quadrant, so that taking all these restriction together we have a 'feasible region' OAPB' within which the solution must lie.

Figure 3.8 The Product-Mix Decision

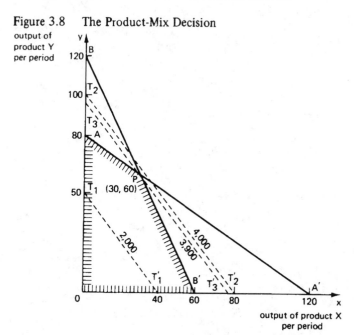

The total net revenue equation must now be considered. As a starting point it can be seen that any combination of x and y lying on the broken line $T_1 T_1'$ will give a total net revenue of £2,000. Point T_1 for example is where y = 50, x = 0 which yields (£40 × 50) contribution and T_1' is where x = 40, y = 0 yielding a contribution of (£50 × 40). Because each point on this line represents the same level of total net revenue or contribution to profit, $T_1 T_1'$ is called an 'isoprofit' line. At the £2,000 level there are many combinations of x and y which lie within the feasible region, and thus satisfy the constraints, but at £4,000, represented by the broken line $T_2 T_2'$, no combination of x and y lies within the feasible region. (Note that the two isoprofit lines are parallel.) This means that the maximum total net revenue is greater than £2,000 but less than £4,000. An infinite number of isoprofit lines exist, but if we were to draw a further line $T_3 T_3'$, parallel to the other two, just touching the outer edge of the feasible region we would find the maximum net revenue, given the constraints. This is in fact £3,900 and only one point on this line is feasible, namely the corner point P which has coordinates x = 30, y = 60. This is the optimal solution, and it means that given the constraints involving machine time, the firm should make 30 units of X per period and 60 units of Y to yield a total net revenue of £3,900 per period, if the objective is profit maximisation. An interesting observation is that the solution lies at a corner point of the feasible region on the graph — something to which we shall return shortly.

The Simplex Method

This approach is non-graphical and is thus not restricted to the two output case under consideration, moreover it is a simple process based upon a mathematical routine (sometimes called the Gauss-Jordan method after its originators) for solving simultaneous equations which is amenable to computerisation. The two constraints in our present problem involve inequalities and the first step in the simplex method is to write these equations using 'slack variables', *viz*.

$2x + 3y + S_a = 240$ equation (a)

$2x + y + S_b = 120$ equation (b)

S_a and S_b can take on any positive value or zero so as to preserve the nature of the constraints, they represent the amount of unused scarce resources — hours of machine a's and machine b's time respectively.

Let us now write the total net revenue, Z, as

$Z = 50x + 40y$ which is to be maximised, or alternatively

$-50x - 40y + Z = 0$ equation (Z)

As this system of simultaneous equations stands, there are five unknowns and only three equations which means that we can only solve for three variables at a time having given some definite value to two of the other variables. In particular, if we let any two variables take on a value of zero, we can solve for the remaining three. We say that such a solution is 'basic' and call the variables we have solved for, the 'basic variables'. The zero valued variables are thus 'non-basic'.

Before proceeding to derive basic solutions for the above system of equations we are going to write them in tabular form by detaching coefficients (Table 3.1).

Looking at this tableau, an obvious basic solution is to let x and y be the zero (non-basic) variables and solve for S_a, S_b and Z.

Having done so, we can read off immediately:

$S_a = 240$
$S_b = 120$
$Z = 0$.

Table 3.1 Initial Basic Solution

	x	y	Sa	Sb	Z		
a_1	2	3	①	0	0	240	Sa = 240
b_1	2*	1	0	①	0	120	Sb = 120
Z_1	−50	−40	0	0	①	0	Z = 0

Basic column vectors

x = 0
y = 0

Table 3.2 Second Basic Solution

$a_2 = a_1 - 2b_2$	0	2*	①	−1	0	120	Sa = 120
$b_2 = \frac{1}{2}b_1$	①	½	0	½	0	60	x = 60
$Z_2 = Z_1 + 50b_2$	0	−15	0	25	①	3000	Z = 3000

y = 0
Sb = 0

Table 3.3 Optimal Solution

$a_3 = \frac{1}{2}a_2$	0	①	½	−½	0	60	y = 60
$b_3 = b_2 - \frac{1}{2}a_3$	①	0	−¼	+¾	0	30	x = 30
$Z_3 = Z_2 + 15a_3$	0	0	7½	17½	①	3900	Z = 3900

Sa = 0
Sb = 0

The encircled ① and its column of zeros is called a 'basic unit column vector' and the presence of these three vectors in Table 3.1 indicates that a basic solution is available. While this is a feasible solution, it is hardly optimal since Z, net revenue, is zero. Sa and Sb are at their maximum values of 240 and 120 respectively which indicates that neither machine is in use when outputs x and y are zero. This solution corresponds to the origin in our graphical solution (Figure 3.8). In fact this solution only serves as a starting point — it is our initial basic feasible solution. From it we can find a better solution, which itself can be examined to find a better solution and so on until the optimal solution is reached.

The Z row in the initial basic solution tells us that we are foregoing (negative signs) £50 per unit by not producing any output X and £40 per unit by not producing any Y. These are the *opportunity costs* (see Chapter 1, Section 1-6) of using the capacity of the machines for any purpose other than the production of X and Y. In the simplex method we seek improvements by finding the largest negative value (smallest absolute value) in the Z row, i.e. −50 and introduce the corresponding variable, which is x in this instance, into the basis. This means that one of the other variables must cease to be basic. In the simplex method, Z always remains basic (even though it was *solved* as zero in the initial solution) so the choice for the variable to depart from the basis lies between Sa and Sb. Let us return to the graphical solution (Figure 3.8) for a moment. Our initial basic solution occurred at the origin but we are now seeking improvement by increasing x from zero, but for the present keeping y *at* zero. This is tantamount to moving along the x axis of the graph and it can be seen that B', where $x = 60$, is the farthest we can go at this stage without leaving the feasible region. At this juncture machine b's capacity is fully utilised, hence Sb = 0. Consequently it is Sb that becomes non-basic when x becomes a basic variable. We say that x is the entering variable (it was non-basic but is now entering the basis) and Sb is the departing variable (it was in the basis but is now departing to become zero valued or non-basic) (see H. M. Wagner [150]). So far then we have studied the initial basic solution and found:

(i)   −50 is the largest, negative value in the Z row so x is chosen as the entering variable.

(ii)   The more restrictive constraint, when introducing x is that pertaining to machine b. We can divide the coefficients of x in a_1 and b_1 into the final column values to find this. *Viz*.

a_1 240/2 = 120
b_1 120/2 =   60

This means that only 60 units of X can be produced before taking up b's capacity to the full, reducing Sb to zero. The lesser of these ratios thus gives the departing variable. The second basic solution thus has y and Sb as non-basic variables with x, Sa and Z as basic variables. Using the tableau to yield this solution involves a 'pivoting' operation, the pivot being at the intersection of the column of the entering variable and the row of the departing variable — marked with an asterisk. The pivot element can be given a value of unity by dividing every element in the row by the pivot value itself which is in this case 2. This gives row b_2 in Table 3.2. To solve for x we subtract or add some multiple of this row from the remaining rows in order to create a new basic column vector. If we subtract $2b_2$ from a_1 this gives us a new row a_2 and if we add $50b_2$ to Z_1 this gives us a new Z row, Z_2 (Table 3.2). Now that x has been eliminated from these other 2 rows, we can read off our second basic solution, *viz.*

> x = 60
> Sa = 120
> Z = 3000

(with y and Sb being non-basic and hence zero).

A further improvement is possible. Examination of the new Z row (Z_2) reveals that we are now foregoing £15 per unit by not producing product Y. There are no opportunities other than the production of Y for increasing Z, so y becomes the entering variable and the column of the pivot element. Returning again to the graphical solution (Figure 3.8), it can be seen that introducing y corresponds to moving along the line B'B. Each unit of Y added contributes £40 to profit, but in order to produce one unit of Y it is necessary to release one hour's production time from machine *b* by reducing the output of X by ½ unit. This reflects the relative requirements of X and Y for machine *b*'s production time (two hours and one hour per unit, respectively), also shown by the slope of line BB' which is 2:1. Each unit of X foregone means a fall in profit of £50, so that a ½ unit foregone means a loss of £25. Consequently each unit of Y added brings a net addition to profit of £40 − £25 = £15 — hence the coefficient of y in row Z_2 (Table 3.2). If we proceed beyond point P when moving along B'B on the graph (Figure 3.8), we shall leave the feasible region, having reduced machine *a*'s spare capacity to zero as well as that of machine *b*. This means that when introducing y, it is Sa which becomes non-basic or zero valued. So y is the entering variable and Sa the departing variable. In the simplex method we show that Sa is the departing variable by comparison of the ratios of

> 120:2 (final column value in Table 3.2
>   : corresponding coefficient of
>   the entering variable)

and 60:½

of which the former is the smaller. Hence the pivot element, which is marked with the asterisk. The pivot is again reduced to unity through appropriate division and y can be eliminated from the b and Z rows by subtraction and addition as follows:

$$\frac{1}{2}a_2 \rightarrow a_3$$
$$b_2 - \frac{1}{2}a_3 \rightarrow b_3$$
$$Z_2 + 15a_3 \rightarrow Z_3$$

shown in Table 3.3.

The third basic solution can then be derived, *viz.*

$$y = 60$$
$$x = 30$$
$$Z = 3900$$

Sa and Sb being non-basic and hence equal to zero, meaning that there is no spare capacity in either machine. There are no further opportunities for increasing Z because there are no negative values in the Z row.

Referring again to the graphical solution to this problem (Figure 3.8) the initial basic solution was at the origin with no production and no profit. The second basic solution took us to point B' and the final (optimal) basic solution to point P. The simplex method takes us from one corner of the feasible region to the next provided that a better result is thereby obtained. Having proceeded from O to B' to P no further iteration is advocated. However, were the coefficients in the total net revenue function to change, the optimal solution could have been at one of the other corner points B' or A. This would be the case if for example the net revenue from X were to increase to £120 per unit, that from Y remaining unchanged, or if the net revenue from Y were to increase to £80 per unit, that from X remaining unchanged. Testing the optimal solution in this way is called postoptimality or sensitivity analysis.

3-6 Sensitivity Analysis

The reason for further analysis is that the solution may only be optimal for a given set of parameter values. If net revenue from an output changes, or constraints become more or less restrictive, a different solution may become optimal. Given the uncertain environment in which decisions are made, it is essential to ask, 'What if so and so happens?', which is the essence of sensitivity analysis (see Chapter 2). In a complicated problem, the simplex method would be applied through a computer and the sensitivity analysis would similarly be computerised. The existing optimal solution, however, can answer many of our questions and it is unnecessary to derive a new solution from first principles with new parameter values.

First let us examine the objective function. If the coefficients change as a result of different net revenue values, it is only necessary to examine the initial and final iterations (Tables 3.1, 3.3) to test for optimality. For example we can find the range of unit net revenue values for X which will leave the present final solution optimal by the following method:

Let the unit net revenue from X change so that it becomes $50 + \Delta$. Row Z_1 now becomes

$$-(50 + \Delta)x - 40y + Z = 0$$

In performing each simplex iteration a multiple of some row was added to row Z_1, consequently row Z_3 in the final iteration will become

$$-\Delta x + 7\tfrac{1}{2}Sa + 17\tfrac{1}{2}Sb + Z = 3,900$$

(or in detached coefficient form as in Table 3.4a).

Table 3.4a Sensitivity Analysis

	x	y	Sa	Sb	Z	
a_4	0	①	½	−½	0	60
b_4	①	0	−¼	+¾	0	30
Z_4	−Δ	0	7½	17½	①	3900

Table 3.4b

	x	y	Sa	Sb	Z	
a_5	0	①	½	−½	0	60
b_5	①	0	−¼	+¾	0	30
Z_5	0	0	7½−Δ/4	17½+3Δ/4	①	3900 + 30Δ

In order to deduce a critical range for Δ we revise Table 3.4a so that the coefficient of x in row Z_4 is zero. This is achieved by multiplying row b_4 in Table 3.4a by Δ and adding it to Z_4 to give Table 3.4b.

For the solution to change there would have to be an unexploited profitable opportunity which would be indicated by a negative coefficient in row Z_5. Thus for the optimal solution to remain unchanged

$7\frac{1}{2} - \Delta/4$ must be positive

and $17\frac{1}{2} + 3\Delta/4$ must be positive.

i.e. Δ must be less than 30

and greater than $-23\frac{1}{3}$

or $-23\frac{1}{3} \leq \Delta \leq 30$.

The unit net revenue from X which is £50 could therefore fall by £$23\frac{1}{3}$ to £$26\frac{2}{3}$ or rise by £30 to £80 without changing the optimal product mix, provided that all other parameters (e.g. the net revenue from Y) remain unchanged.

The validity of the sensitivity test result can be confirmed by returning to the graphical solution in Figure 3.8. If the unit net revenue from X were less than £$26\frac{2}{3}$, the new profit line would leave the feasible region at the corner point A, indicating that 80 units of Y with no production of X were optimal. If the unit net revenue from X were greater than £80, a new profit line again would be involved, and this would leave the feasible region at point B' indicating that 60 units of X should be produced and none of Y for optimality.

Further sensitivity tests will be applied in Chapter 4. The interested reader will find this subject well documented elsewhere (see, for example, H. M. Wagner [150], Chapter 5).

3-7 The Choice of Processes

Let us now consider a rather different issue. Suppose a firm is not so much concerned about the quantities of outputs it should produce but rather the method of production. For purposes of exposition let us imagine that a firm is just making one product. While the complete substitutability of factor inputs depicted in neo-classical analysis is clearly unrealistic, it may that a finite number of alternative processes exist. Each of these would be distinct methods of production, with specific input requirements.

In the example that follows, we shall once again assume that two *scarce* inputs, K and L, are involved and quantities of these *inputs* will be represented diagrammatically on the axes of a graph. Other readily available inputs may also be involved: we shall not represent these in the diagrams that follow, but recognise their presence in assessing the profit contribution or net revenue yielded by a particular process.

Example: Our single-product firm must choose from among three alternative processes.

We shall let q_1 be the quantity produced per week by process 1
q_2 " " " " " 2
and q_3 " " " " " 3.
After taking into account *all* the inputs used in these processes, the firm calculates the unit contributions to profit as

£2 from process 1
£3 " " 2
£2 " " 3

The objective function is then: Maximise total net revenue (or contribution to profit) $P = 2q_1 + 3q_2 + 2q_3$. Limitations on the weekly availability of inputs K and L are 1200 units and 400 units respectively. (These would typically be available machine time, labour availability, etc.) Input requirements per unit of output are as follows:

Process 1   20 units of input K and 10 units of input L
Process 2   40   "   "   "   " 5   "   "   "
Process 3   15   "   "   "   " 20   "   "   "

The constraints may then be written:

$$20q_1 + 40q_2 + 15q_3 \leq 1200$$
$$10q_1 + 5q_2 + 20q_3 \leq 400$$

plus the following non-negativity requirements:

$$q_1 \geq 0, \quad q_2 \geq 0, \quad q_3 \geq 0.$$

The feasible region is shown in Figure 3.9 as rectangle OACB, since any weekly input usage amounting to less than 1200 units of factor K and 400 units of factor L, and lying in the positive quadrant will satisfy the stated restrictions.

Each process can be represented as a ray passing through the origin as shown in Figure 3.10. This shows that 60 units of output per week can be produced by input combinations, X, Y and Z using process 1, 2 or 3 respectively. With fixed technological coefficients a doubling of output from any process is represented by moving along the appropriate ray to a point twice as far from the origin as formerly. Any other proportionate increase or decrease can be similarly represented.

The points X, Y and Z lie on the same isoquant, Q = 60 and we can connect these points to show the complete isoquant ZXY as in Figure 3.10. This shows that Q = 60 can also be attained by mixing processes appropriately as represented by the straight lines XY and XZ, which involve combinations of process 1/process 2 and process 1/process 3 respectively. Processes 2 and 3 could also be mixed to give a weekly output of 60 units as shown by the dotted line YZ. However so far as usage of scarce factors K and L is concerned, combinations along YZ

Figure 3.9   The Feasible Region

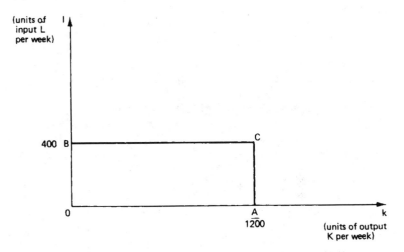

Figure 3.10   Isoquant Diagram

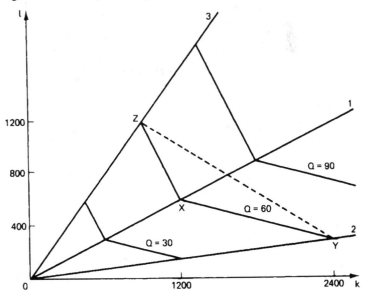

79

are inefficient* compared with those along ZXY which achieve the same output for a smaller input requirement. Consequently isoquant Q = 60 is represented by ZXY rather than ZY. In Figure 3.10 we also show isoquant Q = 30 and Q = 90.

Now that we have introduced more than one process into our linear programming representation of production, the isoquants bear some resemblance to the neo-classical isoquants in that they are convex to the origin.** As we move from segment ZX to ZY, the reduction of input L necessitates substitution of K at an increased rate in order to maintain output at Q = 60. This too is equivalent to the neo-classical portrayal of production. However isoquants in linear programming are kinked because there is always a finite number of processes unlike neo-classical analysis which implicitly assumes an infinite number of processes and perfectly smooth isoquants.

The objective is to maximise profit contribution subject to the constraints. From our analysis so far we are only able to find the maximum *output* given the constraints. (This would be done by entering the feasible region into Figure 3.10 and drawing intermediate isoquants as well as those already present. We could then find the highest isoquant just touching the feasible region.) To maximise profit, however, we must find those input combinations which yield the same amount of profit, i.e. the isoprofit lines. Since each process in this example has a different profit contribution, these isoprofit lines will be distinct from the isoquants.

Given the profit function:

$$P = 2q_1 + 3q_2 + 2q_3$$

it can be seen that in order to yield £120 contribution it is necessary to produce:

    60 units by process 1
or 40   "   "   2
or 60   "   "   3

---

*   At the moment we are relating the scarce inputs K and L to output and ignoring the other inputs which also influence profits.

**   Linear (non-convex) isoquants are possible, but isoquants concave to the origin are not, since points on the latter would always involve greater usage of both scarce inputs than is necessary.
        Points on the dotted line would be more efficient.

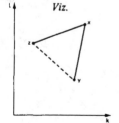

Figure 3.11   Isoprofit Lines and the Feasible Region

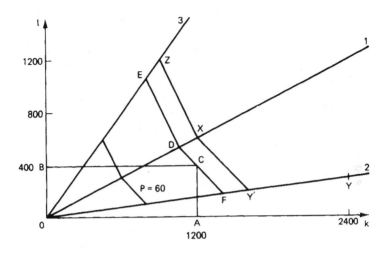

Thus while points X and Z in Figure 3.10 would lie on the isoprofit line P = £120, point Y would not. In fact point Y would contribute 60 × £3 to profit = £180. In Figure 3.11 we draw the isoprofit line, P = 120 as ZXY' where Y' is the point on the ray of process 2 which contributes £120. The isoprofit line P = 60 is also drawn, but it is apparent that the optimal solution lies somewhere between P = 60 and P = 120. The former isoprofit line possesses points well within the feasible region OACB, while the latter lies entirely outside it. It is the isoprofit line EDF with segments parallel to the other isoprofit lines which just touches corner point C of the feasible region. This gives the optimal solution, which is interpreted as follows:

The isoprofit line EDF on which the optimal solution lies is P = 106$^2/_3$, since it lies 7/9 of the distance between P = 60 and P = 120 on any ray drawn through the origin. Rather more of this profit is earned through process 1 than through process 2 since point C lies rather nearer to point D on ray 1 than to point F on ray 2. The precise proportions are 5/3 in favour of process 1 which means that the weekly profit of £106$^2/_3$ comprises £66$^2/_3$ from process 1 and £40 from process 2.

Since each unit produced by process 1 contributes £2 and each unit

81

produced by process 2 contributes £3, the weekly outputs are:

from process 1, $q_1 = \dfrac{66\frac{2}{3}}{2} = 33\frac{1}{3}$ giving a profit of £$66\frac{2}{3}$

from process 2, $q_2 = \dfrac{40}{3} = 13\frac{1}{3}$ giving a profit of £40

Total profit £$106\frac{2}{3}$

This result can be confirmed by the simplex method.

3-8 The Blending Problem

Besides production situations where a choice of processes is involved, there are many instances in which there is a choice of material ingredients. These are typically blends of mixtures like petroleum, chemical and pharmaceutical products, and foodstuffs. In these instances, the constraints are not so much limits on the *availability* of inputs as the *specification* which the final product must meet. Petrol must contain a certain proportion of anti-knock in order to reach a given octane rating. Meat products, like pies, must contain so much real meat if they are not to offend the Trade Descriptions Act. In the following example we shall be trying to find the cheapest way of making a foodstuff which has to meet certain minimum nutritional requirements. Provided that these requirements are met the product will sell at the going market price, so that by minimising cost, we shall be maximising profit.

Example: Brekka-wheat is a 'ready to eat' breakfast cereal. Each family size packet is supposed to contain the following vitamins:

    30 mg. of Niacin
    6 mg. of Thiamine.

A slight excess of either of these vitamins can be tolerated, the important thing is that this specification is met in full. Two grades of cereal G_1 and G_2 are the only material inputs used.

    500 grammes of G_1 contain 20 mg. of Niacin and 12 mg. of Thiamine.
    500 grammes of G_2 contain 40 mg. of Niacin and 2 mg. of Thiamine.
    500 grammes of G_1 cost 3 pence.
    500 grammes of G_2 cost 2 pence.

A further restriction is that the total contents of each packet must weigh at least 450 gm.

Let $g_1 g_2$ be the number of 500 gm. lots of G_1 and G_2 used in the final blend. The problem is to minimise cost:

$$C = 3g_1 + 2g_2.$$

Subject to:

$$20g_1 + 40g_2 \geq 30 \quad \text{(Niacin content)}$$
$$12g_1 + 2g_2 \geq 6 \quad \text{(Thiamine content)}$$
$$g_1 + g_2 \geq \frac{450}{500} \quad \text{(Minimum contents of 450 gm.)}$$
$$g_1 \geq 0$$
$$g_2 \geq 0.$$

Figure 3.12   Cost Minimisation

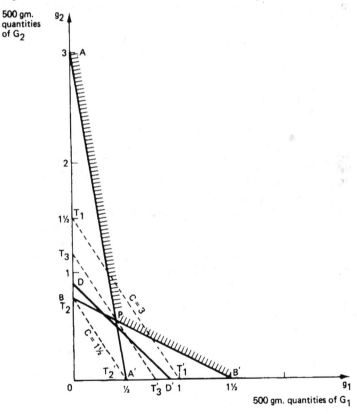

Figure 3.12 gives the graphical solution. The continuous lines AA', BB', DD' show the constraints as equalities. As they are 'greater than' type constraints, the feasible region can be seen to lie above the boundary APB', drawn as a heavy continuous line. It is apparent that satisfying the two vitamin constraints will also satisfy the minimum contents requirement.

Isocost line $T_1 T_1'$ shows all combinations of g_1 and g_2 which cost 3 pence in total. Its intercepts are $g_1 = 1$, $g_2 = 3/2$ found by substituting $C = 3$ in the cost function above and setting g_2 and then g_1 equal to zero. This lies well within the feasible region for a wide range of values of g_1 and g_2. This means that a lower isocost line will be feasible. However $T_2 T_2'$, the isocost line representing 1½ pence, does not possess any combinations which are feasible. If we can find another line $T_3 T_3'$ which is parallel to these first two isocost lines, but lying between them so that contact is just made with the feasible region, then we have found the optimal solution. Such an isocost line touches the feasible region at P giving an optimal (minimum cost) solution of:

$g_1 = \dfrac{9}{22}$ of 500 gm.   i.e. <u>204.55 gm. of G_1</u>

$g_2 = \dfrac{6}{11}$ of 500 gm.   i.e. <u>272.73 gm. of G_2</u>

<u>Cost $= \dfrac{51}{22}$ pence.</u>

<u>Total weight = 477.3 gm.</u>

The Niacin and Thiamine content meets the specification precisely because both of the vitamin constraints are operative at the corner point P.

The simplex method can be used to solve cost minimisation problems like this one, and in fact the graphical solution obtained here was confirmed in this way. The initial tableau would be as in Table 3.5, and we would maximise $Z (= -C)$ in order to minimise cost. The difficulty we face is that if we try to derive an initial basic solution with g_1 and g_2 set at zero, we would find:

$S_1 = -30$
$S_2 = -6$
$S_3 = -\dfrac{450}{500}$
$Z = 0$

As the slack variables have to be ≥ 0 in order to preserve the nature of the constraints, this solution is *not* feasible. It does of course correspond to the origin of our graphic solution ($g_1 = 0$, $g_2 = 0$) (Figure 3.12 which is obviously not within the feasible region).

Table 3.5   Initial Simplex Tableau for Cost Minimisation

	g_1	g_2	S_1	S_2	S_3	Z	
a_1	20	40	−1	0	0	0	30
b_1	12	2	0	−1	0	0	6
d_1	1	1	0	0	−1	0	$\frac{450}{500}$
Z_1	3	2	0	0	0	1	0

In fact a preliminary phase of the simplex method involving artificial variables must be applied to this problem before it can be solved in the usual manner (see A. M. Glicksman [44] pp. 70-4). Our reason for not going into this more fully is that we are not so much concerned with the mathematics of linear programming as its economic content and areas of application. Suffice it to say that there are computer programmes available for solving cost minimisation problems like this one, using the preliminary and usual phases of the simplex method. To test the solution by means of sensitivity analysis could involve changes in the unit costs of the two ingredients G_1, G_2 and changes in the vitamin requirements or total weight.

3-9 The Transportation Problem

The final application of linear programming we shall be considering in this chapter is transportation. Here we are breaking away from the basic theme of production but the transportation problem itself has the same characteristics as the product-mix and blending problems.

There is an objective function: minimise the total transportation cost involved in meeting an assignment — normally to supply various customers with their weekly or monthly orders from a variety of supply points. There are constraints in the availability of supplies which cannot be readily changed, and in the need to provide each customer with a particular quantity. The problem can be represented by a series of linear equations from which we can derive basic feasible solutions and ultimately the optimal solution.

Example: The Brekka-wheat Company has two main factories in the UK, one in Southampton and the other in Manchester. Local demands are supplied directly from these points of manufacture, but there are warehouses at Glasgow, Cardiff and Norwich from which demand in the surrounding areas of these cities is met. Manchester has 200 tons of Brekka-wheat per week available for distribution to the rest of the country and Southampton 300 tons per week.

Weekly demands are: Cardiff   150 tons
                      Glasgow   250 tons
                      Norwich   100 tons

which means that they can in principle be met, given the total weekly supplies of 500 tons. Transportation costs per ton in £s are shown in Table 3.6 in the top left hand corner of each square which relates to a particular route (point of origin to destination).

Table 3.6   Costs of Transportation

	C	G	N
M	2.00	2.50	2.00
S	1.50	4.00	2.00

Table 3.7   North West Corner Solution

	C_{150}	G_{250}	N_{100}
M 200	2.00 150	2.50 50	2.00
S 300	1.50	4.00 200	2.00 100

In Table 3.7 we have added weekly availabilities and requirements and entered a solution which works, i.e. it is a feasible solution given availabilities and requirements. This is the 'North West Corner' solution, so called because the square in the NW corner of the table is completed first, with the maximum amount possible. If there is a surplus supply after filling in this square, as in this example, this surplus goes into the adjacent square, i.e. is allocated to the next customer, and so on. Note that this North West Corner solution has four completed squares and two empty squares. This means that in solving for the six unknowns (amounts to be sent through each route), we set two at zero and solve for the rest. This is therefore a basic solution.* In general the number of occupied squares in any basic solution to the transportation problem will be $m + n - 1$ where m, n are the number of supply points and destinations, respectively. The total transportation cost of meeting this assignment in this initial solution is £300 + £125 + £800 + £200 = £1,425.

An improved solution (lower cost) might be possible through rearrangement. Indeed the observant reader might well have chosen some pattern other than that given by the North West Corner method, and achieved a lower cost already. There is no objection to doing this, it is just that in some problems there might not be an obvious pattern to choose, so it is just as well to have a standard method of deriving an initial solution. Changing the distribution pattern means that one of the presently unoccupied squares will have to be brought into the solution. This is tantamount to bringing another variable into the basis, which of course means that some variable will have to depart from the basis.

Let us consider bringing in route S-C. For every ton sent through this route, one less will be required through route M-C, and if we are to leave route M-N unused for the moment, this means that one extra ton will have to go through M-G. To restore the balance, one less will then be sent through S-G. The cost of sending this ton through S-C is therefore not simply £1.50, because of the redistribution necessary to retain feasability. The true cost is £1.50 − £2.00 + £2.50 − £4.00 = −£2.00 which is in fact a saving of £2.00 for every ton sent through S-C.

---

* The reason for this is that although there are apparently five equations (constraints) viz.
$Q_{MC} + Q_{MG} + Q_{MN} = 200$)
$Q_{SC} + Q_{SG} + Q_{SN} = 300$) Total supplies

$Q_{MC} + Q_{SC} = 150$)
$Q_{MG} + Q_{SG} = 250$) Total demands
$Q_{MN} + Q_{SN} = 100$)

any one of these can be deduced from the other four equations. With only four meaningful equations and six unknowns, we solve for four basic variables at a time.

Before proceeding with this problem let us pause for a moment to think about the significance of the last step. We are emphasising that in any optimisation problem, we must look at the whole problem and never consider an element of a system in isolation. All repercussions of an initial change must always be evaluated in problems of this type. This is something that must be stressed in all aspects of business management and economic analysis. Operations research methods, including linear programming explicitly take account of the systems approach. Individual decisions are taken within a system only after assessing their implications for the system as a whole (see H. A. Simon [133] p. 15).

Continuing with the above transportation problem, it is apparently profitable to revise the distribution pattern, given the cost saving discovered already. However, we have yet to test unused route M-N which could conceivably bring an even greater cost saving. Considering the rearrangement brought about by passing one ton through M-N, assuming that S-C is unused, the change in cost, per ton is: £2.00 − £2.00 + £4.00 − £2.50 = £1.50, which is a cost increase of £1.50 per ton.

Clearly then M-N should remain unused at present and we shall effect our cost savings by bringing S-C into the solution. As all solutions are basic, one variable will have to depart to accommodate the new basic variable. This will happen because once 150 tons are entered in square S-C, the square above, i.e. M-C, becomes unoccupied and the tableau appears as in Figure 3.8, with a total transportation cost of £1,125. This is a saving of £300 which is what one would expect to achieve by reallocating 150 tons at a saving of £2.00 per ton.

Table 3.8 Optimal Solution

	C_{150}	G_{250}	N_{100}
M 200	2.00	2.50 200	2.00
S 300	1.50 150	4.00 50	2.00 100

To test for optimality, it is necessary to reconsider all vacant squares because different cost changes will accrue to redistribution when the pattern of occupied squares has changed. However in this example there are only two unoccupied squares and it is apparent that no advantage can be gained by reintroducing M-C. This is because we have just saved £300 by removing it from the basis. Putting it back in would have to reverse effect. Consequently our test for possible improvement centres around route M-N. Here again there is no opportunity for cost saving. In this particular case the effect of introducing M-N is the same as it would have been at the previous iteration,* *viz*: £2.00 − £2.00 + £4.00 − £2.50 = +£1.50. This means that the solution given in Table 3.8 is optimal. There is no scope for improvement on the total cost of £1,125.

Once again a simplex solution would have been possible, but the method we have just used highlights the significance of each step more effectively. The principles applied are very much the same in either case: a series of basic solutions are derived, each one being an improvement on the previous iteration. Generally speaking the format used in this example is preferred for manual solutions, although the simplex method is more conducive to computer solution.

3-10 Summary

Two distinct views about the nature of production have been proposed in this chapter. The economist's neo-classical theory is based on continuous factor substitutability, e.g. capital equipment can be substituted for labour in the production of certain manufactures. The alternative view adopted in modern economic analysis and in linear programming is that factor proportions can generally only be changed by the introduction of a different process or by the changing of the mix of processes. The modern view seems to be gaining respectability at the present time together with programming techniques in general. Certainly linear programming is a versatile technique and of widespread applicability in many industries. We hope that the brief introduction we have offered here has demonstrated this much. To appreciate this, one only has to think of the international petroleum industry which transports crude oil from all the continents of the world and ultimately distributes the finished products all over the globe. It has to make decisions about the relative proportions of these finished products and the blend of intermediate products which go into them.

---

* In more complex examples this test might have revealed a cost saving even though at the previous iteration the same square indicated a cost increase.

As we shall see shortly the traditional approach and the programming approach give rather different conclusions about cost behaviour. It is thus vital for any firm to examine its own production methods to see which model is closer to the truth. There is no point in using the programming approach to production as a means of analysis if factor input proportions can be varied continuously.*

---

* In agriculture, the number of cattle grazing on a given quantity of pasture can be varied within wide limits. Continuous factor substitution is, however, rare in manufacturing industry.

4 COST ANALYSIS

4-1 Introduction

Cost in its broadest sense means sacrifice, typically a sacrifice of purchasing power, but it is important to think of the wider meaning because it is possible to incur costs without any transfer of cash taking place. Business decisions revolve around private costs which include all outlays made by the firm on materials, labour, land, capital, energy and so on. Social costs, i.e. those sacrifices made by society, to enable businesses to operate include damage to the environment through smoke and waste products, spoilage of the appearance of the landscape, congestion of roads, and disruption of community life. Any organisation with an objective of public responsibility will of course pay heed to social costs such as these, but in so far as they do not influence the profits of a firm directly they tend to take second place to private costs which do have a direct influence on the well-being of the organisation. The usual problems of estimation and informational deficiencies are compounded by the lack of an unequivocal definition of cost. In practice it is impossible to give a straightforward answer to the question, 'What is the cost of producing this item?' This applies to the book you are now reading, the table at which you are sitting and indeed almost any other manufactured product you could mention. Yet for purposes of cost control or managerial decision making it is vital that some financial measure is ascribed to cost.

It is rather easier to provide figures for control purposes than it is for evaluation of alternatives since control relies on comparison of reality with predetermined standards to detect *variations* from the desired state of affairs (see Chapter 1). So long as some benchmark for product cost is set the control system can be workable through the detection of variances. Consequently managers must be very wary when evaluating alternatives, of using cost information prepared by accountants largely for control purposes. As we shall see shortly, one of the most crucial issues is the ascertainment of cost when more than one product is (or can be) manufactured within a given set of productive facilities. As a starting point in this discussion of cost analysis we shall take a brief look at the conventional classification used by cost accountants.

4-2 The Accounting Classification of Cost

(a) Manufacturing Cost

'Direct' material and labour costs consist of the expenditure on inputs that can be assigned to specific physical units of output. It is normally possible, for example, to identify the major components that are integral parts of the finished goods and these give rise to direct material costs. Similarly the wages paid to machine operators and assembly labour can be attributed to specific outputs and are hence direct labour costs. However, certain items cannot be so identified with units of output and these are classified as indirect. Minor materials such as glue, screws and miscellaneous supplies may fall into this category and be regarded as indirect material costs. General material handlers, porters, cleaners, etc. are indirect labour because they cannot be identified with a particular unit or batch of production.

Direct *expenses* are again chargeable to specific units and include lubricants which are identified with a particular operation rather than general maintenance costs. Rental of special tools or equipment might also fall into this category, or designs intended for a once-off job.

Factory overhead consists of all manufacturing costs other than direct materials, labour and expense. By definition then it cannot be traced to specific units of output, yet it may be apparent that the resources consumed do vary with the size and duration of the job. Such a factory overhead is variable. Supplies and indirect labour* fall into this category since generally speaking the bigger the job or output, the bigger the outlay. Electricity and gas may also be treated as a variable factory overhead because while it may be difficult to impute a charge directly to the product, it is apparent that the costs of power do depend on the volume of production. Fixed factory overhead consists of production costs which do not depend on the level of output (i.e. they are fixed) and which cannot be attributed therefore to any unit of output except in the exceptional case of a company devoting all its productive resources to a single job. Rent, rates, depreciation and insurance are all in this category, as are supervisory salaries and any other salaries or wages incurred in the completion of the product and its movement to the point of despatch.

Prime cost is the total of direct materials, labour and expense.

Works or Factory Cost is defined as Prime Cost plus Factory Overhead.

(b) Administrative Expenses

Administrative expenses are another type of overhead and consist of

---

* If indirect labour is salaried rather than hourly paid, the salary would be regarded as a fixed cost, i.e. not sensitive to output changes.

the costs of direction, control and general administration of a business such as: salaries of directors, managers, accountants, secretaries and clerical workers, rent, rates and depreciation of office premises, fittings and equipment, stationery, office lighting, heating, etc.

(c) Selling and Distribution expenses

These form the remaining class of overhead. Costs of securing orders, advertising expenditures and the costs of market research must be included here. Salaries of salesmen and sales managers (normally accounted for here rather than under Administrative Expenses) and the rents, rates, etc. on sales offices also fall under this heading. Other costs regarded as 'selling' costs are those involved in after sales service.

The distribution of goods and services involves the following costs: warehousing and general storage charges; transportation costs, including carriage, maintenance, etc.; despatch workers' wages — both clerical and manual; costs of packing materials, cases, etc.

4-3 Fixed Costs and Variable Costs

Before we can explore the relationships between cost and output it is necessary to distinguish between fixed and variable costs. Fixed costs are those which do not vary directly with output. They are not fixed in the sense that they cannot change with time, but rather that they are insensitive to output changes. In the short run, the company has many expenditure commitments which have to be met regardless of output, if it is to stay in business. Furthermore, there are many sunk costs such as outlays on long-lived capital equipment which are typically depreciated over a machine's expected productive life by the accountant to give a yearly charge which is largely independent of the rate of output.

Variable costs by way of contrast are those which do vary directly with the level of output. In a sufficiently long time period, most costs can be regarded as variable given that existing and planned operations can be reviewed, but even in the short run there are numerous examples of costs which are variable, such as the costs of components, electricity and part of the wage bill. As a general rule in the short run, those costs which we have called overhead — indirect manufacturing costs, administrative costs, selling and distribution costs — tend to be fixed. Direct costs on the other hand are usually variable in the short run. It would be wrong, however, to equate overhead with fixed, and direct with variable. The existence of variable factory overheads provides an immediate refutation of such an equation. We must remember that 'direct' means traceable while 'indirect' or 'overhead' means not traceable. Many administrative, selling and distribution costs will vary with the level of output; for example, some of the wages and salaries, transport, items like packing cases, and so on. Yet the accountant finds that for his purposes it is usually adequate to record these as general costs and allocate them to individual product groups and units at a later stage.

In practice it is not always possible to slot an item of expenditure into the fixed or variable category. Maintenance costs for example will be necessary whenever machinery is operating. However, at higher levels of output there will usually be increased need for lubrication and repair, even though at lower levels of output maintenance costs may be irreducible below some point. Depreciation should strictly measure the loss in value of an asset during the production period. This is in part a function of time, resulting in a given loss in value, but also in part a function of the intensity of utilisation. An every day example of this is depreciation on a motor car. This will suffer a fall in real value through the passage of time even if it remains virtually unused.* However, depreciation will increase as wear and tear take place through increased mileage. The example of maintenance is also very much applicable to motoring, the costs of servicing are in part fixed and in part variable.

4-4 Marginal Costs

The concept of marginal cost is often thought of as being a short run phenomenon (largely because of its connection with the law of diminishing returns which is essentially confined to the short run). However, there is no reason why marginal cost cannot be applied to the long run as well. Marginal cost is defined *at a particular level of output*, as the change in total cost brought about by a unit change in output. It is the first derivative, with respect to output, of the total cost function. Given that any changes in cost must occur in the variable component, it could equally well be defined as the change in *variable cost* brought about by a unit change in output.

The reason for specifying the level of output when stating marginal cost is that it can change from output to output. This would not be the case with linear cost behaviour as implied by the programming view of production functions when a single process is involved. The relationship between fixed, variable, total and marginal cost would then be as in Figure 4.1:

$$T = k + vQ$$
total cost = total fixed cost + unit variable cost × number of units

---

* As measured by the difference between its secondhand value and the replacement cost of a new car.

Figure 4.1   Linear Cost Behaviour

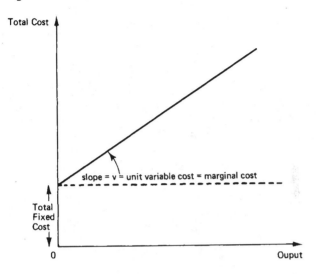

If we return to the neo-classical view of production with its attendant isoquants displaying factor substitution, but at increasing rates for the factor which has become excessive in relation to the proportion of other factors (Chapter 3, Section 3-2), we arrive at the law of diminishing returns which implies non-linear cost functions. Marginal cost then takes on values which depend upon the level of output and normally differs from unit or average variable cost. Let us now examine short run cost behaviour, in relation to the alternative views about production expressed in the previous chapter.

4-5   Short Run Cost Behaviour

First of all let us reconsider the neo-classical approach. If some factor inputs are held constant, it is possible to increase output (total physical product) by adjusting the variable inputs. However, at higher output levels, successive increments of the variable factors being about smaller and smaller increases in total product.* This is illustrated in Figure 4.2a.

---

*   In some representations of production theory, total product is assumed to *decline* after a certain point leading to the so-called 'irrational area of production'. We shall ignore this here but the interested reader may care to consult: Om. P. Tangri [146].

Figure 4.2 Product and Cost Behaviour

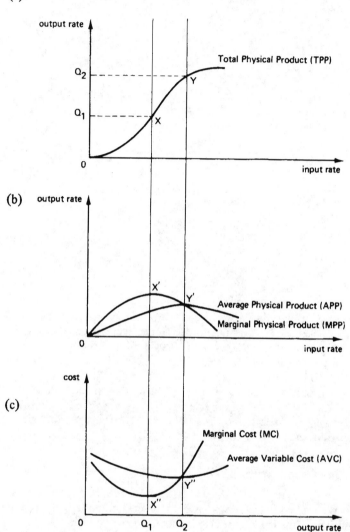

There is a point of inflexion at X in this diagram. (The slope of the function is increasing up to that point whereupon it starts to decrease.) This means that the marginal physical product increases up to that point, reaches its maximum at X in Figure 4.2b and then decreases. The point of inflexion X on the TPP curve and the maximum of the MPP curve X', thus occurs at the same input level. The law of diminishing returns is now in operation so that marginal physical product is falling and at some stage, average physical product will reach its maximum and then start to fall. Since average physical product is total physical product per unit of input, the input at which the maximum of average physical product occurs can be found either by inspection of the TPP curve or by calculus if the equation of the latter is known. Given this particular TPP curve, we find that average physical product reaches its maximum at point Y' in Figure 4.2b. This is also the point at which the MPP and APP curves intersect. This follows from the rule that when marginal exceeds average, the average is rising. When marginal is less than average, then the average is falling. Thus when marginal equals average, the latter is neither rising nor falling and so must be at its maximum or minimum.

In deriving the cost functions (Figure 4.2c) from these product functions, it is assumed that input markets are perfectly competitive so that each unit of input bears the same cost regardless of the total quantities of factors that the firm is buying. Marginal and average variable cost are defined with respect to units of output rather than input. The output axis in Figure 4.2c is not a uniform scale. It is determined by reference to the total product diagram (Figure 4.2a) where for any input level in that diagram we can easily read off the corresponding output level. Having set this scale, it is then apparent that the input-output combination where marginal physical product is at its maximum will result in minimum marginal cost. Similarly average variable cost will fall to its minimum at the input-output combination yielding maximum average physical product. It is not possible to infer anything about average total cost from the product function, without prior knowledge of the fixed costs of production. The ATC curve will lie above the AVC curve at a decreasing distance representing average fixed cost. It will reach its minimum at the point where marginal cost intersects it (see Figure 4.7).

In conclusion, neo-classical production theory predicts 'U-shaped' average and marginal cost curves in the short run. It follows that neo-classical production theory can be tested by observing the cost functions experienced in practice. If they are found to be 'U-shaped', some support will be lent to that theory.

Linear programming on the other hand as we have seen is built on the idea of processes with fixed technological coefficients. Costs

Figure 4.3 Constant Marginal Cost and Average Variable Cost with a Single Process

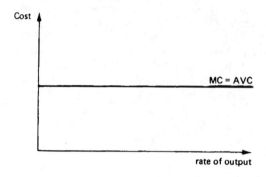

Figure 4.4 Marginal Cost and Average Variable Cost with Multiple Processes

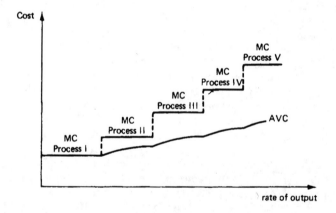

identified as fixed for the short period will still be fixed even if production accords more with this modern view than with the traditional, but the behaviour of marginal cost and average variable cost is entirely different. If only one process in involved, then marginal and average variable cost will be coincident (Figure 4.3). This would correspond to the cost function in Figure 4.1 where marginal and average variable cost are given as v, the slope of the total cost function. The reason for linearity under such circumstances is obvious. Each extra unit of output requires the same inputs as all preceding units, there being no scope for input substitution. If we retain our assumption about the insensitivity of input prices to the quantities purchased by the individual firm, then the linearity of cost functions immediately follows.

It is possible that more than one process is available and that the firm uses a mix of such processes. However, it would seem rational for the firm to use the least cost process initially and introduce higher cost processes when larger outputs are required. Marginal cost then rises in steps as the capacity of each process is reached and a move to the next cheapest one takes place (Figure 4.4). Average variable cost is coincident with marginal cost for the first process, but thereafter lies below it.

4-6 Long Run Cost Behaviour

Whether costs fall and then rise with the scale of operation or remain fairly constant depends to a large extent upon the presence of increasing and decreasing returns to scale on the one hand or constant returns to scale on the other. Increasing returns in the production function lead to falling unit costs and are thus a source of 'economies of scale'. However, increasing size may bring about other economies. B. Lloyd [81] has explored this subject in some depth, emphasising, in particular, internal economies and diseconomies but indicating at the same time that external economies are important too. The former refer to changes in cost conditions that a firm brings about directly through increasing its scale of production while the latter arise from factors in its external environment, in particular the size of the industry to which the firm belongs. External economies include savings in the cost of training skilled workers, the provision of educational facilities and infrastructure in terms of roads, rail and air links and other amenities.

However, it is with internal economies and diseconomies that we are concerned mainly, because an understanding of how a firm's development can influence its costs directly is of immense importance to managers. Following Lloyd let us first consider the question of *Large Dimensions*. We mentioned briefly in Chapter 3 that a vessel's capacity increases at a faster rate than the material used in its construction, because the latter is related to the surface area rather than the volume of the vessel. Consequently, construction costs rise at a smaller rate than the vessel's volume, thereby creating economies of scale. However beyond a certain size, stresses and strains will bring their own costs either directly or indirectly as foundations have to be strengthened and new problems arise which may involve substantial research costs. Eventually, these may exceed the benefits enjoyed and result in diseconomies of scale. Giant oil tankers apparently offer substantial benefits up to a point, but diseconomies seem to occur thereafter, with increased dangers of structural damage through stress in stormy weather and huge losses (both private and social), should collision occur. This has resulted in higher insurance costs, which together with increased charges for docking and storage, have counteracted many of the advantages of large scale oil transportation.

The law of multiples refers to indivisibilities which we have also mentioned earlier (in Chapter 3). Essentially this 'law' tells us that the smallest output for efficient combination of a number of machines is the lowest common multiple of their separate working capacities. Thus below a certain scale of production, inefficient combinations would be experienced, but with costs falling as scale increased. This could be a very important consideration if heavy capital outlays were involved in the acquisition of the larger capacity machines.

Economies from *massed reserves* arise from the need for proportionately fewer standby facilities when several similar machines are being used. The probability of every machine developing the same fault at the same time is in most instances negligible, fluctuations in output may offset each other, the more so the larger the firm becomes. In this context, diversification into a variety of products and markets often accompanies corporate growth and acts as a stabilising device. Except when the economy as a whole falls into a depression, the diversified firms can survive on smaller cash reserves on the assumption that losses in some activities will be offset by gains elsewhere. However, because of the increasing returns from specialisation we discussed in Chapter 3, it is apparent that greater diversification may not always bring the biggest cost savings. Diversification is perhaps best seen as a means of growth and the spreading of risks (see R. Marris [87] and J. Margolis [85]).

Management economies may occur through the employment of specialists in the many disciplines which contribute to management, or in the use of management techniques which are frequently computerised. Computerisation itself may bring economies in the automation of routine activities, and the provision of better information but a firm has to reach a certain size before a computer becomes economically viable. In fact computer rental and the occasional use of external management consultants may be the best options for the smaller company. Diseconomies of scale are often attributed to bureaucracy, the kind of impersonal organisational structure that a large company may breed.

The need for predictable and coordinated behaviour leads to a heavy reliance on controls which involve standard rules and procedures, often referred to as 'red tape', This kind of organisation is often slow to respond to change because of this reliance on standard responses and may fail to exploit new cost saving methods of operation. Administrative problems which often increase with size occupy more and more of the firm's time so that it may pay insufficient attention to strategic matters, i.e. the relationship between the firm and its environment. Departmental budgets tend to grow with one year's budget acting as a precedent for the next. Prestige projects are undertaken and empire building with over-staffing occurs, so that cost control becomes a nightmare.*

By-products and economy in the use of materials in general may offer advantages to a large company. What is waste to a small firm can become a source of profit to a large company particularly if the latter is diversified and can use the by-products of one process as the inputs of another. It is sometimes the case that useful by-products act as a motivating force for diversification, typically within the chemical and allied industries.

Purchasing and marketing economies arise through bulk buying, and the spreading of selling costs. The former effect is enhanced if a large firm also possesses monopolistic buying power but even if this is not the case, bulk buying is normally accompanied by quantity discounts and brings economy in the transportation of materials.

Handling and distribution economies can similarly be achieved in selling final products and the marketing of these can be more effective through national advertising in newspapers, periodicals and on the television.

Financial economies may occur through the spreading of the administrative costs of a new capital issue. In addition size often enhances a company's reputation so that it can borrow money at preferential interest rates. Moreover if the company is diversified so that it is less subject to risks in product markets, its overall cost of capital may be reduced (see Chapter 8 for an explanation of this concept). This however has not been confirmed empirically.

Changing technology may enhance the advantages of large scale production. Lloyd cites developments such as the steel strip-mill and the

---

* In part these tendencies reflect managerial control loss, but O. E. Williamson [157, 158] believes that managers prefer these expenditures since they offer managerial utility in the form of power, prestige and status

conveyor-assembly system in motor car manufacture among those favouring large size. He points to innovations which have had the reverse effect such as the electric motor which has provided a much more flexible source of power than the traditional sources like the steam engine; small electric power units can be used as effectively as larger units. Also the development of freight transport has seen the advance of the lorry rather than the railway, thus shifting the balance towards smaller enterprises in the transport industry.

Even if, on balance, technological change has provided the opportunity for exploiting economies rather than diseconomies of scale, the danger of inflexibility in highly capital intensive processes in only too apparent. This centres around the high output rates that are necessary, for the firm in such capital intensive industries, to break even. Even a small percentage drop in sales can take the firm into a loss making position, so alternative uses for the firm's capacity should be prepared in anticipation of any such event.

There are diseconomies other than those enumerated in conjunction with their corresponding economies of scale. The whole question of risk needs further elaboration. Admittedly the large diversified company can reduce its market risks, but in the absence of diversification, large scale almost inevitably brings increased risk. Any damage which occurs, through fire or some other catastrophe can be much more extensive when the plant is a large one. The risk of obsolescence is also substantial for a firm which has opted for a single large plant. In fact errors of managerial judgement, inaccuracy in forecasting, call it what you will, are far more crucial when major investment decisions are being contemplated. Finally, while in the long run all factors are in principle variable, in practice expansion often occurs with some factors remaining fixed by necessity. So long as land in a particular location or managerial skills or any other factor of production is unable to expand in supply as fast as the other inputs, returns will ultimately diminish.*

The long run average cost curve posited in economic theory is shown in Figure 4.5. This curve is U-shaped showing optimal scale at its minimum cost positions, but of course once the size of the plant is chosen, the scene is set for short period decisions which may involve average costs higher than those indicated by the LRAC curve. The short run cost curves can be entered into the diagram, and then the long run average cost curve is seen to be the envelope of the short run curves. The most important inference that can be made from this diagram is that under the circumstances to which this analysis applies, a firm operating to the left of the minimum point

---

* In a true long run, with *all* factors entirely variable, diminishing returns need never be experienced. It must be emphasised that the law of diminishing returns only applies to situations where the proportions of factor inputs change.

Figure 4.5   Long Run Average Cost as an Envelope of Short Run Average Cost Curves

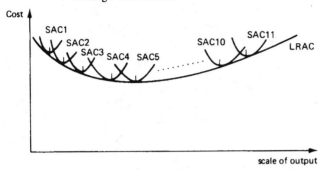

Figure 4.6   Long Run Average and Marginal Cost

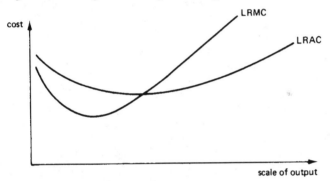

of the LRAC curve will typically be experiencing falling short run costs, but even so costs can be reduced more effectively by switching to a larger scale plant rather than by increasing output from the existing plant. There may therefore, be apparent excess capacity in firms of small scale in the sense that the output level for which the plant has been purchased will typically be lower than that at which minimum unit costs would be enjoyed. On the other hand, once a firm moves beyond the optimum scale plant (i.e. minimum LRAC), short run average costs will be rising. Costs can be saved by reducing output from the existing plant but not as much as by switching to correspondingly smaller plant. Thus if scale is larger than the optimum, firms may be observed to be operating with comparatively little spare capacity.

Every LRAC curve has a corresponding long run marginal cost curve (Figure 4.6). What the LRMC curve shows is the cost of increasing output at a given point by one unit assuming that the least cost combination of inputs (including capital equipment) is used to produce that unit. It is a particularly important concept in public policy towards industry in assessing what is a 'fair' price for a product bearing in mind the capital costs involved in production as well as the variable costs that would be included in short run marginal cost.

4-7 An Alternative View of Cost-Output Relationships

A. Alchian [2] has put forward a series of propositions designed to eliminate some of the 'ambiguities and errors' encountered in cost analysis. He points to three characteristics of output that affect the cost of a production operation.*

(1) The *rate* of output.
(2) Total contemplated *volume* of output.
(3) Programmed delivery *time schedule*.

Emphasis on the rate of output alone can bring misleading conclusions, but Alchian's propositions relate cost to *all* three output characteristics. We shall concentrate on the first five of his propositions which incorporate rate and volume characteristics.

Proposition 1 states that cost is proportional to the rate of production, so that for a given volume of output (and with delivery starting at a particular date) the faster the rate at which output is produced, the higher its cost.

Proposition 2 states that the incremental (marginal) cost is an increasing function of the output rate. Rising marginal cost is thus explained in terms of the rate of output increasing without an increase in the total planned volume of output; rather than in terms of variable proportion of inputs, which is the more usual explanation put forward in economic analysis.

Proposition 3 states that cost increases as the volume of output increases, for a given output rate (and initial date of delivery). This is self-explanatory.

Proposition 4 states that incremental (marginal) cost diminishes as planned colume increases, for any rate of output (and initial delivery date) so that successive increments in planned output add to total cost

---

* Cost is measured here in present value terms (see Chapter 8) and Alchian defines it as 'the change in equity caused by the performance of some specified operation'. However, the reader should be able to appreciate the significance of these propositions without prior knowledge of such concepts.

at a slower rate, provided that the other output characteristics remain unchanged. This implies that cost per unit of output decreases as planned volume increases, which is stated separately as *Proposition 5*.

These are the basic five propositions which Alchian subsequently expands. Staying with these for the moment we can use his arithmetic illustration for clarification, as portrayed in Table 4.1.

Table 4.1 Costs, Volume of Output and Rates of Output

Rate of Output x	Volume of Output V			
(per year)	1	2	3	4
1	100	180	255	325
2	120	195	265	330
3	145	215	280	340
4	175	240	300	355

Source: A. Alchian [2] p. 233.

Proposition 1 Hold V constant at say, V = 4. The faster this volume is produced the higher the cost of producing it, as is illustrated in the final column of Table 4.1.

Proposition 2 Again hold V constant at say, V = 4. As the output per year is increased from x = 1 to x = 2 incremental cost equals $330 − $325 = $5. Subsequent increments in cost are greater: $10 and $15 as output per year is increased from 2 to 3 and 3 to 4 respectively.

Proposition 3 Looking across any row in Table 4.1, it can be seen that cost increases as volume increases, holding the rate of output constant.

Proposition 4 Suppose the rate of output is held constant at x = 2, increments in cost are $(195 − 120) = $75, $(265 − 195) = $70 and $(330 − 265) = $65, as V increases from 1 to 2 to 3 to 4.

Proposition 5 which refers to cost per unit can be explained with the aid of any row in the table. Again let us take x = 2.
The cost of producing:—

  1 unit in total is $120 hence average cost = $120
  2 units in total is $195 hence average cost = $97.5
  3 units in total is $265 hence average cost = $88.33
  4 units in total is $330 hence average cost = $82.5 .

Alchian believes that economies of scale are best explained as the lower cost resulting from a larger planned volume. Economic analysis is sometimes ambiguous as to what 'scale' means and frequently we see it portrayed in terms of rate of output rather than total planned volume. The explanation for propositions 4 and 5 lies in the method of production — a larger planned volume is produced in a different way from that of a smaller one, the former usually involving more durable productive facilities. Alchian, however, is rather noncommittal about why increased expenditure on more durable equipment should result in a greater than proportional increase of output. He says that it 'is a question that cannot be answered, except to say that the physical principles of the real world are not all linear (which may or may not be the same thing as "indivisible")' ([2] p. 235).* The alleged phenomenon of rising marginal cost in the short run is seen here as a reflection of increased *rate* of output. However, in any planning period, short or long, it is possible to vary the planned volume of output, for example through changing batch or lot size. In refuting the principle of rising marginal cost (e.g. in linear programming protrayals of single process situations) it therefore seems necessary to state formally whether it is the rate or planned volume that is variable. Perhaps the lesson of the programming approach to production is that the extent to which rate of output is variable may be slight when modern productive processes are involved.**

4-8 Avoidable and Opportunity Costs

The golden rule for testing a proposal, given resource scarcity, involves two main questions:

> (1)   What are the costs of acquiring the necessary inputs against the value of the resultant outputs, and thus the 'contribution' of the proposal?
>
> (2)   What is the cost of committing the resources already owned by the company to this specific proposal?

It is only if the 'contribution' revealed at Stage I is sufficiently large to offset the costs measured at Stage II that the decision is worthwhile — yielding an economic profit.

The first stage involves marginal analysis or incremental analysis, the former term being restricted to decisions where changes of one unit (of output) are contemplated. What one is doing here is to compare the extra costs against the extra revenues. Sometimes it is easier to detect these marginal or incremental costs by looking at the problem from a different angle. Instead of trying to classify costs into direct/indirect or variable/fixed (the latter requiring a distinction between the short and

---

*   The page number refers to the reprinted article in H. Townsend: *Price Theory*, Penguin, 1971.

** Changing the *mix* of distinct processes may enable the overall rate of production to be changed.

long run), we can simply identify for the decision under consideration which costs are avoidable and which non-avoidable.

The incremental or marginal cost, whether for a short or long run decision, can be determined by finding what will be saved or avoided if the company does nothing rather than implement the decision. The reason for preferring the concept of 'avoidable cost' is its applicability to all levels of decision. It eliminates the possibility of the economist being misunderstood because the statement 'economists advocate marginal costing' is often interpreted by businessmen and accountants as meaning, 'economists make no allowance for fixed or overhead costs'. In fact avoidable cost can include any of the categories identified above in Section 4-2.

'Fixed factory overhead' is, of course, only 'fixed' in a short run sense. If we were to say that in the long run fixed factory overhead is variable, we would be accused of a self contradiction. We can however state without fear of being misunderstood, that in the long run, fixed factory overhead is avoidable. This simply means that the total depreciation, or the capital outlay on a piece of machinery for example, would be zero if the company decided not to replace that machine once its useful life was over. That, however, would be a long term consideration. In the short run by way of contrast, the firm is endowed with equipment purchased in earlier periods and the costs sunk in that machinery cannot be avoided. In deciding whether or not to use machinery in the short run, it is therefore, futile to include depreciation as a cost, but when making a long run decision — e.g. whether or not to replace a piece of machinery — it is vital that the total cost of acquiring that machine be considered.*

If we now move to the second part of the 'golden rule', we see that even if we are not going to include costs like depreciation, other fixed overheads or indeed any fixed costs in short run computations, it is still necessary to ask what the company is sacrificing by committing the resources it already owns to a specific use. It is here that the economist's concept of 'opportunity cost' becomes invaluable. Strictly speaking all costs to an economist should be regarded as opportunity costs, i.e. avoidable costs too should be measured on an opportunity cost basis.** Let us for the moment, however, concentrate on the opportunity cost of using resources already acquired. The opportunity cost principle may be stated as follows: the sacrifice involved in committing resources to a

---

* Replacement is a type of investment decision, see Chapter 8.
** The opportunity cost of material bought on the market and used immediately in the production process is simply its purchase price, since that is the price it would command in any alternative use. However, the opportunity cost of using material from stock may differ from original purchase price as we shall see shortly.

particular opportunity is the return or benefit foregone on the best alternative opportunity thereby displaced.

The way in which this would operate in practice can be illustrated by reference to the example used in Chapter 1 where we first introduced these concepts. Here we assumed that the factory was working at full capacity, so that in order to release production time for a new product Y, the rate of output of the existing product, X, would have to be reduced. The cost of releasing resources in this way is *not* some proportion of the fixed factory overheads. These are already being incurred and the production of Y makes no difference to them. The true cost of using the factory time is the contribution to profit foregone by reducing the output of product X. This was seen to be £2,500 which had to be offset against the contribution of £4,500 arising from the proposed production of Y.

The opportunity cost of productive facilities may in some circumstances be zero. If there is spare capacity and there are no competing alternatives for consideration, then no opportunities are being displaced and therefore, opportunity cost is zero. A decision involving the utilisation of this capacity would then rest on the first stage only — avoidable cost of inputs to be acquired against incremental revenue. The validity of this approach can be seen in the following example:

A factory incurs fixed costs of £20,800 per year which averages out to £400 per week. Under normal circumstances it is in operation for 50 hours per week. At present, however, it is only being used for 20 hours per week because of a fall in demand for the company's major product. Only one prospect for using this spare capacity emerges. This is a new product, requiring 20 hours production time per week and additional inputs (labour, materials and other facilities) which must be hired or purchased at a cost of £200 per week. Proceeds from the sale of this product would amount to £300 per week.

To test the viability of this prospect, we first of all compare incremental (avoidable) cost against incremental revenue. The only avoidable costs are the £200 for additional inputs since the fixed costs will be incurred regardless. Incremental revenue is £300 — this is something the firm will enjoy over and above the revenue it currently earns. The contribution from the proposal is therefore (£300 − £200) = £100 per week. The second step is to look for displaced opportunities, but since this is the only prospect to emerge and it only required 20 hours production time each week, there is no displacement at all. Hence opportunity cost is zero. The proposal is therefore viable on the basis of the first stage. The firm will be £100 better off by accepting it.

There is no disputing the logic of this once we have identified the fixed costs as non-avoidable in the short run. However, conventional cost accounting procedure — so called 'absorption costing' (see C. T.

Horngren [59]) assesses a product's costs to include an allowance for overheads usually levied as an hourly rate. This means that the fixed costs within the overheads will be included in the product's cost. In the present example, the fixed costs of £400 per week could be charged out at £8.00 per hour based on normal utilisation of 50 hours per week.* Under normal circumstances, such a charge would 'absorb' the fixed costs.

The new product which would occupy the factory for 20 hours a week might be costed as follows:—

Variable costs	£200	
Fixed costs	£160	(i.e. 20 hours at £8.00 per hour)
Total cost	£360	

If this figure of £360 were used to test the proposal by comparing it with the revenue of £300, an apparent loss of £60 would be revealed. The error arises from a failure to distinguish between avoidable and non-avoidable costs. The reason for using an absorption costing approach might not be readily understood given this danger of drawing mistaken conclusions as we have illustrated here. However, it is still widely used in the firm's control system. Its usefulness stems from its ability to impute all the firm's costs to individual products, even if this does involve arbitrary allocation and apportionment of indirect costs. We say that such allocations and apportionments are arbitrary because there is no way of telling what proportion of cost is chargeable to each product when joint production or production with shared facilities occurs. Accountants use a variety of apportionment methods for overheads, such as relative direct labour charges, machine time, sales volumes, etc. In a multi-product enterprise it is desirable to have a yardstick by which individual products or product groups can be compared for profitability and this can be done with absorption costing once the sales revenue for each product is known. Some firms even use the cost of the product calculated on an absorption basis as a means of working out prices (see Chapter 7).

However useful this procedure might be within the firm's control system, as a signal of declining profitability within a product group for example, it is becoming increasingly accepted that decisions are better made on a 'contribution' costing basis. Contribution costing uses variable or direct costs and control takes place by observing the contribution — i.e. unit selling price less unit variable cost (or direct cost). As more firms switch to this method, the economist's approach to

---

* Other bases for apportionment can be used — e.g. labour hours, floor space, sales revenue.

decision making will be facilitated.

Standard costing may be used in conjunction either with absorption or contribution costing. It is an attempt to establish what is normal or standard over a given period of time in terms of input costs, speed of production, output per period, etc. Standard cost is then calculated as the unit cost of a product given these conditions. When actual cost differs from standard cost, a variance is said to occur and this can be subdivided into material cost variance, labour cost variance and so on. Favourable variances (actual costs lower than standard) are explained as far as possible in an attempt to detect factors conducive to efficiency. More attention, however, is usually paid to unfavourable variances (actual costs exceed standard) so that corrective action can be taken.

Let us now briefly examine how costs should be interpreted in the long run.* First of all a capacity filling operation such as we have described above may be all very well as a short term expedient but one could not justify the replacement of a factory, or the construction of a new one, without assessing all the costs involved. While in the short run fixed costs might be non-avoidable given the existence of a factory already in production, in the very long run all the firm's costs can be avoided. Avoidable cost in the long run therefore includes far more components than in the short run. A long term project's viability or indeed the viability of the whole enterprise cannot therefore be appraised on the basis of short run variable costs.

How does the opportunity cost argument apply in the long run? When we have detected the avoidable costs (Stage I), we shall already have allowed for the costs of acquiring productive facilities. Stage II of the golden rule only applies to resources already owned. In the long run this is restricted largely to financial resources, and the opportunity cost of using these is the return that could be obtained in the best comparable use. In other words, investments that are only justified if they earn the same return that firms operating in similar markets and subject to similar risks are earning on their investments. Indeed rational shareholders would refuse to buy more stock in a company unable to provide such a rate of return. In Chapter 8 we shall see how the opportunity cost of using financial resources is involved when appraising investments. It is generally referred to as the 'cost of capital'.

4-9 Inventory Valuation

One of the problems in calculating material costs is that frequently material is drawn from stock rather than purchased directly for a

---

* The whole subject of investment appraisal is given extensive treatment in Chapter 8.

particular job. Direct purchases are simple to deal with; the avoidable cost is simply the total purchase price that has to be paid. The opportunity cost doctrine causes no complication in this instance, since when there is a market price for a commodity, this is the price it commands whatever its final use may be. The cost accountant has no such unequivocal figure to offer for the cost of material drawn from stock. He may quote the 'standard' figure which would reflect the expectation of material prices at the time that the standards for the costing system were agreed. In a time of stable prices this may well be the same as the current price, particularly if the standards are updated regularly. On the other hand, in periods of rapid inflation of raw material prices such as were experienced in the early 1950s at the time of the Korean War and more recently in the years 1972-4, standard prices rapidly become outdated.

Companies not using standard costing, value their stocks in a variety of ways and this influences the calculation of cost. The 'first in first out' method of valuation (FIFO) assumes that the earliest acquired stock is used first. The apparent cost of materials drawn from stock is thus historical cost, and in periods of inflation this may be substantially below current cost. 'Last in first out' (LIFO) too is based on historical cost but here the history is more recent; the apparent cost of materials drawn from stock being the price paid for the latest purchases. As compared to FIFO, the adoption of LIFO results in higher estimated costs and consequently a lower reported profit during inflationary times. Another possibility is a weighted average method of valuation which is based on an estimation of the total historical cost paid for the material from which the average unit price can be calculated.

Economists prefer a less widely adopted approach, namely 'next in first out' (NIFO). In other words they are in favour of replacement cost. The reason for this is easily appreciated in the light of our golden rule for decisions and it applies whether the material is immediately replaced or not. Suppose firstly that the material if used would be immediately replaced. The avoidable cost as measured at Stage I is then the money that would be saved if no material were used. This is the replacement cost. Stage II is not invoked since the inventory remains intact as a result of immediate replacement. Now imagine that inventory is not to be restored, at least for the time being. The avoidable cost of material is nil since there will be no difference in monetary outlays on this item whether the firm decides to use it or not. Stage II is invoked here, however, since stock depletion occurs if the decision to use material is implemented. Applying the opportunity cost principle we find that its value in the best alternative use* is what other users

---

* There may in some instances be no alternative use, for example components purchased for a specific purpose or part-finished goods, i.e. work in

would be prepared to pay for it in the market. This is the same figure as the replacement cost. It is therefore essential to check the method of inventory valuation before relying on any material cost figure for evaluation purposes in decision making.

The whole question of income measurement and inventory valuations is an important one in this inflationary age. The formula for calculating taxable profit in the UK does not permit replacement costing. Essentially the costs that go into the calculations are the expenditures actually incurred, i.e. they are historical costs. Suppose a company is suffering from cost increases, and as is customary in many industries, passes these increases on to the consumer. An example of this in 1974, was the huge increase in crude oil prices which inevitably resulted in price increases for petroleum and other oil-based products. Any crude oil in stock which was bought at the old price and subsequently processed into final products selling at the new prices would yield an apparent windfall profit to the company. Some commentators argued that companies had benefited and that one should tax this windfall profit like any other profit that a company meakes. On the other hand the sudden jump in oil prices created additional financing needs for oil companies, because the new stock acquired at the increased price reduced the cash flow, thus calling for tax relief.

Companies of all types have found that as a result of inflation, they have had to pay increased corporation taxes at the same time as their financing needs, as measured by replacement cost of inventories and bigger wage bills have been rising. Moreover the cost of replacing equipment tends to increase over time, but depreciation (see the next section) is also based on historical cost for tax assessment purposes.

There is growing demand for reform in accounting systems in order to rectify the anomalies created by inflation. In any new system, it would be desirable for the cost of goods sold figure to be expressed in the same purchasing power terms as the sales figure against which it will be matched. This would involve indexation, or replacement costing of labour, materials and overheads, including depreciation in order to take account of the rising cost of assets.*

4-10 Depreciation

Depreciation is simply a method of spreading the cost of an asset over its useful working life in the accounts of a company, so as to present a

---

    progress. The relevant cost for decision making does then depend on whether stocks are to be replenished. In the case of obsolete components, i.e. no replenishment of stock and no alternative use, their true cost is zero so far as the decision maker is concerned.

* The whole subject of inflation accounting is well documented elsewhere. See, for example, P. R. A. Kirkham [68].

realistic picture of its financial position. This prevents a major capital programme from apparently causing a sudden drop in the financial wellbeing of the company. Companies depreciate their assets either on a 'straight-line' or a 'reducing-balance' method. The former calculates depreciation as a constant sum each year while the latter imputes a higher figure in the earlier years, falling gradually over time. Reducing-balance is probably more in line with market valuation since where assets are resaleable, the largest drop in value normally occurs in the first year.

At the time of writing, the total cost of a capital project can be included in the company's accounts pertaining to the first year of its life, for tax assessment purposes.* This has the virtue of enabling tax relief to be enjoyed when investment takes place and perhaps acts as an inducement to invest. Depreciation, however apportioned year by year, is limited to the historical cost. A system of accounting for inflation might allow depreciation at replacement cost so as to reduce corporation tax payments and permit firms to retain sufficient funds to meet the anticipated higher cost of new equipment when existing facilities wear out.

Economists are dubious about the validity of the accounting concept of depreciation, particularly if calculated according to an arbitrary formula such as straight line. The economic valuation of an asset is the future discounted benefit or income generated by that project over its useful life. Depreciation of an asset is then the fall in the asset's value so measured per period of time. Economic depreciation is therefore a forward looking concept whereas traditional accounting uses historical cost as the basis. Furthermore, in the short term, economists would only look at the part of depreciation which depends on the use to which the asset is put. This is the 'user cost' which compares the value of an asset at the end of a period of specific use with the value of the asset had it not been used during that period. There are many examples of user cost. If a machine is used instead of leaving it idle, its life may be shortened and consequently its economic value as measured by the (discounted) stream of future benefits. Using a machine may cause future maintenance costs to rise and it may even cause deterioration

---

* Under the 1972 Finance Act, firms throughout the country can benefit from free depreciation in the form of 100 per cent first year allowances; any capital expenditure on plant and machinery (though not on passenger cars), either new or secondhand, may be completely written off for tax purposes against profits in the year in which it is incurred. In addition accelerated depreciation is allowed for industrial buildings, which benefit from an initial allowance of 40 per cent and an annual allowance of 4 per cent. The company can choose to depreciate its assets, over a longer period in its internal accounts if it wishes.

which renders it unsuitable for some jobs it would otherwise have been capable of doing. The fall in value to the owner of the machine will also be reflected in the valuation by other potential owners so that market values may give some indication of user cost whenever comparisons of machines of different production experiences is possible.

In the long run the economist prefers to look at the whole life span of the project so that accounting apportionments into individual years are not necessary. The only part that depreciation plays in investment is in the computation of the tax bill. This point is illustrated further in Chapter 8.

4-11 Linear Programming and Shadow Prices

We now wish to introduce the linear programming techniques we developed in Chapter 3 into our discussion of costs — particularly opportunity costs. Recall that in the product-mix decision we analysed, linear programming techniques enabled us to indicate the optimal output of each product which could be made within a given set of constraints. However the information in the simplex tableau conveys rather more than just the optimal solution. It is also possible to find the opportunity cost of using the firm's productive resources and hence estimate the desirability of introducing a new activity.

Suppose that initially the firm is producing two outputs X and Y. These have the usual programming properties of constant contributions per unit produced and also fixed coefficients with regard to the use of the non-specialised factors (shared productive facilities) of which there are three in this example. X yields a unit contribution of £5 and requires production time per unit of 6 hours in machine A, 4 hours in machine B, but does not require any processing in machine C. The corresponding details of product Y are £4 contribution with 9, 3 and 1 as the numbers of hours production times per unit in each machine. The available production time for machine A each week is 54 hours while B and C have availabilities of 24 hours and 5 hours respectively.*
Writing x and y as the number of units of X and Y and S_1, S_2 and S_3 as the slack variables for machines A, B and C respectively, we have initial and final simplex tableaux as in Table 4.2a (Z is the total profit contribution = $5x + 4y$).** This shows that the optimal output combination (for profit) is 3 units of X per week, 4 units of Y per week, yielding a total weekly contribution of £31.

Let us note that we have solved the problem according to the economist's criteria:

---

*   Resource limitations mean that this is a short run decision.
**   We have omitted the intermediate stages.

Table 4.2a Initial and Final Simplex Tables for Outputs X and Y

		x	y	S_1	S_2	S_3	Z	
Initial	A	6	9	①	0	0	0	54
	B	4	3	0	①	0	0	24
	C	0	1	0	0	①	0	5
	Z	−5	−4	0	0	0	①	0
Final	A	0	①	$+2/9$	$-1/3$	0	0	4
	B	①	0	$-1/6$	$+1/2$	0	0	3
	C	0	0	$-2/9$	$+1/3$	①	0	1
	Z	0	0	$+1/18$	$+7/6$	0	①	31

(a) Avoidable cost has been compared with incremental revenue through the inclusion of the contribution figures and the exclusion of short run fixed costs.

(b) The final tableau shows that no further profit can be achieved by changing the output of X and Y (zero Z row values for x and y columns). If these two products are the only opportunities competing for the productive facilities, the solution is optimal as already stated. Opportunity costs have been used implicitly in reaching this solution by incorporating details of the relative machine times, required by X and Y and their relative contributions.

The coefficients of 1/18, 7/6 and 0, for S_1, S_2 and S_3 respectively in that row, represent the 'shadow prices' or the opportunity costs of using machines A, B and C. These figures mean that if a new venture were to become available, each hour of machine A's time used in that venture would reduce profits by £1/18, each hour of machine B's time used would reduce profits by £7/6, while each hour of machine C's time would be costless, at least so long as there is spare capacity.

One result which follows immediately is that if some new use for the productive facilities came along that required all the available production time, the opportunity costs would be £31 — i.e. the contribution earned at the optimal solution:

Machine A 54 hours @ a shadow price of £1/18 = £ 3
Machine B 24 hours @ a shadow price of £7/6   = £28
Machine C   5 hours @ a shadow price of £0   = £ 0
                    Total opportunity cost   = £31

We can also appraise any new venture which uses part of the production time. Suppose a product M requires

     6 hours in machine A for each unit produced
     1 hour in machine B for each unit produced
and ½ hour in machine C for each unit produced.

In deciding whether to adopt this proposal we first need to consider avoidable cost against incremental revenue, and let us suppose that the unit contribution so calculated is £2. Secondly we require the unit opportunity cost of using the productive facilities.

Machine A 6 hours @ a shadow price of £1/18 = £1/3
Machine B 1 hour @ a shadow price of £7/6   = £7/6
Machine C ½ hour @ a shadow price of £0   = £0
                    Unit opportunity cost   = £1½

The unit opportunity cost of £1½ must be set against the unit contribution of £2 so that each unit of M would add £½ to the existing profit of £31. We can see the impact of this new product by drawing up a new simplex tableau (Table 4.2b) with m as the weekly output of product M. The optimal solution is:

$m = 4$
$x = 5$
$y = 0$

with a total contribution of £33. The 4 units of M have therefore increased the total contribution by £2 as predicted above (4 units @ £½ per unit). Even though further analysis was necessary to determine the total impact of M on the production system, the shadow prices enabled us to find rapidly that the introduction of this new product was worthwhile. Note that in the final tableau (Table 4.2b) we have a new set of shadow prices which we could use to asses the result of any departture from the new optimal solution. Machine C still has spare capacity and a shadow price of 0. Observe too that every unit of Y reintroduced would reduce profit by £½ (the Z row coefficient of y).

Table 4.2b   Introduction of Product M

	x	y	m	S_1	S_2	S_3	Z	
Initial A	6	9	6	①	0	0	0	54
B	4	3	1	0	①	0	0	24
C	0	1	½	0	0	①	0	5
Z	−5	−4	−2	0	0	0	①	0
Final A	0	+1	①	$+^2/_9$	$-^1/_3$	0	0	4
B	①	$+^1/_2$	0	$-^1/_{18}$	$+^1/_3$	0	0	5
C	0	$+^1/_2$	0	$-^1/_9$	$+^1/_6$	①	0	3
Z	0	$+^1/_2$	0	$+^1/_6$	1	0	①	33

4-12   The Primal and the Dual

The shadow prices obtained from the Z row of the final tableau are the solution to what is known as the 'dual' problem. The normal simplex representation is the 'primal' problem and every primal has a dual.

Let us imagine that in the product-mix problem above where just X and Y are being manufactured, that you have to buy machine time by the hour. The entrepreneur who hires out the machines has not yet agreed charges with you, but he knows that you are making £5 unit contribution from X and £4 from Y. He decides to let you fix your own hourly machine rates so long as he receives at least £5 per unit of X produced and £4 per unit of Y produced. This is hardly a worthwhile proposition from your point of view, since it will swallow up all your profit, but assuming that you are determined to stay in production, the best you can do is to work out charges so as to minimise your total payments to this entrepreneur.

If we let p_1, p_2 and p_3 be the hourly rates you agree for machines A, B and C respectively, the entrepreneur's conditions may be written as:

$$6p_1 + 4p_2 + 0p_3 \geqslant 5$$
$$9p_1 + 3p_2 + 1p_3 \geqslant 4$$

(i.e. total charges are at least equal to the contributions earned).

Your objective is of course to pay the least possible so you minimise:

$$C = 54p_1 + 24p_2 + 5p_3 \quad \text{subject to the constraints above.}$$

This is the *dual* problem and its relationship to the *primal* (Table 4.2a) is readily apparent for it can be shown that the optimal solution to the dual is $p_1 = £1/18$, $p_2 = £7/6$, $p_3 = £0$ (by using the simplex method with the preliminary phase). These are the shadow prices for machines A, B and C respectively in the optimal solution to the primal. Both primal and dual have the same solution, namely Z or C = £31. This is an important result because it means amongst other things that we have a choice of approaches in solving a problem. In some instances the dual might be more easily solved than the primal.*

The problem of the fictitious entrepreneur may not provide a very convincing justification for the calculation of shadow prices. Nevertheless we can readily appreciate that if some new opportunity for production comes up for consideration, and it requires inputs of our scarce factors, then the true cost of using the latter are the shadow prices in the optimal primal or the optimal values in the dual. We shall see in Chapter 7 that shadow prices have an important application in the computation of minimum acceptable selling prices of final products and also for intermediate products being 'sold' by one division of a company to another division of the same company. However, all such computations presuppose a knowledge of cost behaviour and it is now time to look at the techniques available for revealing this.

4-12 Empirical Cost Analysis

Firms need cost estimates for a variety of purposes. On a recurrent basis they require such information for budgeting, production planning and pricing, and on a non-recurrent basis they require this information for investment and other strategic decisions. In approaching the question of the relationship between costs and output we can conveniently divide the analysis into the short and long run where to recapitulate we are referring to the *short* run as a period of time during which there is one or more input which cannot be varied (i.e. fixed factor(s)) whereas in the *long* run, firms can vary most inputs and therefore we are concerned with scale properties.

The economist in approaching empirical cost analysis is perhaps more interested to know whether the hypotheses he has put forward in

---

* If the imaginary problem, where the entrepreneur sells production time, were our main primal problem, the easiest way to solve this manually would not be the Simplex method with preliminary phase, but the Simplex method on the problem's dual (i.e. the original product-mix problem solved for x and y).

microeconomic theory about costs and output (the 'U-shaped' AC curve for instance) are confirmed in practice. The businessman, however, is interested to know how his costs will change for any contemplated change in output rate. The difficulty here is that the two-dimensional relationship between costs and output rates is insufficient in practice as there are many other considerations, particularly in the long run. For example, A. Alchian [2] as we showed in Section 4-7, explains that the total planned volume of output and the programmed delivery time schedule are considerations that need to be borne in mind as well as the rate of output, particularly in reference to the long run. A further complication is that the firm may in practice be a multiple plant concern while neo-classical theory proceeds on the basis of a single-product plant firm where the distinction does not matter. As soon as we allow for multi-product and multi-plant firms then the investigator must be clear as to whether he is carrying out studies which relate to firms on the one hand or plants on the other.

Short Run Cost Analysis

We have illustrated in Section 4-5 that the economist argues in neo-classical theory that changes in output in the short run will cause changes in factor proportions so that the marginal product will eventually decline as more and more variable inputs (at constant prices) are applied to a fixed input. Because we are assuming the divisibility of variable factor inputs, the total cost curves of the firm are smooth and continuously differentiable with respect to the rate of output to produce the marginal cost curve. The falling marginal product is accompanied by rising marginal cost and in Figure 4.7 we utilise a similar diagram to Figure 4.2c except that instead of an AVC curve we have drawn a short run average total cost (SRAC) curve, which includes fixed costs per unit as well as variable costs.

Figure 4.7   Short Run Cost Curves

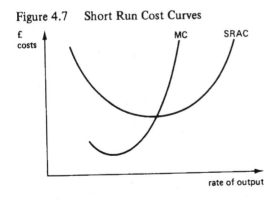

The SRAC curve is assumed to be 'U-shaped' for the reasons discussed earlier, however the empirical evidence (which we shall summarise later in this section) is suggestive of the SRAC curve being non-symmetrical but skewed with the minimum level of AC occurring when the plant is around the capacity level. It may of course be that the AC curve flattens out until capacity working is achieved (see Figure 4.8), at which point it will then become vertical. Another alternative is that before capacity is reached AC starts to rise as the firm finds, for instance, that breakdowns increase. Much really depends upon the definition of capacity (see A. D. Knox [71]). One view is that capacity represents the point where the plant is working twenty-four hours a day, seven days a week. However the practicable capacity level occurs when allowances have been made for breakdowns, works holidays and so on. Capacity is therefore defined in terms of some constraint or bottleneck which prevents the rate of production from increasing beyond a certain point. The classical definition given in economic analysis, namely the output at which short run average total cost falls to its minimum, is not appropriate. For if the programming view of production is followed, there is a distinct possibility that the short run average cost curve will gradually flatten, rather than bottom out over the range of feasible output rates.

Figure 4.8   The 'L-Shaped' AC Curve

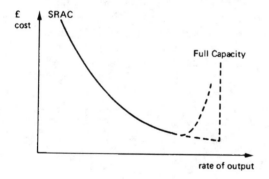

What methods then can be used to determine how costs will vary as the rate of output changes? For short run cost functions there are three methods — intuition, statistical analysis and the engineering approach.

The Intuitive Approach

The firm may rely on the accountant's experience and judgement to determine the short run cost function. Typically he would take a simplistic view and regard total cost as a linear function of output (see Figure 4.1). His task then would be to estimate total cost for at least two output rates and then connect these by a straight line. The intercept then would give the value of total fixed cost per period and the slope would show the average variable cost or marginal cost. From a knowledge of these values, he could then derive the average total cost function.

Statistical Analysis

The statistical approach relies on historical cost data which are not always appropriate given that decision makers require information about how costs *will* behave as output changes, i.e. managers require *ex-ante* rather than *ex-post* data on which to base their decisions. An individual firm could use the statistical approach by referring to its records of cost, and producing time-series data of costs against output from which it could detect the underlying relationship. If a sample of firms is being analysed, cross-section data can be employed as well as time-series. Any such inter-firm comparison should only include firms employing similar technology and scale of plant so that the differences between firms in the sample are restricted, as far as possible, to the rate of output and cost of producing that output. In both cross-section and time-series investigations, problems of measurement exist. This is particularly relevant to multi-product firms where the researcher must choose a common measure of output, and also tackle the problem of how joint costs are allocated to product lines. When we are comparing the costs and output of one firm with those of another then the problem is even more acute as accounting practices will differ, for example, in their treatment of depreciation, material drawn from stock, and so on. Even if we can satisfactorily overcome these problems we have the added difficulty in time-series analysis of changing price levels and changes in scale that have occurred in the past, although all these problems with the exception of changing scale are more serious when we are employing statistical analysis for detecting and measuring scale economies, a subject to which we shall return later in this section.

The technique used in statistical cost analysis is regression analysis but as we illustrate in Chapter 5 when we discuss attempts to estimate demand functions, there is a built-in bias towards linearity in that the basic technique available is *linear* regression. In a straightforward two variable case, e.g. cost against output, linear regression would involve plotting the data derived either on a cross-section or time-series basis, on a graph showing cost as a function of output.

The problem is particularly acute in short run analysis where the normal practice is to plot total cost against output, deducing the average and marginal curves from the total. It would take a substantial departure from linearity for the uninitiated to attempt to draw anything other than a straight line through the ensuing scatter diagram. Statisticians specialising in the estimation of economic relationships, known as *econometricians*, are only too well aware of this pitfall and before pronouncing any relationship as linear always subject it to a variety of tests to ensure that a straight line is in fact the best fit to the data.

Engineering Approach

The third main approach is to use engineering estimates. Unlike the statistical approach which relies heavily on costs actually experienced, the engineering approach is akin to a controlled experiment to derive estimates of what costs would be at alternative levels of output, some of which may never have been experienced. This method presupposes a knowledge of the firm's production function in that the engineer must be able to predict the usage of inputs if he is to be able to predict cost at any output. Again there is the danger that an assumption of a simple production function (with fixed technological coefficients and constant returns to scale) might be used to predict a linear cost function, when the underlying relationship is in reality more complex. Multiple production complicates this estimation method in the same way that it complicates the statistical method, since as we have seen it is virtually impossible to apportion joint cases unequivocally.

The method has the distinct advantage of not using historical data and therefore does not suffer from the problems of having to isolate the separate influences in time-series, but G. J. Stigler [141] points out that the engineering method may overemphasise the plant-cost relationship and neglect the overall contribution of the management of the firm particularly in multi-product firms.

The Empirical Evidence

It is not possible to detail any empirical evidence on the intuitive approach to the short run cost functions because by its very nature it relies very much on the accountant within the particular firm. However, published studies are available involving the other two methods. Statistical cost analysis has been used to estimate cost-output relationships in electricity generation, steel production, passenger transport, food processing and the retail industry, to mention but a few of the applications. The engineering approach has also been used to examine costs in steel production and in a number of other industries. We shall briefly examine just a few of these studies including those of J. Johnston [66] and T. O. Yntema [161] as examples of statistical analysis, and the

C. F. Pratten and R. M. Dean [114] study as an example of the engineering approach.

T. O. Yntema's study of short run cost-output relationships in the United States Steel Corporation dates from 1940. It is based on annual data (time-series) over the period 1927-38, during which annual rates of operation had varied between 17.7 and 90.4 per cent of ingot capacity. Costs were adjusted first for factor price changes by standardising in terms of 1938 prices, and second for the downward trend in costs in relation to volume over the time period under consideration. The *total* output of the Corporation (though produced at several plants using different processes) was compared, after appropriate weighting, with total production costs adjusted as described, and the equation of best fit obtained by least-squares regression was linear and of the form:

$$Y_t = 182,100,000 + 55.73X$$

where Y_t = total cost in dollars, X = weighted output in tons.

The constant term, 182,100,000 represents the fixed costs and the coefficient of X is the MC of a (weighted) ton shipped. The Yntema analysis has led many commentators to argue that short run marginal costs are constant in steel production over the wide range of capacity utilisation experienced in the above period and that it lends no support to the U-shape hypothesis of conventional theory. Yntema's analysis was, however, criticised by C. A. Smith [135] who alleged that the former's methods of data manipulation imparted linear bias to the results. This criticism, however, has not substantially lessened the confidence placed on Yntema's results by other commentators.

J. Johnston [66] also used statistical analysis to examine the short run cost output relationship in electricity generation. Regressions were applied to data from a sample of 17 undertakings over the years 1927-47. The size of capital equipment employed by these undertakings remained constant throughout the period. The unit of output in electricity generation is the kilowatt hour, and working costs consisted of: fuel cost to include delivery and handling charges; salaries and wages for operating staff; repairs and maintenance, oil, water and stores including appropriate wages and salaries. These 'working' costs were primarily variable, though some fixed or semi-fixed components may have arisen, for example, in maintenance costs and fuel costs given that a certain amount of fuel would be necessary to keep the plant banked ready for operation. The 17 regressions in general gave a good fit to the data. In 10 of these, more than 95 per cent of the variance in the cost data was explained. Correlation was high in all cases, on average 0.966 with no instance of the correlation coefficient falling below 0.9 and Johnston's conclusion was that linear functions gave a good fit to the data and supported the thesis of linear total cost with constant average variable cost and marginal cost functions. Marginal cost was not estimated but the evidence was consistent with fairly constant marginal cost over the range 75-90 per cent of capacity operation, but with a possible increase between 90 and 100 per cent.

As an illustration of engineering approach we shall cite the study of Pratten and Dean in their analysis of short run cost-output relations in the UK steel industry. Estimates were made over the range of 75 to 100 per cent of capacity using both published and confidential information from British steel companies. It was plant based rather than a company based study. Wages and salaries were regarded as a fixed cost because of the tight labour market facing the postwar UK steel industry, and materials, fuel and power, were regarded as the principle variable costs. Average production costs were estimated as shown in Table 4.3 and it would appear that unit costs decline as output increases in this range, although at a reducing rate above 90 per cent capacity operation.

Table 4.3   Short Run Costs and the Level of Capacity Working

Level of Working (%) (for integrated steel plants)	Index of Unit Costs (costs at full capacity = 100)
100	100
95	101½
90	104
85	107
80	110
75	113

Source: C. F. Pratten and R. M. Dean [114] p. 80.

The evidence that we have summarised above is broadly suggestive of linear total cost curves with marginal cost being constant over the operating range of output. We must recognise, however, that the measurement techniques — particularly the statistical method — tend to bias the results towards linearity so therefore we need to be cautious in accepting this evidence at face value. Of course when a firm has several processes at its disposal the marginal cost function may rise in steps as shown in Figure 4.4 above. However, that kind of rising marginal cost function is a far cry from the smooth 'U-shaped' function which has failed to emerge from the empirical studies.

Long-run Cost Analysis

Let us now recall the long run average cost curve, or what one economist refers to as the scale curve, of Figure 4.5 above. What it shows is the effect of scale on average costs of production for a series of alternative plants, built at a point in time. This curve is also the envelope of the short run average cost curves as it indicates the lowest possible cost of producing at any rate of output (assuming given factor prices).

A firm, of course, can only be operating at a finite number of scales even if it is a multiple plant firm, but the long run average cost curve has been derived *a priori* as a shallow 'U-shaped' curve initially reflecting economies of scale which continue until optimum plant size is reached and thereafter, diseconomies set in particularly in the management of the firm. There is empirical evidence to suggest that the LRAC is in fact 'L-shaped' (Figure 4.9) or flat, though because the curve is abstract in a sense, empirical evidence can only be analysed after making a series of simplifying assumptions, particularly about the fixity of technical knowledge when making comparisons between firms. Even if some studies do indicate a particular type of cost behaviour, differences between industries and between countries preclude generalisations. The evidence is thus on the whole inconclusive and while we shall refer to some of it, the reader is advised to follow up the references we cite. Our task here is mainly to examine as we did for short run cost analysis the various methods that can be employed in empirical research. The same three methods as with short run cost analysis can in fact be employed as well as 'survival analysis'.

Figure 4.9   Long Run Costs Curves

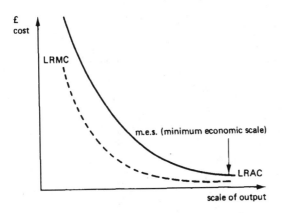

The *intuitive* approach is unlikely to get us very far as accountants will generally not have the experience to enable estimates to be made of costs at alternative plant sizes so we shall only examine the remaining three methods.

Statistical Cost Analysis

The statistical method uses actual data, but the firm is unlikely to have statistical observations of costs in many different sized plants. However, the statistical method has been adopted by academic researchers (see for example J. Johnston) using both time-series and cross-section data. Both types of statistics are difficult to handle, as we discussed earlier, because of changes in price levels over time and particularly because of the differences between firms (plants) in management accounting methods. Johnston in his study of long period costs found that in the time-series studies the evidence was suggestive of a linear relationship between total working costs and output and this was supported by a cross-section study for a sample of 23 undertakings in electricity generation in Britain for the period 1938-9. In addition to working costs it is of course necessary to estimate capital costs, but here the available data were limited partly because of the secrecy surrounding project costs. However, from the information available, Johnston concluded that long run average cost fell rapidly initially, but then assumed an approximately constant value.

Engineering Approach

The engineering method is the most common one used to determine economies of scale. Indeed we can say that this is where the method comes into its own. We pointed out some of the limitations of the approach for short run analysis particularly its overemphasis on plant-cost relationships. This is equally true for studies of scale in that by concentrating on 'plant' it tends to underestimate other economies which the firm may have in management, finance or marketing.

The method as we know attempts to produce *ex-ante* data to indicate what the cost curve will look like at different capacity levels, and as we have commented earlier it is in a sense a controlled experiment in that factor prices, plant location, product characteristics, etc. are assumed to be held constant. To arrive at the data questionnaires are used along with *ex-post* cost information of the firm. One basic criticism of the method advanced, apart from the ones already mentioned, is that because it is concentrating attention almost exclusively on technical returns it may bias estimates in favour of more advanced technology even though managerial problems may be substantial. This argument we do not find particularly convincing.

There is a wealth of empirical evidence derived from the engineering approach including studies by J. Bain [9], F. T. Moore [100], C. F. Pratten [113] and J. Haldi and D. Whitcomb [50]. In addition there are several useful articles which survey the evidence including A. Silbertson [130], C. A. Smith [135] and M. Friedman [41]. Taken together they provide a valuable methodological lesson in empirical research into economies of scale.

The Haldi and Whitcomb investigation into economies of scale in industrial plants in the UK examined purely production cost, i.e. they excluded costs associated with factors such as marketing, general overhead transportation, etc. The conclusion of this study was that economies of scale were typically enjoyed right up to the largest plant sizes in many basic industries such as electric power, primary metals and petroleum refining. The main sources of these economies were in the initial investment but operating labour costs and raw material cost seemed to offer no significant economies. The fact that many companies, particularly in the United States employ several plants which often differ in size was not thought to be inconsistent with these observations. Historical development is one explanatory factor but the increase on transport costs when production is concentrated in a particular location may be another reason for the employment of multiple plants.

Pratten's study covered a number of industries in the UK and the evidence shows that over certain ranges of outputs when using particular processes, economies appear to exist.

> 'The effects of scale vary for each type of plant over different ranges of scale for plants and firms in different industries and for firms following different strategies within an industry. Nevertheless our estimates show that there are substantial technical economies of scale for the production of many products.' ([113] p. 302)

If there are such economies of scale and if they are increasing over time, as Pratten also suggests, then in the UK, given the size of the market, the exploitation of economies of scale may not be compatible with competition. This of course raises public policy issues, which are discussed in Chapter 6, since governments are the guardian of the nation in preventing the abuse of market power — power which in many instances is derived from concentration in industry.

> 'If an economy were built up from scratch, and the benefits of competition were ignored, our estimates of economies of scale suggest that there should be a very high degree of concentration of production of many products.' (*op. cit.*, p. 313)

Pratten's view that there is a conflict between competition and economies of scale is not held by Silbertson who argues that there are comparatively few industries which have significant economies of scale in relation to the size of the UK market.

Engineering estimates do not provide conclusive proof of economies of scale, but they are *broadly* in agreement with an 'L-shaped' LRAC curve.

Survival or Survivor Method

The survivor technique attempts to estimate the long run average cost curve for an industry's product by grouping firms (plants) in that industry into size classes at two or more dates. The proportion of capacity or output (i.e. market shares) accounted for by each size class is examined, and in particular the changes in this proportion over time. It is assumed that the firms (plants) best equipped to survive are those operating at the scale where minimum average cost is experienced, and that over time the size classes encompassing such firms (plants) will increase their proportions of total industry output, i.e. indicating that the size class or size range constitutes the optimum size of firm (plant). The gains enjoyed by these size classes will be at the expense of relatively inefficient firms (plants), whose average costs are higher.

The optimum scale of operation can be revealed by the survivor technique, but on its own, it does not show what the average cost of production is at that scale or any of the less efficient scales of production. It only indicates the shape of the LRAC curve and one of the main drawbacks is that higher unit costs are not the only cause of declining output in certain size classes. By the same token growth in output accounted for by the other size classes is not solely attributed to lower unit costs and the objective of growth is not always stimulated by a desire to reduce unit costs.* Moreover in any sample of firms used in a study employing the survivor technique, it is impossible to treat the environment as given. Each firm will be confronted with rather different circumstances in terms of investment possibilities, product developments** and growth potential. The application of new knowledge and changing technology will also be important factors influencing size in practice, yet to identify economies and diseconomies of scale one must refer to a given technology and state of knowledge. Additionally if firms have restrictive agreements or have control of scarce resources this may improve their ability to survive. Whilst this may effect survivor estimates based on 'firms', this will not be

---

*   J. K. Galbraith [43] and R. Marris [87], as we have indicated in Chapter 1, suggest that growth satisfies managerial needs and that it may conflict with the shareholders' profit aims.

**   Expansion must of course be within the same product type when proportions of total output are compared. Product developments in terms of minor styling changes, etc. are, however, to be expected.

applicable to estimates based on 'plants'. Nevertheless, the basic principle of inefficient firms being eliminated would be a reasonable one in industries where competition is keen and in such instances the survivor technique retains some plausibility. This selection process amongst firms and plants is Darwinian in form, as A. Alchian [3] has suggested in his 'evolutionary approach' to the theory of survival of firms. Firms survive (indicated by the achievement of positive profits) in an uncertain world not just because of behaviour directed towards survival — imitation, trial and error, adaptive behaviour, or venturesome policies — but also sheer luck may have something to do with it. Alchian summarises: 'Even in a world of stupid men there would still be profits' ([3] p. 213).

With the possibility of survival by pure chance, it is difficult to read too much into survival estimates related to economies of scale. Most of the studies that have been conducted have been for the USA though there is a recent study by R. D. Rees [116] on the optimum plant size for UK industries. The major study for the USA is one by G. J. Stigler [141] and we can illustrate this by reference to the data published for the USA automobile industry (see Table 4.4). From this table the percentage of output produced by various company sizes can be determined (Table 4.5) and this shows that in the early forties the largest company enjoyed a rising share of total output while the 2½ per cent to 5 per cent class was suffering a declining share. Generally speaking, large scale seems to have brought economies except in those inflationary periods when prices have been subject to control. Stigler suggests that the long run average cost curve is saucer-shaped in inflationary times, but with no tendency to rise at the largest outputs at other times.

W. G. Shepherd [128] in surveying the evidence of Stigler and others (including the L. W. Weiss [154] study and the one by T. R. Saving [124]) and in providing additional tests of his own on survival of plants in the USA found a decline in the largest size of plant (measured by employment) particularly over the period 1947-58. Out of 133 industries tested, 78 showed a decline and where there had been an increase this had not been reflected in concentrations. The study by R. D. Rees is an important one because it relates to the UK and is the most recent one available to us. The estimates are based on Census of Production data for the years 1954, 1958, 1963 and 1968. Rees recognises the limitations of such data but makes appropriate allowances in his study. Of the 17 industries which had a constant optimum size for the period 1954-68, 'only 9 included the largest size class within the optimum range' ([116] p. 397).

The examples of research that we have cited in this section therefore lend little support to the traditional beliefs held in economic theory

Table 4.4 Percentages of Passenger Automobiles produced in United States by Various Companies, 1936-41 and 1946-55

Year	General Motors	Chrysler	Ford	Hudson	Nash	Kaiser	Willys Overland	Packard	Stude-Baker	Other
1936	42.9	23.6	22.6	3.3	1.5	-	0.7	2.2	2.4	0.8
1937	40.9	24.2	22.6	2.7	2.2	-	2.0	2.8	2.1	0.5
1938	43.9	23.8	22.3	2.5	1.6	-	0.8	2.5	2.3	0.3
1939	43.0	22.7	21.8	2.8	2.3	-	0.9	2.6	3.7	0.3
1940	45.9	25.1	19.0	2.3	1.7	-	0.7	2.1	3.1	0.1
1941	48.3	23.3	18.3	2.1	2.1	-	0.8	1.8	3.2	0.1
1946	38.4	25.0	21.2	4.2	4.6	0.6	0.3	1.9	3.6	0.2
1947	40.4	21.7	21.3	2.8	3.2	4.1	0.9	1.6	3.5	0.5
1948	40.1	21.2	19.1	3.6	3.1	4.6	0.8	2.5	4.2	0.7
1949	43.0	21.9	21.0	2.8	2.8	1.2	0.6	2.0	4.5	0.2
1950	45.7	18.0	23.3	2.1	2.8	2.2	0.6	1.1	4.0	0.1
1951	42.2	23.1	21.8	1.8	3.0	1.9	0.5	1.4	4.2	0.1
1952	41.5	22.0	23.2	1.8	3.5	1.7	1.1	1.4	3.7	-
1953	45.7	20.3	25.2	1.2	2.2	1.0		1.3	3.0	-
1954	52.2	13.1	30.6	1.7		0.3		0.5	1.6	-
1955	50.2	17.2	28.2	2.0		0.1		2.3		-

Source: *Hard's Automotive Yearbook*, 1951, 1955, 1956.

Table 4.5 Percentage of Passenger Automobiles Produced by Various Company-Sizes

	COMPANY SIZE (As Per Cent of Industry)				NUMBER OF COMPANIES	
YEAR	OVER 35%	10-35%	2½-5%	UNDER 2½%	2½-5%	UNDER 2½%
1936	42.9	46.2	3.3	7.6	1	5*
1937	40.9	46.8	5.5	6.8	2	4*
1938	43.9	46.1	5.0	5.0	2	4*
1939	43.0	44.4	9.1	3.5	3	4*
1940	45.9	44.1	3.1	6.9	1	6*
1941	48.4	41.6	3.2	6.8	1	5
1946	38.4	46.2	12.4	3.0	3	4
1947	40.4	43.0	13.6	3.0	4	3
1948	40.1	40.3	18.0	1.5	5	2
1949	43.0	42.9	10.0	4.0	3	4
1950	45.7	41.3	6.8	6.1	2	5
1951	42.2	44.9	7.2	5.7	2	5
1952	41.5	45.2	7.2	6.1	2	5
1953	45.6	45.5	3.0	5.8	1	4
1954	52.2	43.7	0	4.1	0	4
1955	50.2	45.4	0	4.4	0	3

* Or more.
Source: Table 4.4

wither for the short or the long term. J. Johnston [66] referring primarily to the statistical cost investigations summarises:

'Two major impressions (however) stand out clearly. The first is that the various short-run studies, more often than not, indicate constant marginal cost and declining average cost as the pattern that best seems to describe the data that have been analysed. The second is the preponderance of the L-shaped pattern of long run average cost that emerges so frequently from the various long-run analyses.' (p. 78)

If the scale curve is of this shape with no upturn suggesting diseconomies then it does imply there is no limit to the growth of plants and firms, and there is no equilibrium output. Firms can grow, by diversifying if necessary, but there will be constraints on their expansion in practice both from financial limitations and from entry barriers (in some industries).

Despite evidence supporting Johnston's position, any study into short and long run cost conditions necessitates an understanding of the methodology of empirical work. Confusion often arises as to whether the conclusions of studies relate to plants or firms and a joint approach is desirable. Economists working with statisticians, accountants and engineers can provide the information managers need to make their decisions. The importance of accurate cost estimation will be seen over and over again in the chapters that follow, particularly in pricing and investment decisions.

5 DEMAND ANALYSIS

5-1 Introduction

We have stressed in our discussion of the objectives of firms, that although profit may not be the only goal of business enterprise, it is nevertheless the most vital goal if the firm is to survive. As such the decision maker must take notice of the effects of a proposed course of action on both the costs and revenues of the firm. In Chapter 4 we studied the cost conditions of the firm in some detail and we must now explore the revenue function.

It is a basic premise of traditional economic theory that the firm's total revenue function and demand function are known to its decision makers so that it is assumed the firm has the available information on the relationship between its total revenue and the quantity of goods and services it sells; or looking at the matter another way, the quantity that consumers will purchase at alternative prices. The conventional approach is to examine models of individual behaviour and then to analyse the aggregate behaviour in the market. Our present task is to develop an understanding of the factors which influence the sales of a product and to establish a framework for measuring and estimating the influence of each factor. In consequence we shall examine individual consumer behaviour only briefly. Our main focus of interest is clearly directed at the firm in the market and principally we shall concern ourselves with short run analysis with the firm's existing line of products through its usual distribution channels. We recognise that firms are generally multi-product but we do not discuss changes in product-mix* as these are more appropriately dealt with in the context of corporate planning.

5-2 The Theory of Demand — Standard Economic Analysis

We argued in Chapter 1 that the individual consumer was presumed to wish to maximise his total utility or satisfaction subject to a budget constraint. If we had allowed for risk and uncertainty we would have

---
* except that we recognise later in the chapter (p. 141) that firms often make small adjustments in their products. In part this can be seen as a measure to reduce uncertainty as suggested by J. Margolis [85] as well as a conscious aim at diversification.

inserted the adjective 'expected' to indicate that he will not have perfect foresight in choosing between the various alternative courses of action. Normally however complete certainty is assumed.

In this section we wish to cover briefly two alternative models of demand; a cardinal utility model and an indifference-curve model. The cardinal utility model starts with the observation that a consumer obtains satisfaction or utility from the consumption of a good or service. It assumes that the consumer has a continuous cardinal utility function* which indicates the relationship between the consumer's total utility and his consumption of alternative commodities. By cardinal we simply mean that it is possible to measure subjective utility on an absolute scale. Suppose that we have one set of commodities for which the total utility is 100 units and another bundle of goods for which it is 50, then the first group can be seen to provide double the satisfaction of the second.

The cardinal utility function states that an individual's utility or psychic level of satisfaction depends upon the quantities of goods he consumes:

$$U = f(q_1, q_2, q_3, \ldots)$$

Utility maximisation by the individual is subject to his budget constraint which means that expenditure aggregated over all goods 1, 2, 3, ... n just uses up his income:**

$$\sum_{i=1}^{n} p_i q_i = y \text{ (income)}$$

For a given set of prices $(p_1, p_2, \ldots p_n)$ the condition for utility maximisation is given by the proportionality rule:

$$\frac{MU_1}{p_1} = \frac{MU_2}{p_2} = \frac{MU_3}{p_3} = \ldots$$

or $\quad \dfrac{MU_1}{MU_2} = \dfrac{p_1}{p_2}$ etc.

where MU_1 is the marginal utility of commodity 1, or the change in total utility, per unit change in the quantity consumed of commodity 1 (the quantity of other commodities being held constant) i.e.

$$MU_1 = \frac{\partial U}{\partial q_1}$$

---
*   This is not to be confused with the Von-Neumann and Morgenstern cardinal utility index for the analysis of risky choices. See Chapter 2.
**   Saving is a separate decision or it can be represented as one of the goods or services.

Given this proportionality rule for maximisation of utility, it can be seen that relative prices reflect comparisons of marginal utility rather than total utility. The importance of this is that if an individual's consumption is subject to diminishing marginal utility, i.e. each extra unit of a commodity consumed adds less and less to total satisfaction, then we can deduce the direction of the price-quantity relationship for the commodity. If all other factors influencing the demand of a commodity remain unchanged, an individual can only be induced to buy more of it if its price falls (relative to other commodities) and vice versa. Otherwise the proportionality rule will not be satisfied. Thus the price-quantity relationship for a praticular product is assumed to be inverse for an individual consumer (and for the market in total) and this is often described as a law* even though there are anomalies.** This principle can be shown in a variety of ways including a demand schedule where the range of prices and consumer responses (quantities demanded

Figure 5.1

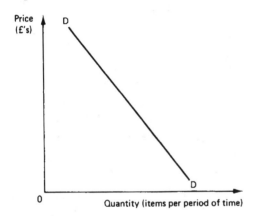

---

* Economic laws are not to be confused with the exact laws of nature. Instead they refer to general principles. In this case the law is derived from introspection.

** A good that has an upward, positive sloping demand curve is often referred to as a Giffen good. Examples usually quoted refer to staple goods such as bread in Europe or rice in Asia. If the price increases a consumer may have to switch to bread from other commodities to stay alive because bread has more calories per unit of expenditure. There are other instances where the demand curve may be upward sloping. These often pertain to articles of ostentation where a higher price encourages a purchase or commodities for which there is an expectation of a future rise in price. Additionally branding and brand loyalty may create an upward sloping demand curve but it is unlikely that the demand curve will be positive throughout its length in any of these instances.

per time period) are tabulated or graphically by means of a demand curve or algebraically in the form of an equation — *viz.* Y = f(X) which states that Y, the dependent variable (quantity demanded) is a function of X, an independent variable (in this case price).

For ease of exposition the normal practice is to use the graphical or pictorial representation of demand by means of the demand curve. This is deduced for individuals and then summed horizontally to produce a market demand curve of the type illustrated in Figure 5.1. As can be bserved this has a negative slope indicating an inverse relationship between price and quantity. As the price falls existing consumers buy more of the commodity in question and more consumers are attracted into the market. We have assumed linearity but this is arbitrary and for convenience only.

If other variables are deemed to change, for example a change in income or advertising expenditure the demand curve would shift and in Figure 5.2 we illustrate this for an increase in household income with a shift to the right causing an increase in total consumption. If we wished to introduce a further variable such as advertising expenditure we would require solid geometry to depict the situation diagrammatically.

Figure 5.2

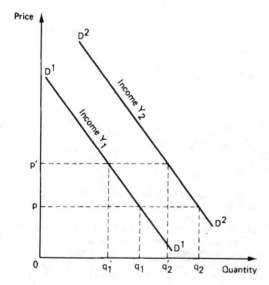

One of the problems with the utility approach arises from the use of *cardinal utility*. Consumers are most unlikely to think cardinally and it was from this criticism that the 'indifference curve' approach developed. Consumers, in this alternative approach are deemed to have complete information and rationality as in the utility approach but the crucial difference is that if a consumer is presented with a finite number of sets of commodities he can arrange them in a 'scale of preference'. If we name these alternatives A, B, C, D, E, ... the consumer can tell whether he prefers A to B or B to A or is indifferent between them. In other words this approach allows for 'weak ordering' because the consumer has both 'preference' and indifference and the relationship between the alternatives is assumed to be 'transitive' in that if the consumer prefers A to B, B to C the he prefers A to C; similarly if he is indifferent between A and B, and B and C, then he is also indifferent between A and C.

The expository device used in this approach is the 'indifference map' which consists of an infinite number of indifference curves and which completely describes a consumer's preferences. The indifference curve represents all those combinations of goods which have the same 'total utility' and curves higher and to the right are positions of relatively greater utility. The scale of preferences which hypothesises a utility function measurable on an ordinal scale thus replaces the cardinal scale and it is not therefore possible to say by how much A is preferred to B.

Figure 5.3

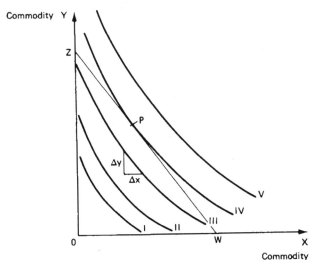

Figure 5.3 illustrates the indifference approach. X and Y are two commodities and I, II, II, IV, V, ... are indifference curves showing a map of a typical consumer's tastes. The properties of these indifference curves are similar to the isoquants we introduced in Chapter 3.

(1) They are downward sloping indicating that as the quantity of X at the disposal of the consumer increases, that of Y must decrease to maintain a given level of utility.

(2) They are convex to the origin indicating that as the consumer buys more of X and less of Y he values X less in terms of Y. In consequence he wants more of X per unit of Y foregone when the quantity of X increases and vice versa. The rate of exchange between X and Y is referred to as the *marginal rate of substitution* and is the slope of the indifference curve. In terms of Figure 5.3, curve III, when the consumer sacrifices Δx of good X and acquires Δy of good Y, the marginal rate of substitution of Y for X can be expressed as:

$$\frac{\Delta y}{\Delta x}.\ast$$

If we introduce a budget constraint and assume the prices of commodities X and Y are known and given by the market then there is a specific quantity of X he could buy (OW) or a specific quantity of Y (OZ). Alternatively of course he could buy some combination of X and Y that fall on the line WZ which we can refer to as the 'price' or 'budget' line. This line denotes the limit of the consumer's purchasing ability, and by relating it to the indifference map we can find the position of maximum satisfaction. In this case it is at point P on the indifference curve IV and here the slope of the price line (expressing the price ratio between X and Y) is the same as the slope of the indifference curve IV (which as we have argued earlier expresses the marginal rate of substitution between X and Y).

Suppose we assume there are only two commodities, X and Y and that the consumer spends all his income on them. If the price of one of these commodities changes economists analyse the effects in two parts.

(1) an *income effect* which will correspond to the change in the level of the real income of the consumer since more income is left over if the same quantity is purchased as previously, but at a lower price;

(2) a *substitution effect* through which the consumer will tend to substitute the relatively cheaper commodity for the dearer one. The substitution effect will always be positive but the income effect depends on two factors. In the first instance whether the commodity in question is a normal or an inferior good (see p. 144) and secondly the

---

* The MRS thus measured is negative, but the modulus, or positive value, of $\Delta y/\Delta x$ is normally quoted as the MRS.

proportion of income which has been allocated to a commodity. The significance of this follows from the fact that if there is a commodity on which a consumer has spent a considerable part of his income and its price falls, the income effect could be significant. For normal commodities both the income and substitution effects noted in the first part of this section will be positive indicating a downward sloping demand curve. Indeed we can indicate how one derives a demand curve from Figure 5.4. We can draw a number of budget lines representing changes in the price of a commodity X. For each budget line there is a particular point chosen by the consumer. This is the point of tangency to an indifference curve and if we join these points the resulting curve is a *price-consumption* or *offer* curve since each of these points corresponds to a particular price of good X. If we were then to plot on another diagram the quantity of good X chosen at each price we would have the individual demand curve for X at a given income level. If income changes, then this causes the budget line to change so that if income increased this would be represented by a new line parallel to the first and tangential to a higher indifference curve indicating an ability to purchase more of both commodities. By analogous reasoning to that involved in obtaining a price-consumption curve we can derive an income-consumption curve, as the budget changes.

Figure 5.4

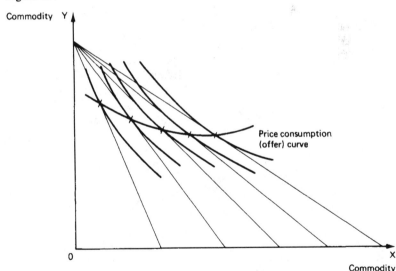

5-3 Factors Influencing Demand

There are obviously many variables which influence the demand for a commodity: its price, the price of substitutes, the income of prospective purchasers and of course the nature of the commodity itself is crucial in determining consumer behaviour. Sales of consumer durable goods, e.g. cars, refrigerators and washing machines are governed by rather different variables from those influencing the sales of non-durable consumer goods, e.g. food, detergents and toiletries. In the case of durable goods a tightening of credit restrictions (by influencing the cost and availability of credit)* would normally decrease the sales of such articles, while the sales of non-durables would scarcely be affected. Sales of producers' goods, i.e. plant and machinery are influenced by economic policy (changes in credit conditions, tax changes)** but the demand for such goods is a derived demand. In other words businessmen are encouraged to add to their stock of capital goods if they can foresee a commensurate growth in the sales of the products which will be manufactured with this equipment. Here therefore the formation of business expectations is crucial particularly in relation to the confidence investors feel in the future developments and growth of the economy in general and in the relevant industrial sector in particular.

To a large extent then each product type must be analysed separately, though the following framework is a convenient starting point for analysis:

(a) Controllable Variables

(i) *Price* As we have seen, economic analysis has concentrated on the price-quantity relationship in its study of demand. The extent to which price is a controllable variable depends upon the market structure in which the product is being sold (see Chapter 6). The firm may be a price setter or leader in which case manipulations of price can be incorporated into the firm's strategies. On the other hand, if the firm's output of the product is small relative to total consumption, it may be

---

* Credit to the personal sector can take many forms including mortgages for house purchase and house improvements, hire purchase, credit sales, budget accounts, advances from banks, loans from other financial institutions, credit cards and the like. The Crowther Report on Consumer Credit estimated that consumer credit (excluding mortgages for housing) finances between 8 and 9 per cent of all consumers' spending; about half of consumers' spending on cars and two-fifths of spending on other durable goods are financed this way. For a full discussion on this topic see *Consumer Credit: Report of the Crowther Committee* [29].

** For instance changes in the level of Corporation Tax and/or changes in the various incentives available for investment in buildings or plant and machinery are likely to change investment expenditure, particularly if firms anticipate buoyant demand conditions.

a price taker or follower and consequently take the prevailing price as given by the market.

(ii) *Promotional Expenditure* Advertising is perhaps the most common type of promotional activity but there are two main types of advertising: informative and promotional. The former usually refers to the provision of information that a particular product exists; the latter implies more persuasive methods often linked with the brand image of the product. Gifts, prizes, special offers and free samples are also widely used and together with advertising their purpose in the short term is to increase the sales of products currently in the firm's catalogue beyond the level consumers would normally purchase. In some cases promotional activities are used as defensive tactics to retain one's share of the market.* This is particularly true when a product market is dominated by two or three large suppliers, when the fear of a price war encourages the use of methods other than price competition (see Chapter 6) to make the products slightly different from one another. This act of differentiation on its own may well increase consumption of the product and this will be reflected in the consumers indifference map as tastes are moulded. It also has the important effect of permitting each manufacturer some discretion over his selling price.

At present we are interested in the effects of promotional activities on the sales of existing products but clearly they are very much part and parcel of the firm's long term strategy in building up brand allegiance and broadening the firm's product line through the launching of new products or minor improvements to existing products. In the latter respect slight improvements in products have the effect of reducing the uncertainty in using price changes and this point, as we have observed earlier, is forcibly made by J. Margolis [85] in his explanation of business conventions.

(b) Non-Controllable Variables

(i) Household Income and Aggregate Demand Although a company has some control over the income of its own employees, these will normally only constitute but a small percentage of the total customers to which the firm supplies its good and services. For this reason household income is regarded as a factor largely outside the control of the manager. J. K. Galbraith [43] argues (in *The New Industrial State*) that the State can provide the environment of steady growth so the firm can itself plan effectively for increasing sales.

The determination of national income takes us into the realms of macroeconomic theory and the part the Government can play in

---

* This can also have the purpose of erecting a barrier to prevent the entry of new firms into the industry. For a discussion of barriers to entry see Chapter 6, Section 6-3, and J. S. Bain [9].

influencing key aggregate variables. But given that the business economist has available to him forecasts of national income (and its distribution) prepared by the Treasury and others (including the National Institute for Economic and Social Research) in addition to the information supplied by the financial press, for present purposes we can leave the task of estimating national income to those bodies and pose the question of how income is likely to affect sales. We know from our previous discussion that increases in income can be represented by an expansion in the budget line or alternatively as we indicated in Figure 5.2 with a demand shift. For normal commodities an increase of income will lead to an increase in demand and this can be determined by measuring the income elasticity which we cover in Section 5-5.

(ii) Export Demand For many firms the home market is only one sales outlet, though usually the most important one. The level of income country by country will be a significant factor in determining exports in the same way that home sales are strongly influenced by the total purchasing power in our economy. This means that export-oriented firms must be aware of economic trends overseas, drawing upon information and forecasts supplied by foreign economic advisory agencies and international bodies such as the Organisation for Economic Cooperation and Development (OECD) and the United Nations Organisation (UNO). The selling price for exports partially depends upon the pricing policy of the firm. However, each government has the responsibility for maintaining the balance of payments near to equilibrium and has the ability to vary the import-export mix through tariff manipulations, import deposit schemes and exchange rate variations. In the latter instance a devaluation which lowers the exchange price of a commodity for export allows exporters to raise their profit margin such that the fall in price actually recorded will not be as much as the depreciation of the currency would suggest: there was evidence of this after the 1967 devaluation in Britain. When the exchange rate is floating this does pose rather a different problem to the firm since there is uncertainty as to the future exchange rate and therefore the export price. The firm may reduce some of this uncertainty by dealing in the forward foreign exchange market.

(iii) Competitive Strategies In some types of market, notably oligopoly, the outcome of one's own decisions is heavily dependent upon the way one's competitors react to the decision. We have seen that a firm can vary its sales by manipulating price, promotional expenditure, and product features. Rival firms will have their own strategies and we must recognise that the sales of one firm's product will be very much influenced by how its goods compare price-wise and in terms of consumer appeal to similar products offered by competitors. The difficulties of handling interdependence in decison making is more fully

explored in Chapter 6.

5-4 Multivariate Demand Functions

As we have seen, the number of demand determinants may be quite large yet if for any given commodity the most important determinants could be isolated and their joint efforts noted on total demand we are in a position to specify a simple but multivariate demand function which could be of the form

$$Q = f(X, X', X'')$$

where

Q = quantity sold of that product per period of time.
X = the variables which are subject to the decision maker's control, i.e. the decision variables.
X' = the factors which influence quantity sold but which are not subject to control by the decision maker.
X'' = the variables which are subject to the control of competitors or opponents.
f = the functional relationship between the independent variables X, X', X'' and the dependent variable Q.

Let us now generalise the equation using $X_1, X_2, \ldots X_n$ for each independent variable irrespective of whether a decision variable, performance factor or competitive strategy is involved. We would write the demand function for a particular brand of beer as:

$$Q = f(X_1, X_2, X_3, \ldots X_n)$$

which means that the demand for (this particular brand of) beer depends on price (X_1), income level (X_2), advertising expenditure (X_3), certain unspecified factors $(\ldots)$ and the price of substitutes (X_n).

If we can specify the exact value of each X and if we know exactly how each X influences Q, we can determine the quantity which will be sold at a given set of values of $X_1 \ldots X_n$. Just as the economist in his use of the demand curve was examining only the impact of price changes on the quantity demanded, holding other variables constant, frequently the decision maker will use a similar approach and will be concerned with studying the effects on his sales of changing price or some other variable in isolation. To this end the concept of elasticity is invaluable, and to this we now turn.

5-5 Elasticity

Elasticity measures the response of a dependent variable to variations in an independent variable. Economists have traditionally studied the price-quantity relationship and the discussion in this section will revolve around price elasticity of demand. It is also possible to use this concept to relate variations in consumption to variations in income* or indeed any other independent variable in the demand function. The concept of elasticity can also be extended to the supply function, to measure the response of supply to variations in price or some other variable.

The elasticity of the demand function, $Q = f(X)$ at a point x is the percentage change in the dependent variable Q brought about by a unit percentage change in the independent variable X.

$$\epsilon_D = \frac{\%\ \text{change in Q}}{\%\ \text{change in X}} \quad \text{or} \quad \frac{\Delta q/q}{\Delta x/x} \quad \text{or} \quad \frac{\Delta q}{\Delta x} \cdot \frac{x}{q}$$

where q and x represent actual or average values of the two variables Q and X and Δq is the change in variable Q brought about by a change (Δx) in variable X. The variable X of course could be price in which case we have price elasticity of demand, but because we have argued in Section 5-2 that a price fall usually leads to a rise in consumption and the converse for a price rise, the price elasticity of demand will be negative. We did also recognise however that there are exceptions to the rule where the demand curve may have a positive slope with respect to price and therefore a positive price elasticity of demand.

(a) Arc Elasticity

Suppose we examine the price-quantity relationship for a particular product keeping variables other than price constant. Suppose that past records suggest that 40,000 units (q_1) of a commodity, Q, will be sold per month when the price is 10p but only 20,000 units (q_2) will be sold per month at a price of 30p per unit. Assuming that the relationship between price and quantity is stable, we can measure the average value of elasticity over that range, or arc, of the demand schedule represented in Figure 5.5.

$$\text{Arc elasticity} = \frac{\Delta q/q}{\Delta p/p}$$

In particular as we are measuring average values over a range of values of price,

---

*   For income elasticity we normally expect a positive relationship between income changes and consumption so that the higher the income the greater the consumption. Some commodities however such as bread, flour and potatoes may have negative income elasticities of demand particularly for poorer families. Such commodities are referred to as inferior goods but this has nothing to do with their quality (see Section 5-2 above).

Figure 5.5

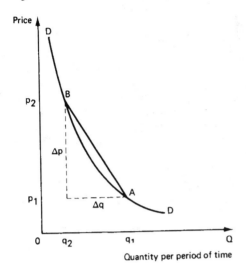

$$\text{Arc elasticity} = \frac{\dfrac{q_2 - q_1}{\text{average value of q}}}{\dfrac{p_2 - p_1}{\text{average value of p}}} = \frac{(q_2 - q_1)/\tfrac{1}{2}(q_2 + q_1)}{(p_2 - p_1)/\tfrac{1}{2}(p_2 + p_1)}$$

$$= \frac{(q_2 - q_1)}{(p_2 - p_1)} \cdot \frac{(p_2 + p_1)}{(q_2 + q_1)}$$

Substituting:

$$\text{Arc elasticity} = \frac{(20 - 40)}{(30 - 10)} \times \frac{40}{60}$$

$$= -\frac{2}{3}.$$

Interpretation: Over the range we have considered, price has an average value of 20p. A change in price of 20p (from 10p to 30p) is thus 100 per cent of the mean value. Quantity, which has a mean value of 30 thousand units changes from 40,000 to 20,000 units, a downward movement of 20,000 units representing 66.7 per cent of the average value over that range. Thus a 100 per cent movement in price brings about a 66.7 per cent change in quantity. A one per cent change in price thus leads to a 0.667 per cent or 2/3 of one per cent change in quantity demanded. Hence the above result.

(b) Point Elasticity

Most demand curves have variable elasticity, that is to say in moving to a new price-quantity combination we have to substitute new values into our elasticity formula to obtain a new result. The arc elasticity then in most cases is an average value over the range stated. To compute point elasticity we consider the exact value at a given price-quantity combination, i.e. the p and q are actual rather than average values and of course are represented by *the point* on the demand curve at which we make our measurement. Given p and q the remaining value we need for the determination of elasticity is $\Delta q/\Delta p$ which is related to the slope of the demand curve.

In deriving arc elasticity, this posed no problems, we simply computed the slope of the chord AB, this being given by:

$$\frac{\Delta q}{\Delta p} = \frac{(q_2 - q_1)}{(p_2 - p_1)} \quad \text{(see Figure 5.5)}.$$

As the two points on the schedule move closer and closer together the slope of the tangent at A becomes a better and better approximation to the slope of the chord. Another way of expressing this is to say that as price tends to zero, $\Delta q/\Delta p$ approaches the slope of the tangent drawn at A. The limit of $\Delta q/\Delta p$ as price tends to zero is written dq/dp and this is hence the value we substitute in our formula for elasticity as a point measure.

Point elasticity then is given by $\dfrac{dq}{dp} \times \dfrac{p}{q}$

where dq/dp is the limiting value of $\Delta q/\Delta p$ (or the value which $\Delta q/\Delta p$ approaches) as price tends to zero. Point elasticity thus determined indicates the percentage change in quantity brought about by a given change in price in the *very close neighbourhood* of a given point A on the demand schedule. The slope of the tangent dq/dp will of course depend upon the region of the demand schedule in which we are operating unless the demand schedule is a linear function, in which case the slope of the demand schedule is constant.

Suppose that the demand function is of the form $q = 100 - 2p$. This can be represented diagrammatically as in Figure 5.6 where the intercept on the price axis is 50 and on the quantity axis 100. The elasticity at the point A (p_1, q_1) is given by the formula:

Figure 5.6

$$p_\epsilon = \frac{dq}{dp} \times \frac{p_1}{q_1}$$

In this case,

$$\frac{p_1}{q_1} = \frac{37.5}{25}$$

and dq/dp has the same values throughout, the slope of the schedule being $-100/50 = -2$, remembering that we are measuring p along the vertical axis and q along the horizontal axis, the negative sign indicating an inverse relationship between p and q.

∴ Price elasticity (p_ϵ) = $-2 \times 1.5 = -3.0$.

Thus for every one per cent change in p in the close neighbourhood of A, q will change by 3.0 per cent in the opposite direction, provided that all other relevant variables remain constant in value.

e.g. Suppose the price moved to 38p, a change of 0.5p.
This is a $(0.5/3.75) \times 100$ per cent change in p. Since the percentage change in q = p_ϵ × the percentage change in price the quantity will, therefore, change by:

$$-3.0 \times \frac{0.5}{37.5} \times 100\% = -\frac{1.5}{37.5} \times 100\%$$
$$= -4.0\%.$$

The quantity demanded will therefore fall by 4.0 per cent of 25 units (= 1 unit) to 24 units.

If the schedule had not been linear in form, the value of dq/dp would have been calculated by drawing in the tangent at A and measuring its slope. Alternatively differential calculus could have been employed, given the equation of the schedule.

Suppose the demand curve shifted to the right due to changed underlying conditions affecting the demand relationship (as we indicated in Figure 5.2) and suppose that the demand function is linear so we have two parallel straight line demand functions. Taking a given price we should note because both curves are parallel, the slope dq/dp is the same on both curves but the factor that has changed is q. The demand curve D^2 exhibits a larger quantity for a given price which means that p/q is lower and hence price elasticity will be smaller.

5-6 Interpretation of Elasticity

In the case of price elasticity of demand, the negative sign which inevitably occurs has already been explained and warrants no further attention. Of much greater significance is the magnitude of the figure we obtain. In many instances it will be impossible to ascribe exact values to elasticity for every single product in a firm's catalogue. A less demanding task is to find out whether demand is 'elastic' or 'inelastic' with respect to price.

(a) Elastic Demand

Demand is said to be elastic when elasticity has a value, ignoring the sign,* greater than unity. The case cited in Section 5-5 where point elasticity was -3.0 was thus an example of elastic demand and referring to the formula:

$$P_\epsilon = \frac{\Delta q/q}{\Delta p/p}$$

we can see that a small percentage change in p is going to elicit a rather more substantial percentage change in q when demand is elastic. The resultant effect is that total revenue ($p \cdot q$) will tend to fall as price rises. This is because a change in price is highly effective in deterring consumption of the product. In the numerical example just mentioned in

---
* For the usual negative sloping demand curves.

Section 5-5 we started at a position of p = 37.5p, q = 25, with a total revenue of 937.5 pence. Raising the price to 38.0p, an increase of 4/3 per cent: produced a reduction in the quantity sold by 4 per cent to 24 units per period with a new total revenue per period of 912 pence. A *fall* in price will of course *increase* total revenue when demand is elastic.

(b) Inelastic Demand

If elasticity, again ignoring the negative sign, is less than unity, demand is said to be inelastic and the propositions we derived for elastic demand are completely reversed. We now find that changes in price have a less than proportionate effect on quantity sold. The effect of a price rise is then to increase total revenue since very nearly the same output is being sold at a higher price than before. Conversely a price cut results in a fall in revenue. The figures we used to explain arc elasticity will show this to be true. Recall that elasticity over the range considered was −2/3, i.e. demand was inelastic (see p. 145). We would then predict that raising the price from 10p to 30p would raise total revenue and this is readily seen to be the case.

At 10p we could sell 40,000 units, total revenue = £4,000
At 30p we could sell 20,000 units, total revenue = £6,000.

5-7 Changes in Elasticity

Point elasticity seldom has a constant value for all possible price and output combinations along the demand schedule. Indeed downward sloping linear demand functions are subject to continually changing elasticity. Let us consider such a schedule of slope $45°$ as shown in Figure 5.7. Suppose originally the price is set at Op_1. The quantity sold per period at this price is Oq_1, and the total revenue is $Oq_1 \cdot Op_1$, given by the area of the rectangle $Op_1 Aq_1$. If the price now falls by a very small amount Δp to a new level Op_2, quantity demanded per period will now be Oq_2 and total revenue, $Oq_2 \cdot Op_2$, represented by the area $Op_2 Bq_2$. The net gain in total revenue by changing the price to Op_2 is therefore given by the area $(q_1 CBq_2 - p_2 p_1 AC)$ which is positive so long as we are operating in the upper region, above the mid point of the schedule. A fall in price thus increases total revenue, showing that demand is elastic in this region. If we now move to the lower half of the demand schedule, we can show that a fall in price Δp from Op_3 to Op_4 induces a change in revenue represented by the area $(q_3 UTq_4 - p_4 p_3 SU)$. This is a net loss in revenue brought about by the price fall, showing that the schedule is price inelastic in this region.

The change from elastic to inelastic in a gradual one as we descend from higher to lower values of P. This means that at one point in

Figure 5.7

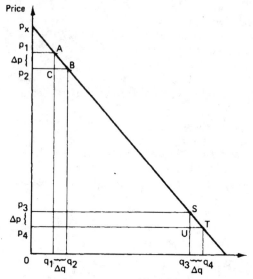

Quantity per period of time

particular elasticity must have a value of unity, or more specifically -1. This in fact occurs at a value $\frac{1}{2}Op_x$ where p_x is the intercept of the schedule along the price axis. Indeed any linear function possesses these properties, as the following example shows: Recall the demand function used earlier, where $q = 100 - 2p$ and represented in Figure 5.6. At the price quantity combination (37.5, 25.0), point A, price elasticity is 3.0, i.e. price elastic. Moving to point S (12.5, 75.0)

$$p_\epsilon = \frac{12.5}{75.0} \times -2.0 = -\frac{1}{3}.$$

Demand is now inelastic. The point where we would anticipate demand to be neither price elastic nor price inelastic ($= -1$) is at a price of 25p. At this price 50 units would be consumed per period.

$$p_\epsilon = \frac{25}{50} \times -2.0 = -1.0$$

which is in accordance with our anticipation.

At the extremities of this linear demand schedule, price elasticity of demand is minus infinity where $p = 0$, and zero where $q = 0$. This result follows from a consideration of the ratio p/q which changes from infinity to zero as we go from one intercept to the other.

Our results could have been expressed in terms of revenue changes

150

with respect to changes in quantity sold rather than price. When the quantity sold is small, any increase in quantity sold tends to increase total revenue until one reaches the point of unitary elasticity. At this point a small change in quantity sold has no effect on total revenue, but thereafter any increase in quantity decreases total revenue, as shown in Figure 5.8.

Figure 5.8

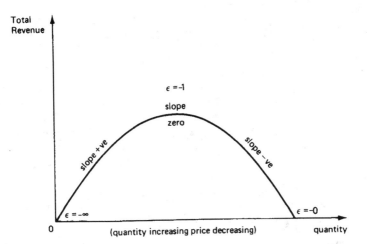

Although many demand schedules exhibit this type of behaviour, namely total revenue rising and then falling with output sold, some relationships, notably exponential functions, give rise to constant elasticity. This will be given further consideration later in the chapter.

5-8 Marginal Revenue

The preceding discussion suggested that a change in price is likely to bring about a change in total revenue except in the rare instance of elasticity being unitary in value, in which case total revenue is constant. Normally then in moving from one price-quantity combination to another we would expect total revenue to change, the magnitude and direction of this change depending upon the elasticity of demand with respect to price in that region of the demand schedule.

As we have shown in Figure 5.8 total revenue can be plotted against price or quantity, convention normally favouring the latter. Diagrams drawn this way show that as quantity sold increases from zero, total revenue will normally rise for a time but more and more slowly until total revenue reaches its maximum value, thereafter each unit sold diminishes total revenue. Another way of stating this is to say that the slope of the total revenue function, drawn as a function of quantity, is initially positive but falls to zero, and then becomes negative. If the slope of the total revenue function at a particular point is positive, this means that a unit increase in quantity sold is accompanied by a rise in total revenue. When the slope is negative, a unit increase in quantity sold is accompanied by a fall in total revenue.

Marginal revenue at a particular output is defined as the change in total revenue brought about by a unit change in quantity sold. The slope of the total revenue function or more strictly its derivative with respect to quantity at a particular point, thus gives the marginal revenue function. If our demand function is typical, total revenue will behave as in Figure 5.8. Marginal revenue is then initially positive, falling gradually to zero, then becoming negative, as quantity sold increases.

We are now in a position to show the relationship which exists between the price-quantity relationship, total revenue and marginal revenue. The notion of marginal revenue suggests that each unit sold has a definite distinct effect on total revenue. Total revenue is the sum of each of these marginal contributions.

Average Revenue is simply: $\dfrac{\text{Total Revenue}}{\text{Quantity Sold}}$

and since Total Revenue = Price × Quantity

we can write, Price = $\dfrac{\text{Total Revenue}}{\text{Quantity Sold}}$

Hence *Price* and *Average Revenue* are the same thing. We can thus regard a demand schedule either as a representation of the quantities demanded over a given price range, or as a representation of the average revenues obtainable from selling different quantities of a product per period of time. The relationship between *Total Revenue* (TR), *Marginal Revenue* (MR) and *Average Revenue* (AR) can be seen by considering the linear demand schedule represented in Figure 5.9. The equation of the schedule is:

$$q = 100 - 5p \ .$$

This can be written as:

$p = \dfrac{100 - q}{5}$ so that *total revenue* (p·q) is:

Figure 5.9

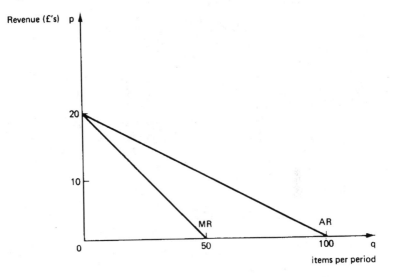

$$TR = \frac{100q - q^2}{5}, \text{ and since } MR = \frac{d(TR)}{dq}$$

then $MR = \dfrac{100 - 2q}{5}$

As q approaches zero, MR approaches the value of £20, and hence the AR schedule at zero quantity. In Figure 5.9 we have drawn the MR function as continuous although in practice output is not continually variable, but only by discrete amounts, i.e., one unit at a time. Average revenue is given by:

$$AR = \frac{100 - q}{5}$$

Comparison with the MR function shows that the latter is twice as steep as the AR function. In general a linear demand function is of the form

$$p = AR = a - bq$$
$$TR = aq - bq^2$$
$$MR = a - 2bq.$$

The MR and AR schedules have the same intercept a on the price/revenue axis (with the above proviso about functions not being continuous). In this example the AR schedule falls at a rate of £0.20 per unit; MR falling at double this rate, namely £0.40 per unit. MR will strictly never reach the value of £20 as given in Figure 5.9 but gets closer and closer to this value as q approaches zero. The point of unitary elasticity is such that total revenue will remain unchanged for very small movements along the demand schedule, i.e. marginal revenue is zero. This occurs when $a - 2bq = 0$. i.e. $q = a/2b$, which is half the intercept of the AR schedule on the quantity axis. The corresponding value of p is given by $p = a - bq$ which on substituting for q gives,

$p = a - ba/2b$

½a .

5-9 Elasticity and Multivariate Demand Functions

When we introduce more than one independent variable into our demand equation, we can still compute elasticity without substantially adding to our difficulties. We have to be careful, however, in using the term elasticity so that we specify which variable this pertains to. For example if we show demand as a function of price and income, we can speak of income elasticity of demand as well as price elasticity of demand. For ease of exposition let us imagine that the demand schedule for a hypothetical product 'Hypro' is derived as a linear function of price and income so that rises in household income would *ceteris paribus* tend to increase consumption of this product. A linear demand function in household income, Y, alone would be of the form $q = a_1 + b_1 Y$ showing that for every £ increase in income per period, demand for Hypro per period would increase by b_1 units. Alternatively we could say that the marginal propensity to consume Hypro is b_1. The demand function in p alone would be of the form $q = a_2 - b_2 p$. We could represent our demand function in price and income diagramatically in two ways. Figure 5.10 shows $q = a_1 + b_1 Y$, the quantity-income relationship at a particular price. Should the price change, the intercept a_1 will rise for a cut in price which would stimulate demand while a price rise would dampen demand, represented by a lower intercept. We would obtain a series of schedules all parallel, assuming the marginal propensity to consume, b_1 remained stable.

Alternatively as in Figure 5.11 we could represent the price-quantity relationship as $q = a_2 - b_2 p$. This schedule would shift outwards for income rises and towards the origin for falls in income. Again the intercept will change for each income level. For purposes of analysis it is preferable to express these relationships in a single equation as follows:

Figure 5-10

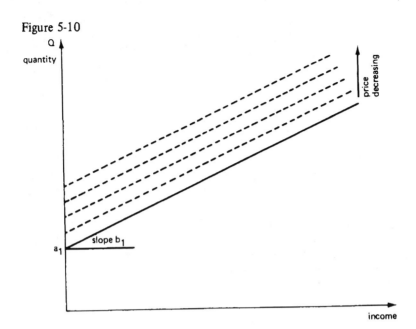

Figure 5-11

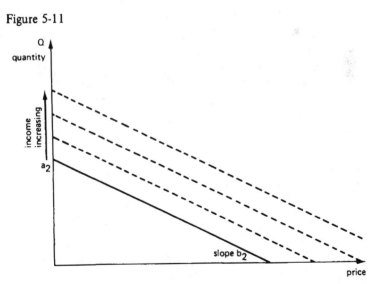

$$q = a + b_1 Y - b_2 p,$$

where 'a' is a constant reflecting the influence of other demand determinants (or the value of q when Y and p are zero). Any changes in its value would indicate movements in unspecified variables. Given an equation of this type, elasticity can be determined for both price and income.

Now suppose for the sake of argument that the sales director of the company producing Hypro is informed by his statistician that the demand schedule is: $q = 4.0 - 0.3p + 0.7Y$ where q is the number of units sold annually in thousands, p is the price in pounds per unit sold and Y is the national income in £000's million.

At present, with an estimated national income of £50,000,000 and the price at £10 per unit the equation predicts that $(4 - 3 + 35)$ thousand = 36,000 units will be sold annually. If current sales are very close to this figure, then the equation appears to have predictive power if we assume that the firm is just meeting demand. If the sales director wishes to know how demand will respond to income and price changes *ceteris paribus*, he could well pose two questions along the following lines.

(i) If the price is reduced, what effect will this have on sales, assuming income remains at the same level? (Here we are considering movements along a single price-quantity schedule.)

(ii) If national income increases by 2 per cent in the following year, by how much will sales increase? (Here we are considering a price-quantity schedule shifting outwards, or alternatively a movement up a single income-quantity schedule.)

The problem is solved by finding price elasticity and income elasticity at the point

(p = 10
(Y = 50
(q = 36

For price elasticity recall that our basic equation is: $\epsilon = (\Delta q / \Delta p) \cdot (p/q)$. If we are measuring point elasticity we are considering the case where price is very small, i.e. $\Delta p \to 0$. Normally we would use dq/dp to represent the value of $\Delta q / \Delta p$ as $\Delta p \to 0$. But we are now dealing with a multivariate demand function which can be differentiated with respect to p or Y, but we can only differentiate with respect to one variable at a time. When we do this we call the process *partial differentiation* and write the limit of $\Delta q / \Delta p$ (as $\Delta p \to 0$) as $\partial q / \partial p$ which assumes that the other variable, Y, remains fixed in value. Finding partial derivatives in this manner is entirely equivalent to studying the price and income relationships separately, as in Figures 5.10 and 5.11 and finding the slope of each at the appropriate price, income, and quantity combination.

Let us now try to answer the questions posed by the sales director. The first question concerning the effects of a price reduction can be answered by calculating price elasticity using the formula:

$$\text{price elasticity} = \frac{p}{q} \cdot \frac{\partial q}{\partial p}.$$

Since the relationship between Q and p is linear the slope of the function, $\partial q/\partial p$ is constant throughout and equal in this instance to -0.3. That is to say, every time price rises by £1, the number of units sold falls by 0.3 (thousands annually). $p = 10$ and $q = 36$, so the price elasticity of demand at this point is given by:

$$\frac{10}{36} \times (-0.3)$$

$$= -\frac{10}{12} \quad \text{or} \quad -0.0833.$$

This means that demand is price inelastic at this point, so a price cut would reduce total sales revenue, the total reduction being dependent on the magnitude of the price cut.

The second question requires us to deduce the effects of a 2 per cent income rise. Income elasticity of demand informs us of the effects of a unit percentage income change. The relevant formula is:

$$\text{Income elasticity} = \frac{Y}{q} \cdot \frac{\partial q}{\partial Y}.$$

Again we have a linear relationship, this time between q and Y, the slope being constant throughout and equal to 0.7. At the point in question, $p = 10$, $Y = 50$ so substituting in the income elasticity formula we obtain

$$\frac{50}{36} \times 0.7 = \frac{35}{36} = 0.9722.$$

A 2 per cent income rise would increase quantity by double this figure, i.e. 1.9444 per cent and assuming price is held constant, total revenue (price × quantity) will also increase by this percentage.

Our forecasting problem is greatly facilitated then by a knowledge of the relevant elasticities and these values can be substituted into demand equation to forecast q. These can, of course, only be determined if the demand schedule has already been estimated as was the case here. The problem of estimating the demand function is then the chief problem of forecasting sales as we shall see in Section 5-12 below.

5-10 Elasticity and Logarithmic Functions

We have seen that multivariate demand functions expressing quantity demanded as a function of price, income and any other relevant variable can be handled for purposes of elasticity computations by means of partial derivatives. However, up till now we have only considered linear demand functions which may well be a close approximation for certain types of product market, but frequently statisticians find that the relationships involved can be better expressed using logarithmic functions and the example quoted below illustrates this. R. Stone [143] in a pioneering study in which he analysed the market demand for products in both the USA and UK derived the following demand function for beer consumption in the UK:

$$q = 1.058 Y^{0.136} p^{-0.727} n^{0.914} g^{0.816}$$

Where q = demand for beer (bulk barrels)
  Y = national income
  p = average retail price of beer
  n = average price index of other commodities
  g = an index of the strength of beer.

This equation is written in exponential form although it can readily be converted into a logarithmic expression:

$$\log q = \log 1.058 + 0.136 \log Y - 0.727 \log p + 0.914 \log n + 0.816 \log g .$$

Thus consumption of beer increases as Y, n or g increase and declines as price rises. We now have a rather awe inspiring formula to contend with, but paradoxically we can determine elasticity with respect to any of the independent variables by inspection. Taking the equation in its original form all we need do is read off the power to which each variable is raised in order to determine the relevant elasticity magnitude. Thus the price elasticity of demand is -0.727, while income elasticity is 0.136. Moreover these values remain constant throughout the full range of values of price and income for which this equation is valid. An alternative method is to convert the exponential form into logarithmic form and inspect the coefficient of $\log p$, and $\log Y$ to give the elasticities of -0.727 and 0.136 respectively.* We can, of course, extend our normal

---

*   Proof of results:

  If $q = 1.058 Y^{0.136} p^{-0.727} n^{0.914} g^{0.816}$

  we can write:—

$$\log_e q = \log_e 1.058 + 0.136 \log_e Y - 0.727 \log_e p + 0.914 \log_e n + 0.816 \log_e g .$$

usage of the concept of elasticity to study the effects of changing the strength of beer, or to isolate the consequences of retail price movements. The latter is similar to 'cross elasticity' which is considered in the following section.

5-11 Substitutes and Complements

The elasticity calculations so far considered all pertain to a particular product taken in isolation. A knowledge of price, income and any other relevant elasticities enables us to predict the change in sales of that particular product. In practice the sales of one product cannot be predicted without a consideration of related products. Two types of relationship exist: where demand is competitive and where demand is complementary. Demand is said to be *competitive*, or the products said to be substitutes, if raising the price of one of the products causes an increase in the consumption of the other product(s), the price of the latter remaining unchanged. Demand is said to be *complementary* if an increase in the consumption of a product causes an increase in the consumption of associated products. A price reduction for product X (causing consumption of X to increase) thus increases the quantity purchased of product Y if X and Y are complements.

If the purchase of one product A has no direct influence on the purchase of product B, the commodities A and B are independent. Indirectly of course the consumption of any product depends upon how its price compares to the price of all other commodities the consumer can buy, but for our present purposes we are only concerned with direct relationships, i.e. where a price change in one product has a direct effect on the consumption of another. We can cite many cases of competitive and complementary demand, and naturally even more cases of near independence. Differentiated product markets, where the difference between product A, product B and so on is often only a case of the brand name and packaging represent the strongest type of competitive relationship. If one cigarette manufacturer increased his price and his rivals kept theirs steady, the products of the latter would tend to be substituted for the former. The car industry too, though offering products with substantial differences must be aware of demand inter-relationships. If Ford motor cars become expensive relative to comparable models offered by Vauxhall, for example, we would expect Vauxhall to make inroads into Ford's market share. The recognition of these inter-relationships particularly between large firms has led to various alternative models of oligopoly behaviour which we discuss in Chapter 6.

Taking the partial derivative with respect to p, $\dfrac{1}{q}\dfrac{\partial q}{\partial p} = \dfrac{-0.727}{p}$

∴ $(p/q) \cdot (\partial q/\partial p) = -0.727$. The LHS is price elasticity, hence the result. The proof is similar for any other measure of elasticity.

Instances of products whose consumption is complementary include cameras and film, cassette tape recorders and cassettes, houses and central heating (though not vice versa). In some cases a manufacturer sells both products and may find it profitable to sell one item at a loss in order to reap the benefits of a large volume of sales of the complementary article. The same applies to retailing, particularly in supermarkets, where certain of the articles sold are loss-leaders. Some manufacturers actually tie their sales of products so that they must be bought together. For a discussion of this practice see Chapter 6, Section 6-3.

To measure the demand relationship between two products, X and Y, we can use cross-elasticities of demand which measure the percentage change in the quantity of Y purchased, brought about by a given percentage change in the price of X. In symbols:

$$\text{Cross } \epsilon = \frac{\Delta q_y / q_y}{\Delta p_x / p_x}$$

The price of Y, p_y, is assumed to be held constant.

If demand is competitive, a small increase in the price of X (Δp_x positive) will encourage the substitution of Y for X (Δq_y positive). Both numerator and denominator in the formula given will be positive giving a positive cross-elasticity. A fall in the price of X will bring about a fall in the quantity of Y consumed, again yielding a positive result for cross-elasticity. If demand is complementary, a change in the price of X will bring about a change in the consumption of Y, but in the opposite direction. Cross-elasticity for complementary goods is therefore negative. If demand is independent, a change in the price of X will have no effect on the quantity of Y purchased. Cross-elasticity is thus zero in this situation. Cross-elasticities of demand are relevant to the problem of defining the boundaries of a market or an industry and we cover this in more detail in Chapter 6.

5-12 Forecasting

Lack of knowledge of the demand curves facing firms has led to various attempts at estimating the price-quantity relationships. The theoretical demand functions shown previously (see Sections 5-2 and 5-3) indicate in simplest form that the amount demanded of any commodity will depend *inter alia* on income, tastes and the structure of relative prices. Various attempts have been made to construct demand curves by statistical methods and these early ventures found the demand curves negatively inclined in agreement with the general law of demand specified in Section 5-2 although one particular finding for pig iron found a positively sloped function (H. K. Moore [101]), possibly reflecting the identification problem.*

Nevertheless there have been many other attempts to learn more about the demand curve for a product because demand forecasts in the short term are essential if production is to be scheduled in such a way that sales can be met without keeping large stocks in reserve. In the longer term they are even more important when managers have to choose the size and type of plant needed for production. We have already seen in our discussion of risk how short term production decisions need a forecast of future demand conditions. In fact any pricing or production decision requires some kind of estimate of both demand conditions in the market as well as cost conditions in the firm and as we indicate in our discussion of pricing policy (Chapter 7) lack of knowledge of market conditions can cause some firms to follow a mechanistic convention of adding a profit margin to a cost base and sacrificing profits which could have been made if the price had been based on market conditions.

Our forecasts will obviously be subject to risk or uncertainty and consequently any forecast can only be either an expected value or a value which is most likely to be achieved given the information provided. In addition to such a point estimate it is highly desirable to indicate the probability and possible magnitude of any error above or below the predicted value. Quite often forecasts are given with a confidence interval, e.g. predicted sales for 1976 may be given as,

£56m. with a 95 per cent confidence interval of ± £2m.

This means that if actual events proceed as anticipated the probability of achieving a sales performance of between £54m. and £58m. is 0.95. Actual sales for 1976 could lie at a level outside this range, but the statistician believes that there is only a 5 per cent chance of this happening. Forecasts are available with varying degrees of accuracy, but to improve results significantly may take such a long time, as more information is sought, that the forecast is no longer valid when it is eventually finalised. Furthermore the cost incurred in so doing may more than outweigh the benefits obtained.

We will now consider some of the methods available which are suitable for making short term forecasts. Some of these methods are also suitable for medium to long term forecasts, i.e. a period sufficiently distant for the company to envisage marketing new products, or purchasing new plant to meet the demand of existing products.

---

* For an elementary discussion of the identification problem, see W. J. Baumol [12].

5-13 Mechanical Methods of Forecasting

Simple Extrapolations

The simplest type of forecast is based on the assumption that future sales per period of time will be the same as the current rate of sales. In other words the firm holds static expectations. Recent sales records would be consulted to determine average sales in the immediate past to arrive at the forecast. Of course, should the data suggest that sales are either increasing or decreasing over time our forecast would naturally incorporate such a tendency. For example if sales had been increasing by an average of 5 per cent each year, next year's forecast would be average sales for the current year plus 5 per cent.

A complication which rapidly becomes apparent is that while sales may have a tendency to rise or fall over the years, there may be fluctuations between the months or seasons within a year. This means that the trend may not be a steady rise or fall, though by isolating average sales we should be able to detect its direction.

Moving Averages

Table 5.1

Monthly Sales 1974	000's packets	Twelve Monthly Total
January	450	
February	440	
March	435	
April	425	
May	360	
June	380	
July	350	
August	360	
September	380	
October	395	
November	450	
December	480	4,905
1975		
January	530	4,985
February	510	5,055
March	510	5,130
April	500	5,205

In Table 5.1 sales are seen to be fluctuating throughout the year. Total sales in 1974 were 4,905 with an average throughout the year of 4,905/12 = 408.75. Each month we obtain a new sales figure which can be used to update the average.

Thus in January 1975 sales for the twelve months up to and including the month itself were 4,985, giving a new monthly average of 415.42. Throughout February, March and April we revise the monthly average to give a series of 'moving averages', as follows (figures are rounded off):

December 409, January 415, February 421, March, 428, April 434.

From this series we can see that sales have an upward trend over time, though we would wish to observe the behaviour of the series over a longer period of time before drawing any firm conclusions. If we were satisfied that the fluctuations of 1974 would be repeated in a similar pattern of ups and downs throughout 1975, we could use moving averages to forecast monthly sales for the remainder of 1975. Comparison of the twelve monthly totals in December 1974 and April 1975 suggests an annual growth in sales of about 18 per cent.

$$\begin{aligned}\text{Estimated sales for 1975} &= 5205 + (18\% \times 8/12)(5205) \\ &= \underline{5830}\,(000\text{'s packets})\end{aligned}$$

Determining an annual growth rate by the comparison of two four-monthly periods is, of course, highly unsatisfactory. Nevertheless, if we can obtain an alternative estimate of the annual growth in sales — perhaps by consulting sales records over a period of several years, a moving average or total provides a convenient starting point for making the forecast. As we saw in the above example, having already obtained a 12 month figure to April 1975, we only needed to add 8/12 of the likely growth rate to yield our forecast for the whole of 1975. Again if we have studied sufficient data to detect a consistent monthly pattern of sales, we can split our annual forecast into individual monthly forecasts. If October normally accounts for 8 per cent of total sales, for example, our estimate for October 1975 would be 8 per cent × 5830 = <u>466.</u>

Exponential Weighting and Secular Trends

A secular trend, which is a trend that causes sales to increase or decrease continually, has a compound effect. If for example sales expand by 10 per cent per quarter and in the first quarter, 100 units were sold, then 110 units will be sold in the second quarter. But the number of units sold in the third quarter will not be 120 but 110 + (10% × 110) = 121. Our figure for the final quarter would be 121 + 12.1 = 133.1. If an even faster rate of growth is envisaged, it is apparent that figures from the early months of a sales period should have less influence than more recent data in preparing a forecast.

Forecasting by moving averages can be refined by using exponential weighting which permits more recent data to have a greater influence on the forecast. Holt's method is a short term forecasting technique which uses exponential weighting (see ICI Monograph [64]). The most recent data receive the largest weighting while the data furthest back in time receive the smallest weighting. The change in weighting is a gradual one and arranged so that successive weights differ by a constant ratio. The final average includes all past sales figures, but the weights attached to the most distant data will be negligibly small, as shown in Table 5.2.

Table 5.2

Period			Sales	Weight	Weight × Sales
1974	quarter	IV	108	0.500	54.0
		III	96	0.250	24.0
		II	80	0.125	10.0
		I	90	0.062	5.6
1973	quarter	IV	92	0.031	2.9
		III	80	0.016	1.3
		II	70	0.008	0.6
		I	84	0.004	0.3
1972	quarter	IV	86	0.002	0.2
		III	76	0.001	0.1
		II	60	-	-
		I	64	-	-
				0.999	99.0

Exponentially Weighted Moving Average

In this illustration, the common ratio between successive weights is 0.5, and data pertaining to periods earlier than 1972, quarter III, can safely be ignored. A common ratio of 0.5 gives a substantial fading out effect useful for purposes of exposition, though in practice a smaller ratio may be more appropriate (see A. Battersby [11]). This type of moving average may be used for forecasting in the same way that simple moving averages are used.

Indicators

So far we have discussed the projection of sales data pertaining to the product itself as a means of forecasting. In some circumstances it may be appropriate to consult other data or forecasts. For example the sales of winter clothes may be related to the weather, as will sales of gas and electricity. Some of these indicators may be highly useful in forecasting. What we must be wary of is using indicators which incorporate a lag; the Brookings Report (R. E. Caves and Associates [24] p. 37) for instance describes how changes in employment follow output changes in the UK economy with a twelve month lag. With government policy heavily focused on unemployment, expansionary measures would be effected a year after economic activity had in reality originally become depressed. Similarly deflationary measures would be effected only after demand in the economy had become excessive leading to inflation and balance of payments deficits. Such deflationary measures taken would thus tend to have perverse results if they took effect when the economy had already moved into a recession as was the case with the July 1961 budget. Expansionary budgets have often exacerbated an already inflationary situation.

Leading indicators,* i.e. series or indices which precede changes in economic activity and sales, are hard to come by and do not always lead by the same interval of time. Movements in share prices, changes in the money supply, purchases of durable goods have all been tried as leading indicators, with mixed success. The use of this method is an improvement on simple extrapolation because at least one is trying to isolate factors which influence demand. However, the observed relationship between an indicator and a predicted series may be fortuitous, or at least tenuous so that the identification of indicators is only a small step in the direction of true econometric forecasting. In addition to this we require a thoroughgoing demand analysis to isolate all relevant variables, and statistical analysis to measure the strength of any causal relationships.

5-14 Statistical Methods of Estimation

Historical sales data are often available to assist in the forecasting or estimation of demand, and demand curves have been isolated by this means. C. E. V. Leser [79] utilised data on price and consumption given by R. Stone [143] to derive a demand curve for soap in the United Kingdom for the period 1920-38. The resulting scatter diagram lent itself to the graphical construction of a downward sloping demand curve. Such a curve is not only interesting because it confirms our

---

* For a discussion of the use of leading indicators, see C. Drakatos [35].

beliefs about demand schedules but also because it may help us to forecast future sales at a given price. Most firms have historical data indicating how sales have moved in the past, together with price movements and changes in advertising expenditure. Current sales performance in different market sectors reflecting different income groups is another source of information which may help to reveal the underlying demand function. The former type of data enable one to conduct a time-series analysis, the latter type of investigation being a cross-sectional analysis. Both forms of data are subject to error. To obtain a series of observations which is sufficiently long enough to be used to give meaningful results poses a major problem and of course the longer the period over which the data have been collected the more likely is the nature of the demand relationship to have changed. Predictions are only reliable in so far as the underling relationship is fairly stable over time. Difficulties in estimating a demand curve* from past data led to this classic remark: 'The most important conclusion from these analyses of the elasticity of demand for automobiles with respect to price is that no exact answer to the question has been obtained.'**

Table 5.3 Estimation of Regression Coefficients

Year	X (Advertising Expenditure £'000's)	$(X-\bar{X})$	Y (Sales £'000's)	$(Y-\bar{Y})$	$(X-\bar{X})^2$	$(X-\bar{X})(Y-\bar{Y})$
1960	5	−5	36	−12	25	60
1	6	−4	39	−9	16	36
2	4	−6	36	−12	36	72
3	9	−1	44	−4	1	4
4	8	−2	48	0	4	0
5	11	1	47	−1	1	−1
6	12	2	51	3	4	6
7	15	5	58	10	25	50
8	13	3	59	11	9	33
9	17	7	62	14	49	98
Sum	100		480		170	358
Mean	10		48			

---

*   See also G. J. Stigler [140] and M. B. Shupack [129].
** General Motor Corporation, *The Dynamics of Automobile Demand*, 1939. Quoted in E. C. Hawkins [56].

Table 5.3 consists of time-series data showing how a company's advertising budget has changed over the years 1960-69, and how the company's sales have behaved during the same period. Given this information a scatter diagram can be plotted and a line of best fit drawn in (see Figure 5.12) freehand or by calculation. This line cuts the Y axis (sales) at 27 (£'000s) and is of slope 2.1. Its equation is therefore:

$$Y = 27 + 2.1X.$$

Figure 5.12 Estimation of Regression Coefficients

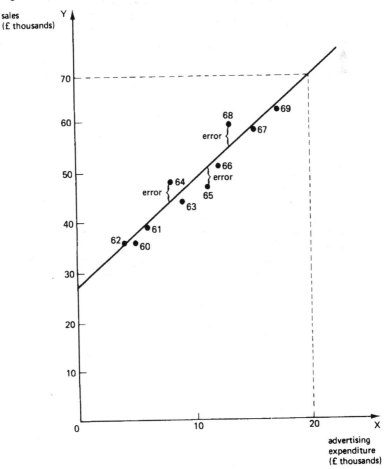

If we believe that this equation is a good fit to the observed data as it appears to be from the graphical analysis, and that the data are not atypical in any way, we can use the equation to predict. For example, we may be required to predict the sales level of 1975 given an advertising budget of £20,000. Substituting in the equation:—

$$Y = 27 + 2.1(20) = 69 \quad (\text{£'000's})$$

The same answer could have been obtained by inspection of the graph (Figure 5.12). The prediction is of course only an estimate, though we would hope that the actual value would not be too far above or below the line of best fit. In practice we would quote the figure of £69,000 as our sales estimate but we would also include a confidence interval to allow for the actual result being greater or less than this value.

The technique of obtaining a linear relationship by fitting a straight line to data in the manner described is known as linear regression. In practice, the statistician would use a formula to derive the relationship rather than try to draw a graph and obtain the best fit freehand. The formula used has been specifically designed to produce the best possible fit to the data, and if the relationship is linear, we are proposing that it is of the form $Y = \alpha + \beta X$. For a given value of X we have a corresponding actual value for Y and an estimated value for Y which we may write as Y'. Any actual value not lying on a 'line of best fit' gives a deviation of magnitude $Y - Y'$ and we call these deviations residuals or errors. They are illustrated in Figure 5.12 by the vertical distance between the point of observation and the line of best fit. Thus for a value of X, say X_i, we have a residual, e_i given by $e_i = Y_i - Y_i'$. The criterion generally chosen to arrive at a regression line is that the line should minimise the sum of squares of the errors (residuals) about the line. Consequently we choose a line to make

$$\sum_{i=1}^{n} e_i^2$$

as small as possible and the line is thus derived by the method of 'least squares'. Thus we use a formula which takes each error, squares it, sums all squared errors and finds the minimum value of this sum.

Taking our linear equation $Y = \alpha + \beta X$, then our job is to find estimates for α and β these estimates being written α', β'. To determine α' and β', our estimates of the intercept and of the slope of the line we go through the following procedure:

(i) Find the mean value of X and Y, $\bar{X}$ and $\bar{Y}$ respectively.

(ii) For each value of X, X_i find $X_i - \bar{X}$ and $Y_i - \bar{Y}$ (see Table 5.3).

(iii) For each X_i, calculate $(X_i - \bar{X})^2$ and $(X_i - \bar{X})(Y_i - \bar{Y})$.

(iv) Find the sum of $(X_i - \bar{X})^2$ and also of $(X_i - \bar{X})(Y_i - \bar{Y})$ written

$$\sum_{i=1}^{n} (X_i - \bar{X})^2, \quad \sum_{i=1}^{n} (X_i - \bar{X})(Y_i - \bar{Y})$$

where n is the number of observed values.

(v) Calculate the ratio

$$\frac{\sum_{i=1}^{n} (X_i - \bar{X})(Y_i - \bar{Y})}{\sum_{i=1}^{n} (X_i - \bar{X})^2}$$

giving us β', our estimate for β.

(vi) Write $\bar{Y} = \alpha' + \beta'\bar{X}$ and determine α', by substitution of the values obtained for $\bar{Y}, \beta'$ and $\bar{X}$.

Thus in our example $\bar{X} = 10$
$\bar{Y} = 48$

$X_i - \bar{X}$ and $Y_i - \bar{Y}$ can be determined as shown in Table 5.3.

For each X_i we can also find $(X_i - \bar{X})^2$ and $(X_i - \bar{X})(Y_i - \bar{Y})$ also shown in Table 5.3.

$$\sum_{i=1}^{n} (X_i - \bar{X})^2 = 170$$

$$\sum_{i=1}^{n} (X_i - \bar{X})(Y_i - \bar{Y}) = 358$$

∴ $\beta' = 358/170 = 2.1$.

Substituting in the formula $\bar{Y} = \alpha' + \beta'\bar{X}$ gives us

$48 = \alpha' + (2.1 \times 10)$
∴ $48 = \alpha' + 21$
∴ $\alpha' = 27$.

Hence our line of best fit.

5-15 Problems of Estimation

The preceding discussion perhaps suggests that the determination of a demand or sales relationship requires little more than a knowledge of statistical formulae and the ability to operate a calculating machine. In practice there are so many problems to overcome that such an analysis needs to be conducted by a statistician or an econometrician (a statistician primarily concerned with deriving relationships between economic variables). Only then can we be confident about using such functions and the predictions derived from them for purposes of company policy.

In Section 5-4 we described the demand function as 'multivariate', demand being dependent on a number of variables which are under the decision makers control, those under the control of competitors, and various external factors. Clearly such a function cannot be estimated by means of simple regression analysis using a scatter diagram, but formulae are available for *multiple* regression, so that in principle an increase in the number of variables need not amount to a problem in itself, the real difficulty lies in the provision of adequate data — relating quantity purchased to product prices, household income, advertising and any other variable which is seen to be significant.

If this information is available, we can then use the least-squares multiple regression technique to estimate parameters for the function:

$$Y = \alpha + \beta_1 X_1 + \beta_2 X_2 + \ldots + \beta_n X_n$$

where Y is a function of n variables $X_1 \ldots X_n$. The formulae referred to above enable us to derive estimates: $\alpha', \beta_1', \beta_2', \ldots \beta_n'$, which can be used to find elasticity with respect to each of the independent variables $X_1 \ldots X_n$. If the equation is estimated in logarithmic form, then each estimate $\beta_1' \ldots \beta_n'$ gives a direct estimate of the respective elasticity measure. We therefore have a means of forecasting should any variable change in isolation, but if more than one variable changes, the appropriate values can be substituted in the equation in order to yield a prediction for Y.

The bigger the number of variables, the more likely is the statistician to use a package computer programme for regression analysis. Calculating the regression coefficients is only part of the analysis since it is important to determine the total explanatory power of the equation and the reliability of each parameter within the equation. Two of the tests normally applied by a statistician are mentioned here briefly. The first of these is the coefficient of multiple determination: R^2 or $\bar{R}^2$ (the latter being adjusted for the degrees of freedom). If $\bar{R}^2$ for a demand equation is calculated as 0.678, then this means that 67.8 per cent of the variation in demand observed in the data is 'explained' by the independent variables in the equation, the remainder being accounted for by the stochastic or error terms. The second test is a check on the individual estimates which proceeds by calculating the standard errors of the regression coefficients. These are normally bracketed below the coefficients in the equation and as a rough guide each standard error should not exceed half the value of the coefficient itself for the purpose of finding 95 per cent confidence intervals. Suppose for example we obtained a regression coefficient of -1.506 for the logarithm of price in a logarithmic function, and the standard error was found to be 0.316. The value of -1.506 is an estimate of the price elasticity of demand,

and we can be 95 per cent confident that the real value lies within the range −1.506 ± 2(0.316), i.e. between −0.874 and −2.138.

Such tests are fundamental in econometric analysis but this brief description is only scratching the surface of what is a highly developed subject in its own right. We have already raised the question of identification in Section 5-12. For the problems of multi-collinearity, least-squares bias, autocorrelation, heteroscedasticity and other econometric problems we direct the readers attention to the standard textbooks on econometrics. Once the reader is familiar with such material we recommend him to consult the econometric studies that have been published on demand forecasting (see A. P. Koutsoyiannis [72]; C. M. Allen [5]; M. J. Buxton and D. C. Rhys [22]; NIER [103]; NIER [104]; D. S. Watson [153]).

5-16 Alternative Estimation Methods

If adequate sales data are available, the statistician can attempt to estimate the demand function and produce sales forecasts using regression analysis. In practice there are many drawbacks to the use of this method as we have suggested in Sections 5-14 and 5-15. Most econometric problems stem from incomplete information and if adequate records have not been kept up or if the product has been newly introduced there is no real basis for estimating the demand function. In any case results obtained from time series data may not be apt for all time periods as changing circumstances may alter the entire nature of the demand relationships. For these reasons, econometric forecasts are often supplemented with information derived from sources other than company records and family budget studies.

Interview Approaches

Interview or the polling of opinions can often serve as the basis of a projection or forecast. One such method is executive polling which analyses a sample of view from the executives of the company. Even when the prime concern of the analyst is a sales forecast, the sample will include executives concerned with other functions of the firm such as finance, production, purchasing and so on, rather than just the sales function. Each executive is required to make an estimate of the likely sales of the company's main products based on his knowledge and beliefs concerning the state of the economy, consumer demand, the strategies open to the company and all other relevant factors.

An average of these estimates can then be taken to yield the sales forecast. It is unlikely that important decisions would be made on the basis of this type of information alone. Statistical or econometric forecasts will normally be preferred, but personal judgement and expertise may be able to allow for factors peculiar to the situation and which have not been taken account of in statistical estimates. Indeed if the executives who are questioned are well informed with the latest available data and reports which are relevant to the situation, our forecasts can be improved by the incorporation of their managerial skills. We must always be sure, however, that the views expressed are the result of well informed judgement and not hunches or guesswork.

The same limitations apply to sales force polling which is primarily concerned with the view of sales executives, product and area managers and sales representatives. While realising that senior managers or executives have a valuable contribution to make, there is a great deal to be said for analysing the views of those in close contact with the market. Immediate orders from major customers can be incorporated directly into the estimates, and departures from current trends can be quickly detected. The advantage of this approach lies in its directness, but it suffers from the drawbacks common to all opinion polling methods, namely the likelihood of hunches and guesswork. In addition, it relies on estimates from employees whose job it is to meet current sales rather than anticipate future trends, at least in so far as the sales representatives are concerned. As with executive polling, information derived by this means may help to substantiate or modify other evidence, but would seldom be relied upon in isolation.

Information may be obtained from distributors of the product (wholesalers or retailers) on what they think the future level of demand will be. This provides only a rough indicator but it has the advantage of representing the views of people directly concerned with the customers. But the most obvious source of information for the purposes of sales forecasts is the opinion of the customers. As in the case of political opinion polls, a representative sample of the population is taken but instead of analysing voting intentions, the interviewer obtains a sample of purchasing intentions. Normally these surveys are carried out by product group, e.g. motor cars, the interviewee being required to state whether or not he intends buying a new car and if he does, what type will be purchased. One must of course be very wary of the interpretation of such data, realising that, as with voting, vague intentions are vastly different from firm commitments! Customers may also be approached about their reactions to forthcoming price changes and alternative types of sales promotion and this information helps the firm to build up a picture of the market.

Market Experiments

Instead of asking the consumer questions, his behaviour can be observed either in a simulated situation or tested in the market place itself. Some companies and researchers have attempted to test consumer reaction to varying prices, different product brands and so on by a carefully planned exercise within the market outlets — usually supermarkets and department stores. Another approach has been to simulate a market situation by establishing 'consumer clinics' in which various product brands and products are available for purchase with money provided by the investigators. Both forms of experiment require careful design and the information they reveal is of more interest to the market practitioner than the economist in that often they only reveal changes in market share between brands in response to price changes. The problems here in a dynamic market situation are of course that there may be other forces at work which are difficult to unravel. One method to minimise this problem is to operate tests in two groups of centres. In one group where price has not been changed, the other where the price changes have been adopted. The former acts as a control and in this way the two results can be compared so that common factors influencing sales (changes in earnings, a national advertising campaign and so on) in a particular period can be isolated. This assumes of course that two groups of shops can be equally matched and this is itself a problem.

Other difficulties over the design of such tests are the lengths of time the test is run for and the type of retail outlets chosen (assuming a willingness on their part to cooperate). If the purpose of the experiment is to obtain predictions for the overall demand of the product then biases in the sample must be recognised and avoided. However use of such experiments can yield up-to-date estimates of price and advertising elasticities, theoretically superior to any inferences drawn from time series analysis because the decision to buy a particular product (or brand of product) is observed in the market place. The market experiment whilst perhaps the most difficult and certainly the most expensive in terms of the commitment of resources offers the most promise in that the researcher is probing the actual buying decision. An analysis of recent work published on market experiments indicates that it is possible given careful experimental design to undertake empirical work in the market or real shop situation (see particularly A. Gabor, C. W. J. Granger and A. P. Sowter [42] and A. P. Sowter, A. Gabor and C. W. J. Granger [137]).

The second form of experimental method, the clinical, controlled method enables variables in the experiment to be manipulated by the researcher to give variations in price, packaging or display and other product modifications. The resultant behaviour of the participants in the experiment is then observed (see A. Gabor *et al.*, *op. cit.*, and E. A. Pessemier [109]). A critical assumption is that the experimental conditions should be psychologically equivalent to the market. Both of these methods can be useful and in general experimental demand analysis is a very fertile approach but there are many drawbacks, as E. C.

Hawkins remarks in his survey of methods of estimating demand.

'Most of the price experiments cited dealt with only one price change, revealing only one small segment of the demand curve. There is no assurance that the results could be used in relation to price points other than those tested.

'Despite these and other problems, the experimental method seems to hold more promise than any other technique for estimating the elasticity of demand for differentiated products under conditions of monopolistic competition.' ([56] p. 138)

In conclusion, econometric methods of estimation and forecasting are becoming increasingly accepted in the area of demand analysis. They are preferable to alternative methods because of their ability to analyse the separate effects of the large number of variables which enter into a demand relationship and therefore allow us to satisfy the *ceteris paribus* assumptions. Human intuition is largely ignored which is an advantage from the aspect of objectivity but a disadvantage from the aspect of flexibility and the accommodation of factors peculiar to a given situation. In the final analysis, we seldom have sufficient data to be fully confident about results obtained from the application of econometric techniques so that any additional information revealed by interviews or market experiments is useful to us even if only to substantiate our statistical results. Of course new products have no sales history so that market experiments and market research are the most likely sources of information about sales.

6 MARKET STRUCTURE

6-1 Introduction

In our economic analysis of the firm we have stressed the importance of both internal and external resource allocation. Traditional economic theory, we have argued, focused on the firm as part of a market system and therefore was concerned more with external resource allocation whereas newer contributions have examined decision making and resource allocation within the firm *per se*. However, decisions whether strategic or operating, cannot be taken without some reference to the environment in which firms operate, in particular with regard to the state of competition, and this therefore leads us into a discussion of the relationship between market structure and business behaviour. This discussion begins with a clarification of the concepts and definitions involved in the study of markets in Section 6-2; followed by a classification of market structures comprising perfect competition, monopoly, monopolistic competition and oligopoly in Section 6-3. We spend the majority of our time here with oligopoly because this is the dominant form of market structure in manufacturing industry. We note that 'mutual interdependence' of decisions is an important consideration and that competition often takes the form of non-price methods particularly with the use of advertising.

The existence of interdependence in oligopolistic markets and the resultant difficulty of developing determinate models has resulted in a failure to develop a general theory of oligopoly. We look at the issue of collusion, both open and tacit, in Section 6-4, followed by an examination of the kinked demand curve model (Section 6-5), and the sales revenue maximisation model (Section 6-6). The latter is an interesting model in that it is an attempt to systematise managerial discretion in objectives as well as to account for some of the features noted in oligopolistic industries, particularly the use of non-price competition. This model does have some drawbacks although it is a useful teaching aid in that it links well with the other models of managerial discretion as well as other models of oligopolistic behaviour notably the kinked demand curve. We then introduce Game Theory in Section 6-7 to illustrate another approach to interdependence and we conclude with a section on public policy towards oligopolistic or dominant firms.

6-2 Dimensions of a Market

The economist views a market as a mechanism by which transactors exchange (though not necessarily in a fixed geographical location) goods and services either through barter or through a medium of exchange such as money. In a market characterised by buyers and sellers in close communication, the interaction of these transactions will determine the market price. Whilst this is a convenient definition of a market, it fails to highlight the multidimensional nature of markets, and this is a serious limitation particularly for public policy in its attempts to exercise control over imperfectly competitive markets as we shall see in our coverage of anti-monopoly policy in Section 6-8. This difficulty is further exacerbated by the fact that all the dimensions may not be operative in all markets so that *a priori* reasoning cannot be used to give a definition of a market in any particular case. Additionally there is uncertainty as to how markets are related to industries, where an industry is defined as a group of firms using a similar production process and/or labour to supply broadly similar customers. We could talk about the motor *industry*, for example, but this covers many 'products', so we follow J. Robinson [120] in using the term 'market' when referring to the nature of competition.

The concept of a 'product' is also difficult to convey in precise terms but one approach is to appeal to cross-elasticities of demand (see Chapter 5, Section 5-11). To recap, the cross-elasticity of demand between two products X and Y measures the percentage change in the quantity purchased of Y brought about by a unit percentage change in the price of X. If the two commodities are independent, cross-elasticity we noted would be zero whereas if the two were close substitutes cross-elasticity would be positive (and negative if the goods were complementary). The case for cross-elasticity as a means of delineation between product markets is a strong one because it stresses substitutability between products. However, it is not an unambiguous concept, as F. Machlup [83] for one has pointed out when he stated that cross-elasticities were 'particularly hopeless unknowns'. A. Hunter [62] likewise has criticised the use of cross-elasticities to delineate products and industries: 'In short, the ideal census industry in which all products and enterprises have, between them, high cross-elasticities of supply and demand is likely to occur only now and again' (p. 54). This is only being realistic, since in practice it is not easy to draw the line between one product and another which is neither *entirely* similar, nor a *perfect* substitute for it. Cross-elasticities can give a guide but we must accept that they will seldom be more than this. However, the concept is still advanced by many economists for the delineation of products and industries, particularly in the USA where they have been used in anti-trust (anti-monopoly) legislation to determine a 'reference' industry.

The *supply* side of a market is an important basis for market analysis; indeed information from Censuses of Production reveal the concentration within an industry so that dominant firms can be identified quite easily. Of course these industry statistics are normally wider in coverage than the markets (that would be identified say by cross-elasticities) and the classification is normally derived from technical considerations. However, it is useful because it focuses attention quickly on usually a relatively small body of suppliers. There are other difficulties which are encountered when examining the supply dimension of markets. Do we consider supply in terms of production for final sale given that some production may be used internally? Additionally are domestic suppliers the only ones to be considered, or imports too? Clearly for some markets either or both these considerations may be irrelevant but given that legislation in Britain has a market share criterion for identifying monopoly power of 1/4 (as under the 1973 Fair Trading Act — formerly 1/3 under the 1948 Monopolies Act) the boundaries of the supply side of the market are important.

The *demand* dimension of markets is particularly difficult to define. We have already mentioned the use of cross-elasticity of demand as a guideline to the delineation of products, but the characteristics of demand may determine the market particularly in terms of the end use of the product. If a consumer wishes to use paper as packaging material, then paper, card, cellophane, etc., may be virtually interchangeable, but on a product or industry supply basis they may be distinct so that the level of competitiveness between the alternative producers is difficult to measure. In the famous cellophane case in the USA the market was broadly defined to include many types of flexible wrapping paper despite differences in price so that the end use of the product here was the characteristic that determined the market. Alternatively, the market may be classified in terms of the type of customer, e.g. by taking sociodemographic factors into account.

If we add to these dimensions the one of geography — particularly important in the USA where there are national and state markets and where judgements in anti-monopoly cases have been made by examining both the narrow and broad geographic implications of a market, we must conclude that it is difficult to invoke economic theory or to be dogmatic over the definition of a market in any particular case. In any investigation of anti-monopoly behaviour the firms concerned will argue the case which is most favourable to them and the task of the investigators is to establish definitions which make economic sense. In doing this, some or all of the market dimensions discussed in this section will be considered but there will always be an element of subjectiveness.

6-3 The Market Structures of Neo-Classical (Traditional) Theory

We can in the first instance classify the different market structures firms are likely to encounter. The usual approach is to view the market structure as a continuum with perfect competition and monopoly at the two extremes. In between these two poles lie various shades of competitive and monopolistic markets. Generally in economics only four structures are taken as representative models though it is recognised that these only represent sufficiently different structures to form a basis for examining the behaviour of firms.

The four market structures recognised are:
- Perfect Competition.
- Monopolistic Competition.
- Oligopoly — pure and imperfect.
- Monopoly.

In this section we begin with an examination of the two extremes, and in passing give brief mention to monopolistic competition, but our prime concern will be with oligopoly. We justify this emphasis because in the first place oligopoly is by far the most significant variety in terms of industrial output and secondly it is the one where determinate models are difficult to formulate on account of the interdependence which confronts oligopolists in decision making.

Perfect Competition

The perfect competition model contains some very restrictive assumptions which will never be satisfied in real life. Historically, however, the model did have some empirical validity and one can also use the perfect competition model to show the link between the firm and the market and it is therefore a useful paradigm. Assumptions made for perfect competition to hold are:

1. *Many sellers and buyers*: (atomistic competition) — each seller has such a small share of the total output that no one firm acting independently can affect the market price so these sellers are price takers. Each buyer is a small part of the total market and no single buyer can influence price.

2. *Homogeneous product* — the products produced by firms are identical.

3. *Freedom of entry/exit* — there is freedom of entry and exit in the industry so that in the long run the supply curve is perfectly elastic.

4. *Maximisation of profits* — is the motivating assumption for firms with buyers wishing to maximise satisfaction.

5. *Perfect knowledge* — of alternatives and their concomitant pay-offs.

With these five assumptions we can examine the short run market and firm equilibrium, once we have introduced the demand and supply functions.

We have explained in Chapter 5 that the normal market demand curve has a negative slope with respect to price, but what induces a firm to supply more to the market? This can be determined by examining the individual firm under the conditions of perfect competition. It is a price taker because it cannot influence price by its own actions of expanding or restricting output so that the average revenue curve of the firm is horizontal and coincides with the marginal revenue curve with both MR and AR equal to the price. This is illustrated in Figure 6.1 where the price determined in the market is 0p and any expansion of output adds the same increment to the firm's revenue. The profit maximising output then depends on the cost curves the firm faces, and under conditions of perfect competition this output will be where marginal cost = price. MC, we can recall, represents the addition to total costs from producing one more unit of output and the MC curve normally takes on the 'U-shape' of conventional theory for this purpose as illustrated in Figure 6.1. But there are two output levels in this diagram where marginal cost equals price represented by $0q_1$ and $0q_2$. At output $0q_2$ losses are maximised whereas at $0q_1$ profits are maximised.*

Figure 6.1   The Firm's Supply Decision

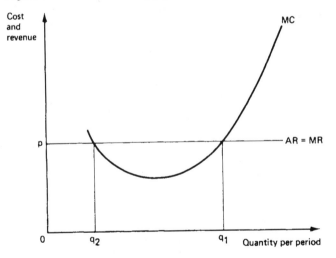

---

*   It can be shown that the sufficient condition for MC = MR to give maximum profit is that MC cuts the MR curve from below.

Thus Oq_1 is the output chosen at market price Op and if this price were to increase, once again the profit maximising output would be where marginal cost equals price so that the upward sloping portion of the MC curve of a perfectly competitive firm is the firm's supply curve.*
To derive a market supply curve (SS) as depicted in Figure 6.2a, we sum the relevant portions of the MC curves of all the firms supplying that market.** Alongside in Figure 6.2b we have drawn the marginal cost and average cost curves of the 'representative' firm, which should be the cost curves facing all suppliers if they have access to the same technical information, pay the same prices for inputs and are all equally efficient.

Figure 6.2a   Figure 6.2b

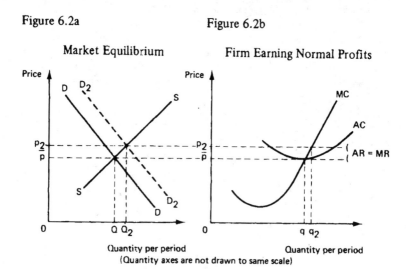

(Quantity axes are not drawn to same scale)

---

*   Strictly speaking the firm would not produce anything in the short run if total revenue did not cover total variable costs. So price must exceed average variable cost for production to take place — hence the relevant portion of the MC curve lies above the AVC curve.

**   The linear supply and demand functions drawn in Figure 6.2a are represented thus purely for convenience and do not correspond precisely to the accompanying diagrams.

The level of profits that the firm makes will depend on the position of the AC curve which in traditional theory is also presumed to be 'U-shaped'.* If the AC curve lies above the price line (i.e. AR and MR) this firm would be making losses and would leave the market whereas if it were tangential to the price line the firm would be making what we term as 'normal' profits, i.e. profits which are just sufficient to retain the entrepreneur in that particular line of business. Although profits would appear from the diagram to be zero (price just covering unit costs), one must remember that the economist's concept of cost includes the opportunity cost of using the firm's resources. Thus if economic profits are zero, this simply means that the firm is enjoying just a normal return on its resources — i.e. what could be earned in a strictly comparable venture (in terms of risk, etc.).

Suppose now that demand increased, represented by a shift in the market demand curve to $D_2 D_2$. Price Op which previously maintained an equilibrium between supply and demand will no longer do so and consequently the price has to rise to Op_2 where the schedules intersect. Once again the total amount supplied to the market per period of time, OQ_2, will be equal to the amount demanded per period. The firm would enjoy higher than normal profits at that price but these 'supernormal' profits would only remain for a short period as new firms were attracted from other industries. Under long run equilibrium where entry and exit can take place, profits are normal for all firms.

The behaviour of the firm under perfect competition is essentially mechanistic since it has no discretion in its pricing policy as it strives to maximise its profits. With the assumption of perfect knowledge of course the firm has no difficulty in selecting the most profitable alternatives and can therefore benefit the community by its efficient use of resources. The price mechanism thus allocates resources in a market economy, by showing where profits can be made in markets for finished goods, and by indicating the costs of production resulting from different combinations of factor inputs (which also have market prices). Because the firm is attempting to equate MC to price, in the short run any change in fixed costs or corporate taxes will not cause the firm to change its profit-maximising output.

Monopoly

The economist's definition of an absolute monopoly is a market where one firm is the only supplier of a product and its close substitutes. The cross-elasticity of the monopolist's products with others is zero so that the demand curve facing the monopolist is the market demand curve,

---

* In practice linearity might be a better approximation for MC, with AC continually declining, though at a slower and slower rate (see Chapter 4).

and if this is negatively sloped as theory suggests, the firm must lower its prices in order to expand output. The AR and MR curves are therefore no longer coincident, for as we illustrated in Chapter 5, Section 5-8 the MR curve lies below the AR curve and has twice the slope of the latter. It is only in the limiting case of perfect competition with a horizontal AR line that AR and MR are equal throughout for the firm.

The price/output behaviour of monopolists can be illustrated by supposing that a perfectly competitive market were monopolised overnight and that there were no savings in costs — a reasonable assumption given the speed of monopolisation. Figure 6.3 sets out the price/output positions for both perfect competition and monopoly.

Figure 6.3   Price and Output Under Monopoly

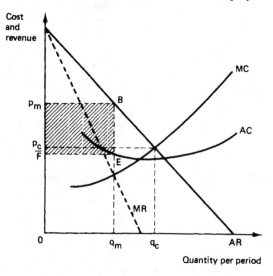

Under perfect competition the price established would be $0p_c$ with an output of $0q_c$ because equilibrium occurs where supply equals demand and since the supply curve is the sum of the marginal cost curves it follows that in equilibrium MC equals price. Under monopoly the profit maximising rule is for price and output to be determined by the intersection of MC and MR. Here the output is $0q_m$ and the price is $0p_m$ (the AR schedule showing the price at which output $0q_m$ can be sold) and thus the output is lower and the price is higher than under perfect

182

competition; this forms the classical case against monopoly. The shaded area in Figure 6.3 — p_mBEF — represents monopoly profit and the identification of such supernormal profit in a firm gives an indication of the use of market power. The welfare implications are that since the monopolist restricts output and charges higher prices than would prevail under perfect competition, he causes allocative inefficiency. Anti-monopoly policy has normally aimed to remove this allocative inefficiency. If we dropped the assumption of monopolisation 'overnight' then cost conditions under monopoly and perfect competition may well diverge in that the monopolist may be able to exploit economies of scale, which could shift the cost curves to such an extent that the monopolist could produce a larger output at a lower price. The monopolist might also be able to engage in research and development and thus innovate whereas smaller units perhaps could not command the necessary resources. Equally possible of course is that the monopolist may opt for an easy life, buy up patents and inventions to safeguard its position, or even misallocate resources internally rather than strive for the optimum proportion of factor inputs. This gives rise to internal inefficiency, or 'X-inefficiency' in H. Leibenstein's [78] terminology and it is another way of using market power which may exist side by side with allocative inefficiency in the market (see Section 6-8 below).

There are two other controversial practices which monopolists and other large dominant firms may engage in: tie-in-sales and price discrimination.

Tie-in-Sales

Sometimes two items which in principle could be sold separately are in fact sold together with a restriction that one or the other or both of the items cannot be purchased separately. There are at least three reasons why firms may adopt a tie-in-sales policy:

1. there may be economies in producing and/or selling (e.g. in distribution) the products jointly in which case consumers can benefit from an agreed tie-in-sale;
2. the firm may have a monopoly in one item and may seek to extend its power over another by tying this item in the sale. This can facilitate price discrimination and may raise entry barriers.
3. Tie-in-sales can be used to evade price control of one product (say where there is a legal maximum price) and the purchaser is required to purchase a non-fixed price item.

Tying arrangements nowadays tend to be voluntary and informal particularly as anti-trust action in the USA has made them illegal on the basis that they may substantially reduce competition. In Britain evidence of tie-in-sales was furnished by the Monopolies Commission Report on Industrial Gases in 1956 [96] in the case of the British

Oxygen Company.

Price Discrimination

The purpose of price discrimination is to extract as much profit as possible from a market, but the term 'price discrimination' can mean any of three things:

1. Where the same products are sold to different buyers and where the costs are no different. This can be illustrated by reference to the simple market demand curve drawn in Figure 6.4. If each unit could be sold for the maximum amount purchasers are willing to pay rather than a uniform price say of Op_1, the total revenue to the firm could be raised. Total revenue without discrimination would be given by area $Op_1 Bq_1$, but with price discrimination this could be raised to $OABq_1$. Of course it is an extreme case to assume that such complete price discrimination could be adopted (often referred to as first degree price discrimination). Instead the market may be segmented in some way. This could be done geographically by charging one price for the home market and another (or others) for export markets. In one market the firm may face more active competition than in others so it will pay the firm to charge less, cross-subsidising

Figure 6.4   Price Discrimination

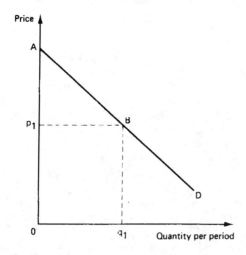

from another more lucrative market. In some cases this may even involve selling in some markets below cost (what is referred to as dumping).* This may be done to achieve a foothold in the market or to earn desperately needed foreign exchange or to get rid of surpluses (as with agricultural products). Alternatively the nature of the product may encourage price discrimination. For instance electricity cannot be stored so it is possible to discriminate between domestic and industrial users, as there is no possibility of re-transfer. Another example relates to the original and replacement equipment for motor vehicles. When the Monopolies Commission reported on electrical equipment [97] it observed a marked difference between the prices charged to manufacturers of cars and those charged on the market for replacement parts. The report held that these price differences were mainly designed to prevent entry into the initial equipment market and could not be justified by cost differences. However, it could reasonably argued here that the Monopolies Commission may have underestimated the countervailing power of motor vehicle manufacturers. In general if segmentation of markets is possible with restrictions on resale, and if elasticity of demand differs from segment to segment of the market, price discrimination will enable the firm to increase its revenue for a given output.

2. Where basically the same product is sold to different buyers but at prices which vary more than the cost differences. An example of this is the use of a deluxe rating on some consumer durables.

3. Where a uniform price is charged to customers but where there are cost differences which are not reflected in prices, e.g. uniform inland postal charges regardless of distance, and delivery charges on some makes of new cars. This is covered in Chapter 7, Section 7-9, when we discuss the problem of basing point and pricing.

The practice of price discrimination implies that some market power (even if not absolute monopoly power) is being exercised, since in a competitive market, price differences would be eliminated, consequently price discrimination *prima facie* is a reflection of monopoly power. Indeed there is evidence that price discrimination can be used to support a monopoly position, the classic example for the USA being Standard Oil which is reputed to have built its monopoly by price discrimination aimed at eliminating competition, and potential entry. A similar example can be given for the UK in the case of the British Oxygen Company in the same report that we mentioned earlier [96].

It is, however, only fair to point out that price discrimination does not always represent a deliberate policy to increase profit and use

---

* This practice is against the General Agreement on Tariff and Trade (GATT) rules.

monopoly power, quite often it may reflect the difficulty of finding non-discriminatory prices particularly where there are some differences in costs, like those of delivery (Case 3).

Monopolistic Competition

This is a market structure advanced by E. H. Chamberlin [25] which basically retains all the assumptions of perfect competition save the homogeneity of product. Products are differentiated for example by trademark, packaging, design, colour, or in the conditions surrounding their sale. Product differentiation may create barriers to entry* which could therefore violate the third assumption of the perfect competition model. This, however, is unlikely because so long as the firms are small, few absolute cost differences will persist and it may therefore be relatively easy to set up in business and produce a broadly similar product.

Figure 6.5   Monopolistic Competition — Long Run Equilibrium

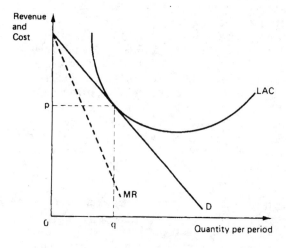

---

*   Product differentiation, particularly by trademark and the brand image conveyed therein, may deter new competition from entering the market. In practice the barrier to entry effect is more likely to be significant in less competitive markets.

Because of product differentiation, each firm has some control over its market and will face a negatively sloped average revenue curve for its product rather than the horizontal AR line facing the firm under perfect competition where the prevailing price had to be followed. On account of the *relative* ease of entry, in the long run AC will be tangential to the AR curve (as shown in Figure 6.5) so that only normal profit is earned. The reader will notice that the price/output combination given by the tangency of AC and AR does not occur when AC is at its minimum (as would happen in perfect competition when entry and exit were complete). Firms are producing at outputs lower than those conducive to minimum average cost so one of the predictions of the monopolistic competition model is that there will be excess capacity. Examples of monopolistic competition are not all that easy to find and the assumption of atomistic competition is seldom satisfied. The retail trade is a reasonable example where it is often possible to set up a small general dealers shop with a small amount of capital and to compete with others through service and the establishment of a good reputation. Even here, the assumptions are not fully satisfied, since direct competition between a group of retailers is limited by geographical location and the market structure may more properly be regarded as oligopolistic. In consequence then whilst the monopolistic competition model was a useful attempt to bridge the gap between monopoly and perfect competition, a study of oligopoly behaviour is likely to prove more fruitful and it is to this that we now turn.

Oligopoly

An examination of the size structure of firms in British industry reveals a skewed distribution with a relatively small number of large companies accounting for a very large proportion of employment, sales (or net output) and total assets. The extent of this phenomenon is usually measured by the concentration ratio and normally two levels of concentration are recognisable — overall and industry concentration (see M. A. Utton [148]). The former measures the proportion of sales or employment or assets of the whole of manufacturing industry accounted for by the largest companies. This is typically indicated by the top 100 or 500 companies (for instance Fortune's Top 500 US industrial companies), and the most recent statistics for Britain (see S. J. Prais [112]) indicate that 45 per cent of manufacturing net output in 1970 was accounted for by the largest 100 firms compared with 42 per cent in 1968, 37 per cent in 1963 and 31 per cent in 1958. Industrial concentration, however, relates to concentration in a particular trade or industry and is usually measured as the proportion of industry sales or net output of the top five firms in that industry. Whilst industrial classifications change over periods and often cover several product

Table 6.1   Average of Five-Firm Concentration Ratios, 1958-68

1963 and 1968: 295 products		1958 and 1968: 157 products	
Average	Change	Average	Change
1963 = 62.0%		1958 = 56.2%	
1968 = 66.0%	+ 4.0%	1963 = 59.4%	+ 3.2%
		1968 = 64.5%	+ 5.1%

Source: D. Elliott [39].

groups, concentration ratios (as given in Table 6.1) are useful in that they provide *prima facie* evidence of oligopoly and possible use of market power.

Table 6.1 based on 1968 Census of Production data (published in 1974) indicates that the average level of industrial concentration has risen over the period 1958-68, confirming estimates from academic sources (see P. E. Hart, *et al.*, [54]) that had been made over this period. If we break the averages down into broad industry groups we can obtain a rough indication of industry concentration as shown in Table 6.2. Further examination of the Census data reveals that if the rate of growth in concentration experienced during the 1958-68 period is maintained, something of the order of two thirds of products will have concentration ratios (based on net output) of between 80 and 100 per cent by 1993. Thus as overall concentration, industry concentration and concentration in specific product markets is increasing, a study of big business behaviour is vital to economists and students of management alike. The rest of this chapter examines models of oligopoly behaviour and discusses some of the attempts to control oligopoly and monopoly through public policy.

Oligopoly relates to fewness of sellers (duopoly where there are only two) and it can take the pure form (where there is an homogeneous product) or the more usual imperfect form where there is product differentiation. The distinguishing feature of oligopoly is not just the number of sellers but rather the mutual interdependence felt by oligopolistic firms in their decision making. We illustrated above how firms under conditions of perfect competition were price takers and free to pursue their output policy without recourse to considering the activities of other firms operating in the same market. An absolute monopolist with complete control of a product and its close substitutes, is also free to pursue an independent line of policy. When we come to oligopoly, however, a firm must have regard to the activities of other firms in the

SIC* order	Description	Number of products for which ratios available	1968 sales (£m) of products for which ratios available	Average concentration ratio (%) 1963	1968	Change	Coverage of ratios for each order (%)
II	Mining and quarrying	5	136.8	57.4	65.0	+7.6	15
III	Food manufactured including tea and coffee	33	2,420.1	78.1	78.9	+0.8	85
III	Beer, spirits, etc.	6	1,193.7	74.4	77.1	+2.7	98
III	Cigarettes, tobacco products	3	1,393.0	99.2	99.4	+0.2	100
IV	Coal and petroleum products	8	1,010.5	91.5	93.5	+2.0	87
V	Chemical and allied industries	39	1,952.4	74.0	75.5	+1.5	78
VI	Metal manufacture	8	975.8	72.9	74.3	+1.4	31
VI	Metal manufacture (including steel)	20	2,831.0	70.6	79.8	+9.2	93
VII	Mechanical engineering	35	1,521.7	60.3	62.4	+2.1	64
VIII	Instrument engineering	5	109.5	60.1	62.3	+2.2	82
IX	Electrical engineering	27	1,546.0	68.1	77.2	+9.1	80
X	Shipbuilding and marine engineering	1	60.1	34.6	57.4	+22.8	14
XI	Vehicles	8	1,724.0	85.2	89.1	+3.9	57
XII	Metal goods n.e.s.	21	1,301.0	55.0	57.6	+2.6	76
XIII	Textiles	28	2,040.8	41.5	49.7	+8.2	72
XIV	Leather, leather goods, fur	5	139.0	33.8	37.7	+3.9	90
XV	Clothing and footwear	14	792.1	30.1	37.0	+6.9	91
XVI	Bricks, pottery, glass, cement, etc.	16	662.1	65.6	75.5	+9.9	82
XVII	Timber, furniture, etc.	9	543.5	28.0	28.4	+0.4	67
XVIII	Paper, printing and publishing	10	970.3	54.5	56.2	+1.7	54
XIX	Other manufacturing industries	14	674.7	53.5	57.0	+3.5	68
	Total (excluding steel products)	295	21,167.3				

* Standard Industrial Classification

Source: D. Elliott [39].

industry who are supplying for the same market. This is not to say that at all decision levels this will be the case but certainly for many strategic decisions governing the future course of the firm — such as the launching of new products and the associated advertising and promotional expenditures firms should take account of the anticipated reactions of rivals. Pricing decisions, although frequently classified as operating decisions* may also give rise to interdependence. In fact there may be a complex interplay of anticipated strategies and counter-strategies which firms engage in, a topic which is examined later in this section in terms of the theory of games. Firms can either ignore interdependence — particularly for operating decisions (as we illustrate later in the Baumol sales revenue maximisation model) or make some specific evaluation as to how rivals will react to a given policy change; this evaluation is sometimes called the 'conjectural variation'. Alternatively they may try to reduce the uncertainty of interdependence by collusion (see G. Stigler [142]) either tacit or formalised (perhaps through a trade association).

The presence of interdependence in oligopolistic markets makes the formulation of a general model of oligopoly practically impossible. All one can do is to examine on a systematic basis, the characteristic types of behaviour encountered in oligopoly. The first feature which is often apparent is the use of non-price competition. The use of price as a competitive instrument is often rejected because of imperfect knowledge of the market demand curve besides the problem of predicting competitive reactions. This may lead to price stability: a point taken up in the kinked demand curve model elaborated later in this section. Price changes** can be seen as an aggressive step whereas changes in the advertising budget (in imperfect oligopoly) are more difficult to detect; difficult to replicate and often seen as less aggressive. It is hardly surprising therefore to see extensive use of advertising (probably beyond the level which would maximise joint profits for the oligopolists, since although total revenue from the market would normally increase, much of the advertising effort is self-cancelling). A consideration often neglected in oligopoly is that of barriers to entry which may impede or block new competition not by legal impediments or by outright exclusion, e.g. by a trade association, but by purely economic forces. It is to this that we now turn our attention.

Barriers to Entry

In the perfect competition model developed above in Section 6-3, freedom of entry and exit was assumed. Firms making supernormal profits would find these removed in the long run as new firms were attracted

---
*   e.g. Ansoff's [6] classification, see Chapter 1, Table 1.1.
**   The firm may however use price rebates etc. as a way of effecting price changes without openly declaring a price change.

into the market in the absence of any barriers to prevent or restrict entry. Likewise those firms making below normal profits would leave the market perhaps finding alternative employment for their resources. In the monopoly model entry is effectively prevented as the monopolist so defined is the sole producer of a commodity and its close substitutes now and in the future. In the case of oligopoly 'entry conditions' require further analysis and while the analysis could be restricted to situations where entry is prevented the bulk of industry would thereby be omitted.

In recent years increasing attention has been paid to the conditions of entry into an industry, where these relate to purely economic forces as opposed to legal restrictions such as patents. It is recognised that potential entry as well as actual entry has an impact on the market in that the *threat* of entry can influence the price/output behaviour of existing firms. The motivation for entry will at least in part be the rate of profit. Current supernormal profit may be the signal which attracts a new entrant but of course what is of crucial importance is the level of profit he anticipates he could earn given his own cost conditions, *vis-à-vis* those of his potential competitors; the demand conditions for the product(s) of the industry, and the reactions of existing firms in the industry.

Existing firms may have cost advantages which act as barriers to entry, and the bigger these are, the more can price exceed average cost in established firms without inducing entry — i.e. the higher the 'limit price'. Product differentiation may act as a barrier to entry since it gives established producers advantages over potential entrants. Product differentiation will reflect two sets of factors. In the first place there is the basic product itself; for instance consumer products are more amenable to differentiation than capital goods. The second factor relates to the policies of existing firms with respect to advertising, product design, etc. As we indicated earlier in this section, non-price competition — particularly advertising — is a feature of oligopoly so that for a firm to break into a market it will probably have to promote a sufficiently different product to compete effectively with rivals, and to wrest buyers away from their established suppliers. Because such promotional activities incur a cost to the entering firm, in effect a capital requirement to reach an effective level of promotion, product differentiation as a barrier can be conveniently grouped as an absolute cost advantage to existing firms.* The term 'absolute' means that existing sellers have average cost curves that are significantly lower throughout their entire range than those of potential entrants. Other possible sources of such an advantage include specialised managerial or technical

---

* For a useful comment on advertising as a barrier to entry, see the Monopolies Commission Report on detergents [98].

knowledge; control of crucial patents or of resources and sales outlets (through vertical integration).

Economies of scale may also act as a barrier to entry since new firms will invariably command only a small share of the market initially. If economies of scale are significant, the entrants will therefore find it difficult to compete with established firms who are large enough to exploit these economies. If the entrant tries to compete by acquiring a large scale plant in the hope of gaining an ultimate foothold in the market this may add a significant amount to the output of the industry and with it the uncertainty as to the reactions this would provoke from existing firms. The interdependence of decision making — such a hallmark of oligopoly — is reinforced in this situation since it relates to how potential entrants think established firms will react to entry and how established firms think potential entrants expect them to react to entry.

In a pioneering study, J. Bain [9] examined the existence of barriers to entry, particularly those relating to product differentiation and other absolute cost barriers. He evaluated a cross-section of twenty industries in the USA and found that in six industries with high barriers to entry, five of these had product differentiation barriers but other absolute cost advantages he found to be generally not significant. With regard to economies of scale, only in two out of the twenty industries did extreme scale economies pose any serious problem for new entrants. The product differentiation barriers centred around advertising in markets for consumer goods, and distribution policies were also important when vertical integration was present.

The most significant imponderable for an entering firm is the *post-entry* price, since there will be some price at or below which new entrants would face losses. The absolute cost advantages of established firms and then their response when entry takes place will determine the profitability of entry. Clearly empirical observations on the conjectures of existing and potential firms is desirable but in the absence of any systematic evidence we must determine these *a priori*. The normal proposition forwarded to determine existing firms' reactions is that they will maintain output in the face of entry and allow price to fall because this would be the most damaging to new entrants. This proposition is usually termed the *Sylos postulate*, which was coined by F. Modigliani [93] in his review of Sylos Labini's book *Oligopoly and Technical Progress* [73]. The significance of this postulate is that it produces a determinate solution to the oligopoly problem where there are no product differentiation barriers (in other words homogeneous oligopoly), but it is questionable on the grounds that it does not necessarily represent the strongest reaction that could face potential entrants. Existing firms might, for example, *increase* their output either by using plant that has been designed for a smaller output or by using excess capacity in the industry. Indeed excess capacity may itself be interpreted as a barrier to entry if entrants anticipate that existing firms will react by expanding output (see J. T. Wenders [155]). As firms expand output they will be forcing prices down to the entry blocking price as given by the cost differences.

The type of reaction which firms adopt or think their rivals will adopt will be conditioned very much by the demand conditions for the product. If industry demand is expanding, entry is likely to be easier as existing firms will feel less threatened and of course if the industry is one where innovation and technical change are rapid, entry could be gained by a new entrant who possessed an absolute cost advantage over the existing firms.

6-4 Collusion

As we stated earlier, oligopolistic structures invite collusion and there are three principal reasons which we explore here. In the first place a well organised collusive agreement between all firms in an industry allows firms to act collectively *as if* they formed a monopoly. This could then lead to joint profit maximising where the monopolistic profits are shared between the firms in the agreement. Secondly, by acting together the uncertainty of oligopoly is removed so that firms know what other firms are doing with regard to production, price, etc. Thirdly, a collusive agreement can by establishing a joint pricing policy attempt to forestall entry of firms into the industry.

Whilst collusion may offer those advantages to firms there will always be the incentive for independent action, particularly from a low cost firm. If a firm does break away from a collusive agreement it would normally be faced with a more elastic demand curve than the total market demand curve, thus creating the possibility of achieving higher profits, provided that other firms do not follow. In practice many agreements have broken down as firms have pursued an independent course of action and now that governments do not favour collusive agreements (in contrast to the favour and promotion of agreements in the 1930s) our discussion in this section relates to situations where there is no government legislative control (for a discussion of government policy on monopoly and restrictive trade practices, see Section 6-8 of this chapter).

Broadly there are two main forms of collusion; perfect collusion through a centralised agency (or cartel) such as a trade association, and tacit collusion typically achieved by means of the leadership in price given by a dominant firm.

(a) Perfect Collusion

Perfect collusion can take various forms and at the extreme the cartel can determine production quotas, or prices and the distribution of profits to member firms. The fixing of quotas on prices can follow very rigid rules, for example, where costs of member firms are collected and a price based on these. There are two other less formal alternatives. One involves direct negotiation among member firms, which may create tension within the cartel, in the fixing of quotas; the other utilises a price list from a base year to which adjustments are made in order to take account of cost increases, changes in profit margins, etc.

There is little evidence in the literature on the actual operation of collusive agreements though a recent article by M. Howe [61] illustrates the workings of trade association pricing in the wire ropes industry. This is a very interesting study as it illustrates some of the mechanisms by which prices were actually fixed as well as the defence and criticisms of these methods. Up to the judgement of the Restrictive Practices Court in 1964 against the operation of the trade association price fixing in the wire rope industry, there were three trade associations; the Linked Coil Ropemakers' Association (LCRA), the Mining Ropes Association (MRA) and the Wire Ropes Manufacturers' Association (WRMA). It is sufficient for our purposes to examine only one of these associations and we have taken the WRMA which was responsible for the pricing of 'engineering ropes' and special ropes (excluding marine ropes to the Admiralty).

The WRMA used as a basis for its price list for engineering ropes costs of selected key products (forty in all) from a cross section of twelve member firms that accounted for about 75 per cent of the output of the industry. The sample of firms that submitted cost data was not chosen with any specific criteria in mind and was more of the legacy of historical circumstance. The trade association had over time developed a fairly formal procedure by which average total costs of those 'key products' (normally bulk produced ropes) were collected by a Secretariat for a six monthly price review. Inevitably the cost data were not standardised in that accounting conventions differed between firms and some firms submitted standard costs reflecting their own normal capacity utilisation and others historical costs. Additionally there was a discretionary right of firms in the sample to submit 'notional' costs where they had not produced any output of a particular key item in the relevant period. Before 1958 the cost data were usually averaged out but then the basis for the price review was provided by taking the average of the six lowest costs for each key item. These data also formed the basis of calculating costs on non-key itemed products. To these costs a target profit margin was added which in 1961 was $16^{2}/_{3}$ per cent on sales or 20 per cent on costs (and the price list extended to 40,000 items, including size, construction, quality, etc.). There was also a flexible provision built in to allow for across the board price changes where costs had changed uniformly.

The arguments put forward in favour of this method of pricing were that it was 'cost' based and therefore fair to customers and that the profit margins in the whole industry were not excessive. On mining ropes the margins varied between 6 per cent, 9 per cent and 12 per cent on sales and similarly on locked ropes. Some arbitrariness and rigidity is to be expected in pricing, particularly when the number of products and varieties is large, as was the case in this industry. However, this still does not justify the non-standardisation of costs and the evidence revealed by Howe indicates very large differences between members in the sample of firms. Additionally the use of notional costs was arbitrary and in some instance biased the cost base upwards.

This study thus reveals the actual workings of a price fixing agreement but what is significant is not the method *per se* but the effects that the agreement may have. The usual charge made against collusive agreements is that they protect the least efficient and can be a discouragement to innovation and restrict the force of potential competition by preventing the entry of new firms. On the credit side such agreements bring about an interchange of ideas, costs and technical information which may be a spur to efficiency.

Agreements of this type are likely to break down where the industry is one in which there is rapid technological change and/or where some firms have a significant cost advantage and hold different expectations about demand conditions in the industry. Whilst collusion may explain relative price rigidity and the removal of uncertainty of competitive reactions in oligopolistic markets, price is only one dimension of the problem and where opportunities do exist for independent action the evidence is that collusive agreements will often lapse. Now they are tightly controlled by legislation even down to 'open price agreements' where there is no formal structure of centralised pricing but tacit collusion via the circulation of price lists.

(b) Tacit Collusion

Tacit collusion may take the form of price leadership and there are essentially two variants. The first relates to an oligopolistic market structure where conventionally one firm (often termed the *barometric* firm) announces price changes which are closely followed by the other oligopolists. This firm need not have any cost advantage or be a dominant firm in terms of output, so long as its decision to change prices reflects changing costs conditions experienced by the industry in general. The second model relates to leadership by a dominant firm (with respect to output) who is also a low cost producer. The dominant firm sets the market price and it is then left to the smaller firms to choose appropriate outputs. The small firms are then in an analogous position to firms in perfect competition in that they are price takers. In practice many instances can be documented of price leadership both in the USA and the UK and in some instances it follows the break up of a formalised collusion system as illustrated in the wire rope industry referred to above.

6-5 The Kinked Demand Curve

The stability of prices of oligopolistic industries noted in some statistical studies in the 1930s, such as in the US sulphur industry (where between 1926 and 1938 the price of sulphur remained at $18 per ton apart from two deviations of 3 and 2 cents per ton for two years) led to the advancement of the theory that the demand curve for the product of an oligopolist is kinked. It was proposed independently and virtually simultaneously in 1939 by R. L. Hall and C. J. Hitch [52] and P. M. Sweezy [145]. The two versions are somewhat different, particularly as the Hall and Hitch approach incorporates the full-cost principle of pricing (see Chapter 7), however we shall present the kinked demand curve model as it is currently formulated.

We begin by assuming that the product of the oligopolistic firms in the industry is nearly homogeneous and that advertising expenditures are zero and that a price level in the industry has been established by convention or perhaps a previous collective agreement. The question explored in this theory is what the rival firms will do if one firm decides to increase or decrease its price. Some conjecture has to be made otherwise the demand curve facing an oligopolist cannot be defined. Figure 6.6 illustrates two demand schedules, one of which (DD') is operative for a price increase, the other (dd') being operative for a price cut. The dotted line dd' represents the demand curve for the firm's product assuming that his competitors follow the firm's actions. As one would expect, it has quite a steep slope indicating that the firm is unlikely to gain or lose a substantial amount of sales from changing its price if competitors quickly follow suit. The continuous line DD' indicates the demand curve facing the firm if rivals do not follow the firm in changing price. This curve is of course far more elastic than dd' since a unilateral price change will have a significant effect on the sales of a company. The proposition is that rival firms will follow a price decrease in order to protect their market shares, but will not match a price increase (although Sweezy recognised that they may follow a price rise albeit slowly or not to the full amount) since they can then make inroads into the market share of the higher price firm. This pattern of expected behaviour on the part of the its competitors will produce a kink at K_1

Figure 6.6 Derivation of the Kinked Curve

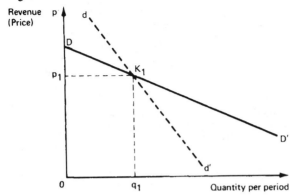

Figure 6.7 Changes in Marginal Cost

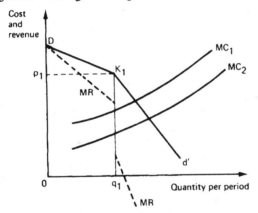

in the firm's composite demand curve ($DK_1 d'$) and the firm's marginal revenue curve will be discontinuous (as illustrated in Figure 6.7). The upper portion of this MR curve is related to the average revenue curve DD' and the lower portion relates to the curve dd'. The magnitude of the discontinuity depends on the differences between the slopes at the kink of the upper segment DK_1 and lower segment $K_1 d'$.

The homogeneity of the product and the number and size distribution of rival firms, will influence the relative slopes of the two portions. The more homogeneous the product the more elastic will be the upper segment of the kinked demand curve since buyers will be more willing to shift their purchases. The number of firms selling in the market is also likely to affect the slopes of the demand curves in that when there are a small number of firms, each is more likely to follow a price increase and the larger the number of firms the less likely is each firm to follow either a price increase or decrease. The presence of a dominant firm particularly with a cost advantage may well lead to a situation of price leadership (mentioned in Section 6-4) rather than the kind of interdependence depicted by the kinked demand curve approach.

If the firm's short run marginal cost curve passes between the two MR curves, fluctuations in MC will not affect the profit maximising price/output combination (Figure 6.7). This remains at price $0p_1$ and output $0q_1$ for one can see that if the firm attempted to produce at an output higher than $0q_1$ the MC would be greater than MR and conversely if the firm were to produce a smaller output than $0q_1$. The prediction that movements in the marginal cost curve, brought about by changes in short run variable costs, may leave the prices of firms unchanged is accompanied by the prediction that changes in short run fixed costs will have no impact at all on prices. This follows from the observation that a change in fixed costs has no direct impact on marginal cost or marginal revenue. Since the profit maximising output occurs at the intersection of these marginal functions it will remain unchanged, as will the price. Of course this response to changes in fixed costs is predicted by any model in which short run profit maximisation (achieved by marginal analysis) is assumed. Since the predictive power of a theory is an acid test in positive analysis, the acceptability of these market models in positive economics will depend on how well these conclusions about price rigidity stand up to the facts. So far as we are concerned in normative analysis, our purpose in exploring these models is to gain an insight into some of the key variables in markets, which managers must consider in making decisions. So far as students of management are concerned, predictions made for a hypothetical profit maximising firm are not particularly important.

Just as the kinked demand curve appears to explain price rigidity despite changes in cost conditions it also illustrates that price stability may remain over a longer period even if demand conditions change. This is illustrated in Figure 6.8. If the demand for the product of the firm increases this will cause a rightward shift in the demand curve and as the assumption made in the model about rival firms' behaviour is not a function of a firm's sales it can be supposed that the price of $0p_1$ is likely to persist.

Admittedly if all oligopolists in the industry faced similar increases in demand or costs then it would be likely that the general level of prices in that industry would rise and a kink would then be re-established at a higher price. However, the kinked demand curve model cannot explain the derivation of the initial price $0p_1$, it is a datum for this model. It could well be a relic from a previous collusive agreement,

Figure 6.8 Shift in Demand

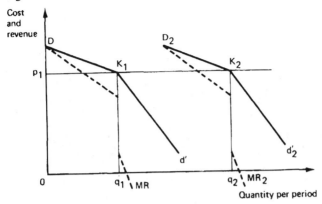

from some informal arrangement* or it could be the result of some action by a recognised dominant firm in the industry. Likewise there is no explanation of why prices that have once changed should settle down again and produce a new kink. This cannot therefore be regarded as a model of price output determination in oligopoly but rather an explanation of why prices may remain stable.

Another basic criticism of the approach centres around the conjectural variations; is it plausible to suggest that rivals will behave in this way? If the firm has no information about the likely reaction of its rivals it may assume the worst** and therefore anticipate their following price cuts but not price increases. K. J. Cohen and R. M. Cyert [28] suggest that such behaviour may be a realistic assumption in industries which are in their early stages of growth or where new firms have entered the market. In both these instances inter-firm knowledge may be low but the obvious retort is that over time, firms should acquire experience and be capable of a more accurate assessment of their rivals' reactions. This weakens the case of economists who claim that the kinked demand curve can account for persistent price rigidity. Moreover the circumstances of the 1930s may have been particularly conducive to rigid prices because in depressed business conditions firms are unlikely to increase prices as they know competitors will be unwilling to follow. Price reductions would be equally unlikely because of the fear that others might follow with the consequence of a price cutting 'war', which in the end would benefit none of the firms. When demand is buoyant, however, in periods of boom, a firm will be more confident of others following. There will be no incentive to cut prices in response

---

* Full-cost pricing, as observed by Hall and Hitch, may be seen as such an informal arrangement.
** Thus adopting a Maximin approach (see Section 6-7 below).

to a move by one firm since the other firms will probably be producing to capacity at the prevailing price so that a kink may still materialise in the demand curve but pointing towards the origin instead of away from it as in Figures 6.7 and 6.8.

The final and most telling criticism of the kinked demand curve is that even in the 1920s and 1930s, the period of alleged price stability for which this model was designed, there is no evidence that firms did react to each other in the way described. G. Stigler [139] analysed responses to price changes over the period in question for seven oligopolies in the USA. Rival firms seem to have followed price increases as readily as price cuts both in industries where there was strong price leadership (e.g. cigarettes and steel) and where there was no strong pattern of leadership (e.g. automobiles). Moreover in the case of steel, price rigidity simply was not experienced, in fact rigidity of prices seemed to be stronger in instances of near monopoly than it was in oligopolies. Even when price rigidity is experienced in oligopoly, price leadership or some other form of tacit collusion often provides a better explanation than that offered by the kinked demand curve model.

6-6 Sales Revenue Maximisation

The sales revenue maximisation hypothesis of W. J. Baumol [14] is an attempt to break away from the rigid assumption of profit maximisation but apart from changing the objective function, Baumol retains the neo-classical assumptions, for example with regard to the knowledge possessed by the firm. Baumol's model is inductive in the sense that it followed what he refers to as 'spotty observations' of the behaviour of large firms. These firms seemed to favour sales — even to the point of increasing sales and sacrificing profits.

The model hypothesises that the size of a firm's operations, as measured by total sales revenue, shares with profit in the objective function. This is simplified in the model by putting total sales revenue as the maximand but subject to a profit constraint.* Implicit in this assumption is the belief that managers may have discretion in the pursuit of objectives. Baumol himself applied his model to oligopoly and in particular to large firms that exhibited some separation of ownership and management. His proposition represents an attempt to bridge the gap between the neo-classical (traditional) theory of the firm and the reality of actual business behaviour so as to provide a determinate model of oligopoly behaviour. Baumol does not claim to have provided a universal model for oligopoly and he admits that it may even be inapplicable in certain instances. What it has done at least is to provoke a

---

*   The profit constraint would represent the minimum profit necessary to satisfy shareholders and to provide for the company's internal financing.

flood of comment in the academic literature and in that regard at least it justifies our coverage here, but more fundamentally it has aroused interest in business objectives and behaviour, matters which are of direct concern to any study of management.

The model is illustrated diagrammatically in Figure 6.9 where Baumol's original curves are drawn, including a total cost curve which is unlike that normally presented in neo-classical theory, but this is not a significant aspect of the model.

Figure 6.9 The Sales Revenue Maximising Firm

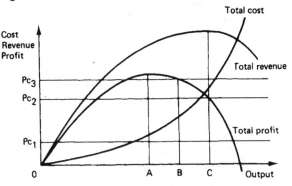

The profit maximising and sales revenue maximising outputs are OA and OC respectively. However, Baumol's model is one of constrained sales revenue maximisation though the constraint may not always be operative. If for instance the profit constraint is drawn at Pc_1, then this does not limit the maximand since the total sales revenue function reaches its peak at an output OC where profits are above this minimum required level. At Pc_2 the required profit just equals that given by maximising the sales revenue whereas if Pc_3 is brought in then the output produced would be lower (OB) than the unconstrained sales maximising output of OC.

The informational properties of this model are the same as for the neo-classical model in that it is assumed that cost, revenue and profit functions are known and hence the profit maximisation or sales maximisation positions and departures from them. Although the sales revenue maximiser is seen to produce at a higher output than the profit maximiser, e.g. at OC or OB (depending upon the profit constraint), rather than OA, he would not use other than the optimal (least cost) combination of factor inputs to produce that output. This follows because if a sales maximiser operating at a profit constraint were to

201

achieve any cost savings, he could then use the liberated resources to produce and sell more.

Baumol recognised that a typical feature of oligopolistic behaviour is the use of non-price competition in the form of advertising expenditure, modification to products, inducements to purchase and other promotional expenditures.

Figure 6.10 Advertising and the Sales Revenue Maximising Firm

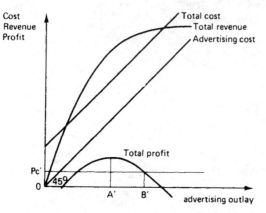

In Figure 6.10, advertising expenditure is introduced. The vertical axis represents total revenue, total cost and total profits. Advertising expenditure is represented on the horizontal axis. The total revenue curve is drawn on the reasonable assumption that increased advertising will always expand physical sales although diminishing returns to increased advertising may well set in after some point. The advantage of advertising of course is that sales can be increased while price remains constant. Total costs (production, selling and distribution) are drawn as a function of advertising expenditure and the 45° line serves its usual purpose of transferring data, in this case advertising outlay, from the horizontal to vertical axis. The total profit curve is of course the difference (at each level of advertising expenditure) between TC and TR.

The profit maximising output is OA' and if we introduce a profit constraint of Pc' then the level of advertising expenditure is constrained at OB' and as we have assumed that advertising always increases sales (albeit at a decreasing rate) marginal revenue is always positive. It it not possible therefore to have an unconstrained sales maximisation under this new assumption and the profit constraint will always be binding. Sales maximisers will normally advertise at least as much if not more than profit maximisers since they will sacrifice profits up to the point where the constraint becomes effective.*

Baumol's model has the advantage of being richer than the neoclassical models without losing any of their tractability. Managerial objectives and advertising are incorporated into his model and it is still possible to analyse responses to changes in certain parameters. The most interesting prediction, which clashes with that of the conventional models, is that increases in fixed costs or the imposition of a lump sum tax, will cause the price/output decision to change. This prediction arises because the sales maximiser is always operating at the profit constraint so that when profits are reduced by any external influence he has to trim his output (by increasing price or reducing advertising) to a level nearer that of the profit maximiser. The latter, however, finds that the total profit function is still maximised at the same output as before and there is therefore no case for change.

The main criticism of Baumol's approach is that the key problem of interdependence is only handled implicitly — through the abandonment of price competition in favour of advertising and so on, behaviour which reflects interdependence. The first fundamental critique of the Baumol model was that by W. G. Shepherd [127] who argued that instead of the model being applicable to a wide range of oligopoly situations, it is a specialised theory of sales maximisation applicable to monopolies, to firms in conditions of monopolistic competition and to some minor oligopolists. In Shepherd's eyes the model is only applicable for non-collusive firms; firms where decisions are non-interdependent with those of competitors and firms which are in a position to include sales maximisation as one of the objectives of the firm.

By introducing interdependence using kinked demand curves and assuming a single product situation Shepherd illustrates that the same output decision is reached regardless of whether the objective is sales maximisation or profit maximisation. If there is a very definite kink, reflecting strong interdependence (Section 6-5 of this chapter), the kink will occur at the point where total revenue is at a maximum and it *may* cause the marginal revenue curve to extend below the output axis.** We have italicised the word 'may' purposely as Shepherd assumed that if the kink was very sharp the MR curve would necessarily extend below the output axis. J. R. Davies [33] however, points to the limitations of the kinked demand curve approach. Since it is unable to offer any account of how or where the prevailing price is set,

'... it provides no basis for expecting the price elasticity of demand

---

* There is of course an implied assumption that the increased liquidity to cover increased sales will be available.

** Total revenue reaches its absolute maximum where MR = 0 or where MR changes from being positive to negative.

for a product to fall* as the interdependence among firms producing the product increases. Indeed it could be argued that the fewer the firms and the stronger the interdependence, the greater the probability of finding price along an elastic range** of the demand curve.' ([33] p. 201)

C. J. Hawkins [55] criticises Shepherd's approach, because once advertising is introduced as a variable there is no longer a single total revenue function. Thus even if both profit maximiser and sales maximiser operated at the kink in their respective demand curves, these would typically differ with the sales maximiser achieving a bigger output and total revenue commensurate with a larger advertising outlay. Hawkins however agrees with Shepherd that Baumol's model is applicable only to a limited number of cases and that in general there is likely to be little difference between the behaviour of sales maximising and profit maximising firms.

There are various ways of testing this model, including 'casual empiricism' or informal observations of big business behaviour such as those which led Baumol to propose the model. Then there is the predictive power of the model such as the response to changes in fixed costs which intuitively seems to be borne out in practice in the form of price increases. Formal testing along these lines is problematical since firms often raise prices when production costs in general (and not fixed costs alone) are rising and and also because there is an alternative response in the form of reductions in advertising expenditure. The approach that several empirical studies have adopted, in rather different guises, is to test the assumption that decision makers will prefer sales to profits. One of these was a study conducted by J. W. McGuire, *et al.* [82] following evidence cited by authors such as P. Patton [106] and D. R. Roberts [117] that 'managerial income' was directly related to company size. McGuire's study used data on executive income (the salary of the chief executive and allowance for stock options) and sales and profits for 45 of the 100 largest (as given by Fortune) US industrial corporations for the period 1953-9. McGuire found that the chain of causation was from sales to income though he recognised that a relationship between executive income and profit may have been obscured. But R. T. Masson [89] argued that the McGuire study and those conducted earlier did not correctly specify executive compensation and in fact omitted a large element of their income. He conducted a revised version of the study and found from his sample of industries that

'... the firms in these industries do not pay their executives for sales maximisation, that the financial incentives of the executives do

---
* and hence no argument for MR extending below the output axis.
** i.e. a range where MR is positive.

indeed affect stock market performance and that the coincidence of executive financial return with the stock performance of the firm benefits the stockholders.' ([89] p. 1290)

He recognised that there were flaws in his study, particularly in the sample of industries used, but his work coupled with that of W. G. Lewellen [80] whose study revealed from a sample of large manufacturing firms that separation of ownership and control need not lead to managerial objectives so widely divergent from those of shareholders, suggests that this particular line of empirical research does not give much credence to the Baumol model.

Another means of testing the motivational assumption was that of M. Hall [51] who examined the hypothesis implicit in Baumol's model that firms sacrifice profits in favour of sales up to the point where the profit constraint is operative. To achieve these extra sales the firm can choose to cut prices or increase advertising. Of crucial importance is the need to give an operational definition to the profit constraint; something Baumol recognised to be a major analytical problem though he did specify it loosely in terms of '. . . that stream of profits which allows for the financing of maximum long run sales' ([14] p. 188), and he stated subsequently that this could be expressed as a rate of return on capital. Hall argued that as a simplification the desired level of profits would be the same throughout a given industry so he used industry mean profitability in his study.

Hall, like McGuire, used Fortune's directory and he selected the largest 400 of US industrial manufacturing firms and confined the sample to industries with concentration ratios of 50 per cent or over, and to firms with a fairly assignable industrial classification. Hall felt that he had selected a group of firms whose market structural characteristics were not unfavourable to the practice of revenue maximisation with a profit constraint. By estimating a constraint he attempted to explain variations in revenue by departures from the profit constraint for the period 1960-62. In general his findings gave no support to the sales revenue maximising thesis but they did not support the profit maximising thesis either.

Both types of test have been subject to criticism, questioning both the suitability of the data and the econometric technqiues used to analyse the data. Their inconclusive results are not surprising but they illustrate that assumptions about firms' behaviour warrant further consideration, especially their objectives, as do the conceptual and econometric issues involved in testing models of this type against industry and/or firms' data.

The sales revenue maximisation model of Baumol has theoretical flaws and empirically it has been found wanting. However, the fact that it has provoked comment has clarified many thoughts on the nature of business behaviour. Sales as well as profits may play an important part in decision making and business behaviour. Another virtue is that the model does provide a useful link with growth models of the firm such as that of R. Marris [87] and Baumol in fact does develop a growth model in a later publication [13].

6-7 Game Theory as an Approach to Oligopoly

The Two-Person Zero-Sum Game

So far in the models designed to explain and predict oligopolistic behaviour interdependency has been superficially treated — for example by assuming the worst response from one's competitors as in the kinked demand curve model, or by assuming collusion — either formalised or tacit.* These models have concentrated on restricted aspects of oligopoly, price stability being the most usual, whereas there are many dimensions which could and perhaps should be considered in a theory of oligopoly. Game theory provides a means of evaluating the alternative courses of action open to a firm or other kind of 'player'. These alternatives can contain price changes, advertising, modifications to products and other inducements to purchase. More importantly, interdependence is *the* key variable in the theory of games.

However, game theory has not been widely adopted as a way of resolving competitive situations. Its use has been more in revealing the anatomy of the decision making process itself and making the evaluation of alternatives more meaningful. Game theory is applicable where there is a situation of conflict between two or more parties, where the actions of one interact with the actions of another — as in oligopoly. It originated in the work of J. von Neumann and O. Morgenstern [105]. There must be a finite number of players and alternative strategies (or courses of action). The outcome in adopting a particular strategy depends on the actions of others and the choice of strategies is assumed to be made simultaneously by the parties involved. The type of game applied to oligopolistic behaviour is usually a zero-sum game and indeed much of the analysis in the literature of game theory has been for that type of game where the loss of one player is the gain of another, so that the sum of all the gains is zero.

Another simplifying assumption used initially is that only two players are involved; hence the 'two-person zero-sum game' so commonly described in game theory. Instances which may conform to this type of game are: duopolists competing for market shares, and a trade union

---
* Baumol's model involves tacit collusion in that non-price competition is an important feature in it.

bargaining with an employers' association for shares in the company's revenues. If however, the prime variable was *total* duopoly profit or the *total* benefits for distribution to wages and profits, then one would no longer be dealing with a zero-sum situation.

Suppose now that in a duopoly, the two firms are fighting for shares of the market and each has various alternative strategies open to it. Firm A considers that it can mount a promotional campaign in which it has three alternatives (represented by rows in the pay-off matrix of Table 6.3) of: (1) temporary price reduction; (2) gifts; (3) different packaging. Firm B has four alternative lines of action, namely a promotional campaign based on advertising on (1) TV; (2) radio; (3) newspapers; or (4) magazines. Table 6.3 summarises the various strategies for both firms and also the pay-offs or consequences of each action in terms of market share. In this instance we have taken A's market share for each pay-off though of course B's pay-offs are $100 - A$'s for each strategy pair. Firm A we have termed the 'maximiser' since clearly it wishes to increase its own share of the market and B is called the 'minimiser' since by minimising A's share it is maximising its own share.

Table 6.3 The Two-Person Zero-Sum Game (A's market shares %)

		B_1	B_2	B_3	B_4
A (Maximiser)	A_1	40	85	25^S	30
	A_2	25	20	22	80
	A_3	65	25	23	24

B (Minimiser)

(S – denotes saddle point)

One of the restrictive assumptions of game theory is that all players know not only the various strategies open to themselves and their rivals but also the relevant 'pay-offs'. This clearly may not be the case and in a market situation where there are great uncertainties and where interfirm knowledge is low, game theory would be inapplicable.

Maximin and Minimax Strategies

Taking the pay-offs as given in Table 6.3, the cautious approach is to assume the worst, and act on this basis. Thus for A the worst possible outcomes from his strategies are as follows: strategy (1) 25 per cent; strategy (2) 20 per cent; and strategy (3) 23 per cent share of the market. A can make the best of this situation by selecting the strategy with the highest of these minima, i.e. the 'maximin'* which is strategy (1). The worst for B occurs when A achieves the largest pay-offs. For B's strategy (1) this would be 65 per cent, for (2) 85 per cent, for (3) 25 per cent and for (4) 80 per cent. The best of these for B is 25 per cent (from strategy 3) and this is called the minimax. Note that exactly the same kind of pessimistic behaviour is assumed for B. He chooses the 'minimax' because the matrix is in terms of A's pay-offs. In this particular instance with A playing strategy A_1 and B strategy B_3 we have an equilibrium situation, with A's maximin coincident with B's minimax; so that the pay-off A obtains from its maximin strategy is exactly the same as the pay-off B expects A to get when B employs a minimax strategy. We call this equilibrium point a 'saddle point' (marked 'S' in Table 6.3) and it is the largest of our row minima and smallest of column maxima. This maximin/minimax offers protection to both parties and when a saddle point exists, it results in stability. In this particular example both are utilising a single or 'pure' strategy, and the same solution could have been found by using the principle of *dominance* which we introduced in Chapter 2. Recall that a particular pure strategy would not be used when it is always inferior to another.

A strategy for the maximiser is dominated when the pay-offs throughout that row of the matrix are exceeded by or are equal to the corresponding pay-offs from another strategy. Dominance can only be established after the comparison of *all* pay-offs between two strategies. For the minimiser, it must be remembered that the pay-offs are expressed in terms of his opponent's values. That is why he is the minimiser! Dominance for his strategies is established again by comparing all the pay-offs, in turn between the two strategies, but now the strategy which is eliminated is the one which has the higher (or equal) values throughout. For example, in Table 6.3, taking firm B, strategy B_3 is better than strategies B_1 or B_4, but not better than B_2 because the 22 per cent in B_3 is inferior to the 20 per cent in B_2. B_1 and B_4 can therefore be eliminated; so if we now take firm A, each strategy now has only two outcomes and on this basis strategy A_1 is superior to both A_2 and A_3. If he does play A_1, B will of course react by playing B_3, as 25 per cent is clearly superior to 85 per cent so far as B is concerned and thus we are back to the saddle point. Solution through dominance is not always feasible but even in its absence it is sometimes possible to find a saddle point via maximin/minimax.

When a saddle point exists there is no virtue in either player

---

* See Chapter 2, Section 2-6, for the use of this decision criterion in decision theory.

deviating from his pure strategy, since the opponent can immediately retort with a countermove to the first player's detriment. Maximin behaviour is therefore entirely rational in this situation where there is every reason to expect the worst. Its adoption in decision theory is however questionable (see Chapter 2, Section 2-6). However, if no saddle point exists, then by definition there is no unique optimal strategy pair, and a player may be able to improve his pay-off by mixing his strategies, so long as his opponent doesn't know which one he is going to play at any point in time. Playing a mixed strategy in card games like poker can be profitable. This is achieved through 'bluffing' whereby a player does not always opt out when he is dealt a poor hand; sometimes he will bet heavily in these circumstances in order to prevent his opponent(s) from outguessing him. If we look at Table 6.4, we can see that the game depicted there has no saddle point. Dominance however, rules out strategies B_3 and B_4 but no further dominance of pure strategies is possible.

Table 6.4 Matrix with no Saddle Point (A's pay-offs)

(Total points at stake = 20)

		B (Minimiser)			
		B_1	B_2	B_3	B_4
A (Maximiser)	A_1	10	0	12	20
	A_2	0	11	1	7

The remaining strategies are A_1, A_2 and B_1 and B_2. It would be unwise for A to play either A_1 or A_2 singly, since B would reply with B_2 or B_1 respectively, to reduce A's pay-off to the minimum possible (zero in either case here). Similarly it would be unwise for B to play a pure strategy. Instead both players should mix randomly, but the theory of games shows that there is an optimal *proportion* in which these strategies should be mixed for each player.

To find the proportion for A, let strategy A_1 be played a fraction p of the time and thus strategy A_2 a fraction $(1 - p)$ of the time. If B played B_1, the expected pay-off for A would be $10p + 0(1 - p)$ and if B played B_2, the expected pay-off for A would be $0p + 11(1 - p)$. p is set optimally for A when B is unable to act systematically to give A a reduced pay-off. This means that whether B plays B_1 or B_2, the expected pay-off for A should be the same.

Thus
$$10p + 0(1-p) = 0p + 11(1-p)$$
$$\therefore 10p = 11(1-p)$$
$$\therefore 21p = 11$$
$$\therefore p = 11/21$$
and $$1 - p = 10/21$$

So A should play strategy A_1 $\underline{11/21}$ of the time and strategy A_2 $\underline{10/21}$ of the time. His expected pay-off will be $\underline{110/21}$ regardless of how B reacts and this figure is called 'the value of the game'. Mixing would be futile if A played strategy (1) on eleven consecutive occasions and then played strategy (2) on ten consecutive occasions. The idea is to mix randomly in the indicated proportions.

B's optimal mixed strategy can be similarly derived. Let q be the proportion of strategy B_1 and thus $(1 - q)$ be the proportion of strategy B_2. If there are, say, 20 points at stake in this zero-sum game, B's pay-offs will be 20 minus those of A. B's expected pay-off when A plays A_1 is

$$20 - [10q + 0(1-q)]$$

and when A plays A_2, the expected pay-off for B is

$$20 - [0q + 11(1-q)] \ .$$

Optimality for B occurs when:

$$10q + 0(1-q) = 0q + 11(1-q)$$
i.e. $$21q = 11$$
Thus $$q = \underline{11/21}, \quad (1-q) = \underline{10/21} \ .*$$

B's expected pay-off, regardless of how A plays is

$$20 - 110/21 = \underline{310/21}$$

A quicker way of arriving at this solution is to compare the row *differences* for the one player, and the column *differences* for his opponent. In Table 6.5 for instance the difference between the two pay-offs for strategy A_1 is $(10 - 0) = 10$ and for strategy A_2 is $(11 - 0) = 11$. Reversing the figures as shown in Table 6.5 indicates that A_1 and A_2 should be mixed in proportions 11:10 respectively, i.e. $\underline{11/21}$, $\underline{10/21}$.

A similar operation on B's strategies reveals differences in pay-offs of 10 and 11 which on reversal indicate mixing in proportions 11:10 or 11/21, 10/21 for B_1 and B_2 respectively.

---

*   The fact that A and B both mix their respective strategies in the same proportion is a reflection of the figures used in Table 6.5 and is not a general feature of mixing strategies.

Table 6.5

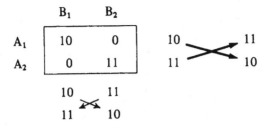

Any two-person zero-sum game that can be reduced to a 2 × 2 game by dominance* can be solved. This is not an arbitrary method but one which has a sound mathematical basis. More complex games can sometimes be solved through linear programming.

As soon as we leave two-person zero-sum games, we find that game theory is far less able to provide unique solutions. Duopoly is a limiting case of oligopoly and in practice the latter involves more than two firms. Moreover firms can influence the total pay-off in terms of sales or profits. It is only market shares that can be handled within the zero-sum format.

Non-Zero Sum Games

For the moment let us retain the 'two person' assumption but relax the 'zero-sum' assumption. Suppose once again that there is a duopoly consisting of two major firms A and B. These two firms are not just concerned about their market shares but also total sales revenue and profits. Costs have recently risen so that both firms can contemplate moderate price rises without increasing the possibility of attracting new entrants.

Table 6.6 The Non-Zero Sum Game

A \ B	Same price	Raise price	
Same price	40 (40)	100 (0)	A's pay-offs
Raise price	0 (100)	80 (80)	

(B's pay-offs in parentheses)

---

* Sometimes dominance is not immediately apparent on a strict term by term basis (i.e. pure dominance) but a graphical method can sometimes reveal inferior/superior strategies.

Table 6.6 shows two alternative strategies for each firm; retaining the same price or raising it. The pay-offs reflect the satisfaction (utility) that A will enjoy from each outcome, bearing in mind its profits, sales and market share. B's pay-offs are shown in parentheses. The figures are entirely arbitrary with utility of zero indicating the worst result and utility of 100, the best. The figures of 80 and 40 merely represent intermediate pay-offs.

The best result for A would probably be for B to raise his price while A kept his own unchanged, particularly if spare capacity existed. The worst result for A would come about if he were to raise his own price in isolation. Of the other two strategy pairings, A and B raising price together would be preferred to both keeping prices unchanged. Provided that firm B is similar to A in all aspects, the pattern of utility values immediately follows.

It can now be seen that the total pay-off can vary from cell to cell of the matrix. The game is therefore no longer a zero-sum game. Moreover there are two optimal solutions, one for independent action and one for collusion. Independent evaluation would indicate dominance of 'same price' over 'raise price' for each player. This gives pay-offs of 40 (40); but if both parties could be induced to raise prices together the joint optimum of 80 (80) could be attained. This would require collusion in some form and in view of the fact that both firms have been suffering from cost increases, the full-cost pricing rule* might serve as a means of achieving tacit collusion.

When only two firms are involved, the scope for tacit collusion may be such that joint optima can be reached. However, as the number of firms increases, the more difficult it will be to reach any joint optima. A widespread use of cost based pricing methods or strong price leadership may however enable firms to pursue their joint interests even when three or more large firms are present in the oligopoly.

Game theory certainly adds a new dimension both to positive and to normative economic analysis. However, decision makers would seldom in practice be confronted with two-person zero-sum games and it is only for this restricted category that the theory of games can indicate optimal pure or mixed strategies. The drawbacks encountered in decision theory are only too apparent here as well (see Chapter 2, Section 2-10). These centre around the construction of complete pay-off matrices and human decision making capacities.

---

* See Chapter 7, Section 7-2. If both firms used this rule, cost increases would be 'passed on' to the consumer in the form of price increases.

6-8 Market Power, Anti-Monopoly Policy and X-Inefficiency

In Section 6-3 we illustrated the classic case against monopoly in terms of a lower quantity produced and a higher price giving rise to monopoly profit. In practice of course cost curves are likely to be different for firms under monopolistic conditions and we explained in that section that economies of scale may offset some of the allocative inefficiency of market power. Another reason why costs may be different in firms with monopolistic power is the existence of internal inefficiency for which H. Leibenstein [78] coined the phrase 'X-inefficiency'.* The whole area of market power requires very close scrutiny. In this chapter reference has been made to the growth in market power both in terms of overall size and concentration within industries. Potential market power exists whenever a firm (or group of firms) is in a sufficiently dominant position in a market to be able to exert a significant influence on the terms of sale of the goods or services.

In Britain two types of approach have been made in the field of anti-monopoly legislation. Preventive measures have been taken to prohibit behaviour likely to reduce competition, particularly with regard to agreements amongst producers. This has been embodied in legislation in the 1956 Restrictive Trade Practices Act which established a Register of agreements and a Court to try the cases brought before it. Seven gateways were available to firms to prove that their agreement did not not contravene the public interest. These included that the abandonment of the agreement would lead to unemployment or a reduction in exports. The 1964 Retail Prices Act abolished retail price maintenance but again provision was made for hearings at the Restrictive Practices Court. The 1956 Act was extended in coverage in 1968 to open price agreements. Implicit in these measures is the belief that such practices are *prima facie* against the public interest and should be prohibited unless cogent arguments are placed before the Court as to why they should be retained. On the question of dominant firms and mergers a more pragmatic approach of investigation and reporting on firms has been adopted. However, here it has been more difficult to identify market power and to establish a consistent and meaningful policing system.

How do policy makers identify market power? Theory would argue that a high rate of return on capital is an indicator of the use of market power and case histories of growing firms point to various predatory and other tactics which firms may engage in to increase their power. The latter are easier to identify and therefore to condemn but when one comes to profitability, the usual measurement problems arise and of course high profits could be due to factors other than the use of

---

* Organisational slack (Cyert and March [32]) and Management slack (Williamson [157, 158]) have a similar meaning.

market power. Even if profitability is measured on a consistent basis using historic costs or replacement costs what are the figures to be compared with to determine whether or not they are 'high'? Since 1956 the Monopolies Commission has used a series of different guideposts* with which a profit of a firm on a reference product has been compared and the argument advanced by C. K. Rowley [121] is that if the Commission had had the various estimates that are now available for evaluation purposes their decisions would have been different.**

Market power, as we indicated earlier in Section 6-3, is concerned with allocative efficiency and the available empirical evidence† indicates that the social welfare gains emanating from the pursuit of an effective anti-monopoly policy directed against allocative inefficiency in the market are likely to be small. This is because if we assume that a dominant firm has optimum resource allocation *within* the firm, then the effects of the use of market power are related only to the price/quantity differences resulting, and these effects may be outweighed by economies of large scale production. If the question of efficiency in *internal* resource allocation is introduced then a different picture emerges. The argument runs as follows: dominant firms free from strong competitive pressures will allow costs to exist above the minimum possible level. Higher costs may arise from both workers and management as they substitute their own objectives — status, prestige, a quiet life and other non-monetary rewards. The X-inefficiency argument is thus closely related to that developed in those managerial and behavioural theories of the firm which introduce the concept of management or organisational slack. The evidence O. E. Williamson put forward in his attempt to test his expenditure preference model of the firm indicated that when firms met harder times they reacted by cutting into 'management slack' to reduce costs. If Williamson had also been able to show that X-inefficiency increased on the return of 'good' times, the Leibenstein thesis would have been strengthened.

It is difficult to be precise about the size of X-inefficiency, particularly as the evidence Leibenstein collected is international, covering a variety of economies, industries and types of firms. However, what evidence there is does point to the existence of some X-inefficiency which must be included on the debit side together with allocative inefficiency

---

*   For a useful analysis of this see C. K. Rowley [121].

**   This viewpoint has been challenged by A. Sutherland [144] although the exact details of the arguments do not concern us here other than they illustrate the difficulty of framing criteria to pursue an anti-trust policy with respect for the market power of dominant firms. This difficulty increases when attempts are made to frame criteria with which to evaluate mergers (under the 1965 Mergers Act) and in particular those involving conglomerates.

†   Some of this is to be found in H. Leibenstein [78].

to be offset against any favourable benefits that market power may bring such as economies of scale. It would seem that widespread removal of X-inefficiency would lead to greater output for the nation but the evidence at present available is not systematically related to market power so in this context we cannot be definite about the relationship between market structure, X-inefficiency and economies of scale. What we can say is that X-inefficiency probably exists in any real world situation where competitive pressures are weak. Although it may appear more prevalent in large firms, the larger firm even with market power may be in a position to raise internal efficiency by various incentive schemes to both managers and workers.

Perhaps policy dealing with dominant firms should retain the present pragmatic approach embodied in legislation and allow the Monopolies Commission to undertake cost-benefit studies of industries, i.e. whereby the gains from scale are weighed against the losses resulting from X-inefficiency and allocative inefficiency. Certainly it is no longer adequate to judge a dominant firm's use of market power solely on its price/output behaviour and resultant profitability. A consideration of internal resource allocation would seem desirable as well, but whether or not gains and losses should be aggregated is another matter since society would obviously like to enjoy the benefits of scale economies without the disadvantages of allocative and X-inefficiency, if this could be achieved through anti-monopoly policy.

In concluding this chapter, it can be seen that a firm's decisions are constrained and influenced by the kind of market structures its products are sold in. Most markets fall between the two extreme structures of perfect competition and monopoly and that is why most of this chapter has been devoted to oligopoly. We were unable to offer a general model of oligopoly but pointed to some of the key characteristics that have been explored in a number of market models. Interdependence and the avoidance of price competition are among the most fundamental of these characteristics, together with collusive practices and the forestalling of entry. Management must be aware of all of these factors when making decisions and this applies to pricing which is considered below in Chapter 7.

7 THE PRICING DECISION

7-1 Introduction

Much has been said already in Chapter 6 about price and output decisions in the context of market structure. We have explained that the number of competitors, their product differentiation activities, the degree of interdependence between firms and the possibility of potential entry all constrain the pricing decision. Valuable though the conventional analysis of markets may be, it is often thought that its contribution to pricing in practice is at best indirect. A. M. Alfred [4] for example writes: 'Company pricing policy is an area where the academic world has long since retreated in despair of ascribing consistency of principles or rationality of practice' ([4] p. 1).

In the present chapter we shall examine some of the findings of empirical pricing studies, to see if there are any consistent principles that are applied in practice, and more importantly to suggest ways in which new principles might be introduced in order to satisfy more fully the objectives of firms. Before embarking on this task, however, it is important to note that despite the attention given to pricing in conventional economic analysis, in the Ansoff classification referred to in Chapter 1 (Table 1.1) pricing emerges as an operating decision. Of course operating decisions can, and do, have a substantial impact on the success of the firm within a given strategic setting, but even so, it is debatable whether pricing is even a major operating decision for many firms. In the study of J. G. Udell [147], which included 200 American firms, it was found that one half of these did not place pricing in the five most important decision areas influencing their marketing success. Certainly one must accept that price is but a single variable in the multi-dimensional world of the businessman. His strategies consist of varying mixes of product developments, advertising and other promotional activities as well as price, and his objectives include target sales levels, market shares and aims other than profit both for the short and the long term. Moreover it must be recognised that the information available to firms will limit the sophistication of analysis, in particular the extent to which both cost and demand considerations can enter the pricing decision. Perhaps then we should not be too surprised if we find that pricing decisions often rely on simple rules of thumb. However, it is our impression that many firms are too dependent on such methods and that it is time they attached more importance to the pricing decision and paid heed to the lessons of economic analysis. Before proceeding to the main theme of this chapter let us briefly look back to Chapter 6 where many of the foundations for our analysis of pricing were laid.

It was explained in that chapter that in a competitive market the firm has to be a 'price taker' whereas in monopoly the firm supplies the whole market and can fix either price or quantity, setting the other consistently. For instance by restricting output the price would tend to increase, assuming the market demand curve had a negative slope. The motivational assumption for both perfect competition at one extreme and monopoly at the other is profit maximisation with the competitive firm achieving this when it equates marginal cost to price and the monopolist when it equates marginal cost to marginal revenue. When we turn our attention to oligopoly a rather different picture emerges with a variety of models to cope with uncertainty caused by the mutual interdependence of firms. Each model stresses one or more characteristic aspects of oligopolistic behaviour, though a feature commonly referred to is the use of non-price competition particularly by advertising and other promotional expenditure, indicating that price decisions are just part of the strategy of marketing. This is particularly true of more recent models like that of Baumol [14], rather less so of the traditional models. Price changes in such a market structure could often be seen as an aggressive move if there had been no change in the general cost levels affecting the whole of industry. We did recognise that there are other means to price competition than manipulating the *price per se* so that although there may be apparent price rigidity, price competition may still take place by variation in discounts and rebates and possibly through differences in quality and weight.

Collusive price/output agreements of the type described in Chapter 6 Section 6-4, are now illegal and firms are required to set prices independently. This is now in Britain conditioned by the price controls and at the time of writing a rigorous 'prices code' is in operation. This prices code, which allows price increases on the basis of some proportion of *cost* increases, is reminiscent of wartime pricing which would often be based on costs plus a regulated profit margin. In fact pricing in practice is often a reflection of full cost and not marginal analysis of cost and revenue as depicted in conventional theory.

7-2 Pricing in Practice

A series of pricing studies in the UK and the USA in both large and small firms reveals behaviour apparently inconsistent with profit maximisation, although some of these studies reveal elements of marginal analysis and a concern for long run profits.

The first major attempt to find how firms did in fact fix their prices was the Hall and Hitch [52] study of 1939 that we first referred to in Chapter 1. They analysed answers to questionnaires from a sample of thirty-eight businessmen of whom thirty-three were in manufacturing industry. Thirty of these respondents used a full cost pricing system (average direct costs plus average overhead costs plus a profit margin at some output level) all or some of the time with twelve adopting a rigid adherence to this principle. Their calculation of 'output' varied with some taking a particular percentage of capacity whilst the majority took some normal operating level to determine output which was based on actual past levels or some forecast of the future. Hall and Hitch combined their full cost pricing model with the kinked demand curve theorem described in Chapter 6, although G. Stigler [139] for one has indicated that the two are basically incompatible.

The Hall and Hitch study was a pioneering attempt and initially their findings were greeted with scepticism. However the emphasis that many firms give to costs as the pricing base has been widely confirmed in other studies; for instance I. C. Pearce [108], R. M. Barback [10], D. C. Hague [46, 47, 49] and R. C. Skinner [134], all of which relate to pricing in Britain. The work of D. C. Hague has been of particular importance because of the span of time encompassed by his studies. The first of these was in 1949 [46] and was based on interviews with businessmen which revealed pricing according to average cost as the dominant pattern. This was confirmed in a study published in 1957 [47] relating to price policy in the rayon industry in Britain in the inter-war years. Of particular interest was the policy adopted by Courtaulds where price was used as a strategy to expand output at a time when some of that company's competitors were arguing for a rise in prices because of increases in costs. The most important pricing study of Hague's was that conducted at the Centre for Business Research [49] where thirteen case histories were examined. This represents the first in-depth study of pricing decisions in Britain,* and it probes into the objectives pursued by the companies and the resolution of conflict between those objectives. In this regard there is a close parallel with the findings of Cyert and March's work [32] which indicated that conflicts between objectives were only partially resolved, precluding decisions which satisfied all objectives simultaneously. Instead, objectives were attended to sequentially. We shall further examine Hague's work in Section 7-3 when we consider the mechanism of pricing in more detail.

---

* There was however a very useful study by Barback [10] in 1964 which examined small/medium firms in some detail. He found that the profit objective was shared with other objectives and that cost based pricing was the most usual despite some pricing apparently according to marginalist principles.

A rather different study of pricing was that of Skinner [134] which investigated by means of a postal questionnaire (with follow up telephone enquiries where this was necessary for clarification). The questions were quite detailed and 70 per cent of the respondents claimed to use a cost-plus pricing system although prices appeared to be sensitive to competition and demand conditions as well as to cost and the desired profit margin.

The fact that firms may not have sufficient information about demand conditions is indicated in an interesting study of a single pricing decision, namely the choice of a price to launch the Jaguar XJ 12: R. Harrison and F. M. Wilkes [53] showed that the approach was essentially cost based and this seems to be the case for many of BLMC's other pricing decisions. While BLMC had accurate data on costs for the XJ 12 its marketing information was poor and it adopted a safety first policy of pricing on the basis of costs (at a target production figure of 20,000 units per year) preferring to gauge demand from orders (which built up to a two year waiting list by the end of 1972).* British Leyland were obviously sacrificing profits in that prices could have been raised to bring demand in line with their ability to supply. In time it would normally have done so as it had done with previous cars such as the XJ 6 and Rover 3500 S. In a period of Government control over price changes, this kind of sequential approach to the pricing decision is not possible; companies have much less scope for price experimentation of any kind. In any future launch it is vital that more account is taken of market demand when the price is set, and assuming that inflation persists, the company can always hold the price or increase by less than the general rate of price increases if demand begins to flag.

The studies mentioned so far relate to the UK and with the exception of British Leyland are in the main of small to medium sized firms. One of the classic studies of pricing practices of large firms was that carried out by the Brookings Institution in the USA of which the main strands of the evidence are reproduced in an article by R. F. Lanzillotti [74]. The study was confined to pricing in 'Big Business' with a sample of twenty companies all taken from the two hundred largest corporations in the USA and a half of these were from the hundred largest. The sample covered a wide range of market structures featuring some firms with almost complete control of the market and others very much aware of their competitors. The general conclusions are that firms do have pricing objectives which are related to long run profit goals but that

'... no one single objective or policy rules all price-making in any

---

* The reluctance or inability to forecast demand and the reliance on short run feedback data is commonly observed, e.g. Cyert and March, *op. cit.* [32].

given company. In fact in many companies a close inter-relationship exists among target return pricing, desire to stabilise prices and target market share.' ([74] p. 931)

and '... pricing policies are in almost every case equivalent to a company policy that represents an order of priorities and choice among competing objectives rather than policies tested by any single concept of profits maximisation.' ([74] p. 939)

7-3 The Pricing Mechanism

Empirical studies reveal a cost based approach in most manufacturing industry with the calculation of average costs as the first stage in the pricing process. This of course does not necessarily mean that a rigid cost-plus pricing system is in operation but the fact that pricing normally begins from a cost base usually means that cost has a predominant part to play in pricing whereas really the firm ought to consider both costs and market information in determining price.

Figure 7.1 Full-Cost Pricing

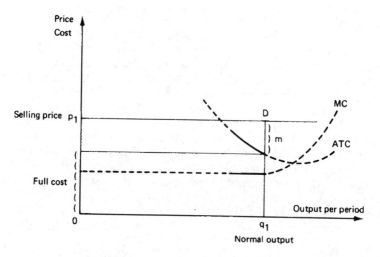

In Figure 7.1 we are assuming the firm has some normal level of output $0q_1$ in mind. This can be related to past capacity utilisation or be some expected level of output. Full costs include direct costs and overheads (and consequently both variable and fixed costs in the short run) and to these are added the margin 'm' to arrive at the final selling price of $0p_1$. However, there are several crucial questions here, particularly the measure of cost which is not a definite unequivocal concept as we illustrated in Chapter 4. Accounting measures suggest a precision in the allocation of costs but in a multi-product firm common costs are often arbitrarily allocated so that the costs of individual products cannot be uniquely defined. Additionally cost estimates may be actual costs, expected costs or standard costs. If they are 'actual' they will relate to the immediate past and will comprise the unit costs of labour and materials plus some unit allocation of overheads. Expected costs are forecasts of costs based on estimated prices of inputs, output rates, etc.; as are standard costs which relate to some normal operating level of output which normally reflects the long run average rate of plant utilisation. Short run movements in plant utilisation are then reflected in variances from standard. Of course firms will have some experience of operating at this normal output level so they should be in a position to calculate standard costs fairly readily and additionally have some idea of the sensitivity of demand to small variations in price around that determined on the basis of the standard.

This method of pricing implies in the short run that firms can fix independently both output and price. At the normal level of output the firm fixes a margin above average cost to provide for profits, and assumes that it can sell that output at the resultant price, yet there is circular reasoning here in that sales volume cannot be estimated without reference to competition and potential demand which will depend on price, and the latter is calculated from unit cost which in turn cannot be determined without reference to the sales volume.

The 'full-cost' pricing method does not explicitly take account of demand and only by chance will the normal sales volume coincide with the demand at the calculated price. If the firm sells all its normal output and its stock of finished goods is at its normal level, then we can say that the demand curve passes through D in Figure 7.1, and if the margin represents a profit level which equals or is greater than the target level set by the firm then the firm will effectively be in a position of stability. If the profit level is too low this might set into motion efforts to reduce costs and perhaps some improvements in the product. It is of course unlikely that the firm will be able to fix a level of output and a price to coincide with the demand curve facing it and it may face either excess demand (where the demand curve is to the right of point D) or a shortfall in demand (where the demand curve is to the left of point D). The firm can gauge from its inventories and order book what the state of demand is, since if stocks of finished goods are low and the order book is lengthening then it is clear that demand exceeds the available supply. It would probably keep the price at the same level unless it felt that this imbalance would persist for some time, in which case it could consider an expansion of output or a price rise to take advantage of the high and persistent demand. In the case of pricing of the Jaguar XJ 12 mentioned earlier, a two year waiting list developed at the end of the first year launch with an active black market on the car. This position was similar to the Range Rover and Rover 3500 S and in both these cases British Leyland raised their prices: that of the Range Rover by over 20 per cent in two years and in the case of the 3500 S by 12 per cent within a year.

In the converse situation where there is an excess supply and output has to be cut back the firm may have to reduce its price in order to bring about equilibrium, yet a strict application of full-cost pricing would lead to the raising of prices, since average costs would have risen as fixed costs per unit increased.* In situations of depressed demand, competition would preclude the passing on of higher unit costs to the consumer and indeed prices would tend to fall. However, in oligopoly collusion, either by the development of cartels or less formalised price leadership by a dominant firm in the industry, can transmit price increases even when there is excess capacity in the industry.

Full-cost pricing is sometimes seen as a convention to enable firms to make satisfactory profits in a world of ignorance and uncertainty. Firms can reduce their uncertainty still further by imitation of the conventions of other firms.** Thus firms are unavoidably using a pricing method which is different in procedure to marginal analysis but the results may be the same, particularly if flexibility is embodied in the percentage mark up so that it takes account of the external environment of the firm, in particular market demand. However, marginal analysis and full-cost pricing can never be fully reconcilable but we would not go as far as Lanzillotti in arguing that they must always be inconsistent.

What full-cost pricing offers is a relatively easy and safe approach to pricing in the absence of knowledge of demand. It will give greater price stability than marginal analysis which involves variation in prices in

---

* Provided that average variable cost, over the region of the change in output, is constant as is normally assumed by cost accountants.

** A. Alchian [3] argues that firms may imitate successful firms in order to reduce uncertainty and to ensure survival. Lanzillotti [74] found that several companies in his study of pricing modelled their general target return policy along the lines of that of Dupont or General Motors.

response to market forces. Firms prefer relatively stable prices and even if they had the information to use marginal analysis they might be unwilling to adopt it because of the costly changes in price lists as well as other inconveniences. Consumers too may prefer stable prices and in oligopolistic industries price changes by one firm may be seen as aggressive moves by its competitors. Certainly price changes require consideration of rivals' actions and may also involve reference to potential competition as we illustrated in Chapter 6, Section 6-3.

The key questions still to be answered relate to the determination of the profit margin and its possible variation through time due to changing cost, demand and competitive comditions. Taking the first question — what determines its size? This is presumably related to the firm's objectives and in some cases the evidence suggests that firms somehow translate long run objectives into profit margins for the product range. Some objectives are vague and non-operational, but others will be specific so that the firm can accommodate them in its pricing formula.

7-4 Objectives in Pricing

We have explained in Chapter 1 that the traditional motivating assumption of profit maximisation has been criticised. Admittedly profit will enter the objective functions of most firms, but even if it wanted to, a firm could not maximise profits because it would not have the necessary information. If the firm is a multi-product one it will be difficult to calculate costs or revenues and it will be uncertain about how its profits will change in response to its pricing decisions. There may be uncertainty about competitors which will require some conjecture being made about their reaction and of course the whole decision process takes place within a complex organisation which is a coalition of different interest groups who may have conflicting interests. Cyert and March [32]* argue that firms contending with these difficulties may 'satisfice'. However, even if firms could maximise profits they may not wish to do so either because of some sense of social responsibility or because managerial objectives may be pursued, (assuming separation of ownership and management) at the expense of higher profits. Thus on both counts, cognitive (they cannot) and motivational (they wish not), the assumption of profit maximisation in traditional theory is criticised and empirical studies have revealed that on the whole firms do not use optimisation methods such as marginal analysis and do not appear to attempt to maximise profits. The observation of full-cost pricing is a case in point, although it is worth noting that some studies, particularly

---

* Because of the departmentalisation of firms multiple objectives may arise. Cyert and March suggest sales or market share, production, and inventory as well as profit.

that of J. S. Earley [38] published in 1956, are suggestive of a more widespread use of marginal analysis than is customarily believed. In his sample of 100 'excellently managed companies' (as defined by the American Institute of Management) the majority followed pricing, marketing and new product policies that were essentially marginalist. Of course these companies did have costing systems that provided the necessary information on which to base their 'marginalism-on-the-wing' as Earley referred to it. Studies in the UK, for example, that of M. Howe [60] reveal marginal analysis in certain instances in pricing decisions though in the main Howe found in his study of the cost accounting procedures of twenty-eight firms that full costs were the final step in the pricing process. There is some evidence which suggest a greater awareness of marginal analysis with respect to export pricing and in the extensive inquiries of D. C. Hague referred to earlier, many respondents stated that they attempted to maximise profits or stressed that they were in business to make profits. However, it is difficult to attach any real significance to the phrase 'maximisation of profits' even though explicitly in operational research techniques, e.g. linear programming, maximisation of profit (or minimising of costs) does have a definite meaning within the restrictive assumptions made.

If pricing is directed towards some profit objective, but not profit *maximisation*, and this shares with other objectives, some of which may not be entirely consistent with profit, it is obviously impossible to derive any universal propositions from the empirical evidence. The latter, however, makes it fairly definite that the profit objective is held clearly in mind when pricing decisions are made. Feedback reveals on a continuous basis whether profit targets are being achieved so that if a firm is prepared to adopt a flexible mark-up on cost it can make appropriate responses.

Many firms have a global figure of profits in mind and indeed many company chairmen give a forecast of anticipated profits in their statements to shareholders. However, an absolute figure of profits is not very useful operationally so many companies prefer to use a percentage return on capital and while in principle this is the most useful guide to profitability, it can also be the most misleading.

In the first place the return is usually expressed as a target and this will probably be related to some long run profit objective, even though the actual profit attainable may vary from year to year. Measurement problems invite more damaging criticism and these include difficulties over measurement of costs, and capital employed which are usually glossed over. We encountered some of these issues in Chapter 4, in particular the question of the valuation of fixed capital, inventories and the depreciation policy employed. Up to 1960 few British companies attempted to revalue capital assets but since then there has been an increasing use of replacement cost valuation of capital and depreciation. As we illustrate in Chapter 8, the rate of return which should be used as a measure of profitability is a discounted cash-flow return and there is increasing evidence now of its use in British industry.

Where an attempt is made to calculate industry-wide rates of return on capital, or to make comparisons between firms or industries, the measurement problems multiply, yet for monopoly policy one guide to the exercising of market power is profitability greater than the normal (with adjustment for risk). The classical case against monopoly (see Chapter 6, Section 6-3), is that surplus profit is accompanied by a higher price and lower output than would be experienced under more competitive conditions. The Monopolies Commission (see C. K. Rowley [121]) has used a series of ex-post returns as guidelines, and the original ones for 1960 were based on historical costs. Since then there have been successive refinements, including the incorporation of replacement cost valuations.

The profit objective of a return on capital will often be expressed as a target figure. There is, however, some dispute as to whether the use of 'targets' is simply a business convention reflecting imitative behaviour of firms, or a target which has survived from a previous collusive agreement or whether it can be taken to be an objective in its own right. We take the view that it does represent an objective and our treatment throughout adopts this approach.

The margin added to full unit cost in the pricing formula is related to the company's target rate of return in the following manner:

$$\text{Target rate of return} = \frac{\text{Annual profit target}}{\text{Capital employed}} \times 100\%$$

$$\frac{\text{Annual profit target}}{\text{Total budgeted costs for year}} \times 100\% = \text{percentage margin on cost}$$

(The total budgeted costs will be based upon an estimate of sales volume.) For example, the TRR Company has a target rate of return of 20 per cent (before taxes). Capital employed is estimated to be £1 million, so that the annual profit target is £200,000.

Total budgeted costs for the year are £800,000
so the percentage margin on cost is $\frac{£200,000}{£800,000} \times 100\%$

= <u>25%</u> .

Whether or not the target rate of return of 20 per cent will be realised depends upon whether the anticipated sales volume can be achieved at the prices charged on the basis of cost plus 25 per cent. Despite the apparent precision of the calculation of this mark-up on cost, the omission of demand information means that the attainment of equilibrium is still fortuitous.

The Hague [49] and Lanzillotti [74] studies confirmed target returns though they stressed that their use in the pricing process varied. In the Lanzillotti study the average target was 14 per cent (after taxes) and he found some desire to stabilise prices perhaps by virtue of the structure of his sample which included many oligopolistic firms. Some companies used the target more as a benchmark than a rigid guide, particularly as in most cases it was regarded as a long run objective. In the UK study by Hague targets typically ignored tax and only one firm used different target rates of return within a product line though it is perhaps unrealistic to expect firms to do this, particularly where products may be produced jointly. Some firms apparently using a target rate of return pricing claimed to be profit maximisers while others were clearly satisficers. Those identified as maximisers in the study included some firms who were encountering falling demand and who were virtually compelled to take opportunities to improve profits through changes in the margin over cost. Whilst it may have been the case that some of the other firms wished to maximise profits Hague concluded that in many cases their actual behaviour was more indicative of satisficing, with margins insensitive to demand changes except when objectives were threatened. While all firms in his study used target rates of return they also set target profits as an absolute sum of money and many had a conception of what was a fair and just profit given risk conditions and what was necessary to maintain long run growth.

This conception of a fair profit is important in all firms in Britain now. In the first place large firms with market power fear anti-monopoly action, and smaller firms are often conditioned by what the industry is achieving, for example, when they make contracts with Economic Development Committees (EDCs). Additionally the existence of legislation on prices with an elaborate price code implies criteria of just and fair prices. Of course these must be high enough to compensate shareholders and to provide for the financing needs of the company. This concept of a threshold level of profits is built into managerial theories of the firm, such as those of Baumol [14], Williamson [157] and Marris [87] and also relates to Cyert and March's concept of a satisfactory profit.

The maturity of the product can be important in determining the target. It is usually found to be higher for new products to recoup development costs but management may choose either to skim the market at a higher price or to go for a penetration price. In using a skimming price they try to exploit the inelasticity of demand in the market and may be forced later to reduce the price or maintain it at a given level (which in inflationary conditions is equivalent to a price cut). In penetration pricing they seek a low price to generate a large volume of sales and a base for future sales. In both instances accurate market information is necessary.

We have stressed the fact that a single objective is unlikely to exist in a firm and a 'market' objective is usually set in terms of sales volume, sales value or market share. It was of course Baumol [14] from his observations of business and consulting experience who proposed a theory of the firm based on sales revenue maximisation, discussed in Chapter 6, Section 6-6. Targets for sales are confirmed in both the Lanzillotti and Hague studies. Lanzillotti for instance found that a market share objective was almost as important as target return on investment, particularly from products where the firm did not already have a patent or an advantage gained from innovation. In other products where they possessed market power they were anxious to maintain a market share but not necessarily to expand it. In the Hague study too a market share objective was set by most firms, though the importance which a firm placed on it varied with the type of product, the market structure, and trading conditions. With the exception of one firm, all set targets for the volume of sales to be achieved in specific periods and some also set targets in terms of sales value.

Other objectives which firms pursue are often vague or non-quantifiable yet they may still condition the firm's behaviour. The sort of objective we have in mind includes the desire to be the recognised leader in the industry, technology, or more generally to maintain high utilisation of plant and to maintain employment. In part of course this objective can be contained in the sales target referred to above. When multiple objectives cannot be satisfied simultaneously the firm might attend to them sequentially and rank these objectives in order of preference.

In trying to improve pricing decisions, the problem of multiple objectives must be borne in mind and the other practical difficulties we have described. These include relating short-term decisions to long-term needs, imperfections in information, especially knowledge of demand, and the consequent reliance on feedback data. These are the characteristic problems of *time* and *knowledge*. In oligopoly, the anticipation of rivals' reactions is a further complication, and so we could go on. Nevertheless it is our belief that there is scope for introducing the economist's approach into the pricing decision so as to remove some of the anomalies brought about by full-cost pricing.

7-5 Product-Analysis Pricing

W. Brown and E. Jaques [21] have proposed a method of price

determination which is directly opposed to full-cost pricing. The 'product-analysis' approach aims to produce market oriented prices which reflect consumer valuations of the product rather than the firm's cost experience. The rationale behind this approach is that a consumer is not interested in the firm's cost experience and that he would be unwilling to pay a higher price to one firm simply because it had incurred higher costs than its competitors, or because its overhead allocation method had resulted in a particularly heavy loading of overheads on to a particular product group. On the other hand the consumer would be willing to pay a higher price to a firm that sold a better product in terms of performance, reliability, or appearance.

To a certain extent better products do cost more to produce but this is not always the case. Suppose there are two firms producing for the same market. Superco is a highly efficient organisation enjoying low production, selling and administrative costs, while Inferco is troubled by high costs in all parts of the organisation. Moreover, Superco are innovators, their products are more technologically advanced than Inferco's and they have a reputation for greater reliability and after sales service. Clearly the products of Inferco cannot be sold at a higher price than those of Superco, yet full-cost pricing with a constant industry-wide profit margin could lead to this anomalous situation. In fact the only way in which Inferco can continue operating in the same market is to accept a lower price. This is precisely what product-analysis pricing advocates.

It is perhaps in pricing for contracts that this approach would have its widest application, particularly where products are custom-built so that no two items are sold at the same price. A simple pricing rule is required for this kind of situation and clearly full-cost, convenient though it may be, generally fails to meet the requirements an economist would stipulate. Given that most firms require a simple pricing method even if they are producing for mass markets, the product-analysis approach obviously has wider applicability than just to contract or jobbing situations.

The first step in product-analysis pricing for a particular type of product is to determine the significant properties of the basic product range and the additional features that the customer may order. Some measure of power such as an engine's cubic capacity might serve as a means of classification and the weekly throughput of a machine as another. Attributes which influence market value are the only relevant ones and it is vital that the analyst gives this matter careful consideration. For the Jaguar XJ 12 cited earlier, the significant properties would be acceleration, top speed, seating capacity, comfort and a style with consumer appeal, all of which would be compared with rival models. Product-analysis pricing necessitates a thorough demand analysis in order to find the price at which products with various characteristics can sell in the desired quantities. The target level of sales is ideally that volume which will satisfy the long run objectives of the firm, including profit, so that the cost of producing and selling that volume must also be considered.

The full-cost pricer might try to pick holes in this alternative approach because it does not guarantee a profit, whereas the full-cost method certainly gives the illusion of guaranteeing a profit in that adding a profit margin to cost hopefully contributes to the firm's income. We have already explained the circular reasoning involved here. Suffice it to say that if the price is calculated in the absence of demand information or consideration of competition of the market, there is no guarantee that the resultant sales will match the level assumed at the start of the calculation. It may be that the calculated price is so high relative to the valuation by consumers that items remain unsold and losses are made.

To ensure a profit when the product-analysis method is used, the firm must monitor its costs carefully. Let us suppose now that the firm has assessed the price of its major product in accordance with a desired sales volume, after careful consideration of the product's principal features, *vis-à-vis* the substitutes offered by competitors and the other products in the firm's own product line. The next step is to determine whether or not at that price, the firm will benefit from selling that product. This involves a consideration of the alternatives open to the firm. If in the short run there is no alternative use for the firm's capacity, so long as the price exceeded variable costs, the opportunity would be worthwhile since a positive contribution, otherwise not available, would be enjoyed by the firm. If however, other opportunities for using the firm's productive capacity were available, a positive contribution from one product would be no guarantee, on its own, of acceptability. The firm would have to consider the total problem, perhaps using linear programming in order to optimise overall performance (see Chapter 3). The shadow prices determined from linear programming indicate the opportunity costs of using productive facilities and provide a means of testing the acceptability of an addition to or replacement in the product range (see Chapter 4).

Product-analysis pricing then is essentially a market oriented approach to pricing which tries to find the price the consumer is willing to pay given the nature of the output in terms of significant properties and the onus is then on the firm to make a profit at that price by control of costs. An example of tailoring cost to the market price might arise in the pricing and costing of a holiday tour. Suppose that the Traveleasy company knows from its experience of the market and competitors' prices that a holiday at the Adriatic resorts of Italy should be priced at about £150 for 15 days. This is slightly higher than competitors' prices because of Traveleasy's reputation for comfort and good service. Cost estimates for aircraft, hotels, transport to and from the hotel and administration, (separating the variable costs from the fixed) enable the contribution to profit to be calculated. Suppose that the contribution is only £50 per person and the required figure is around £60, the latter being based on the return obtainable from holidays of similar duration and similar flight distance. Traveleasy could try to trim costs by £10 per head perhaps by providing a lower grade hotel or by offering half-board instead of full-board. In doing so the tour operator would have to ascertain the reduction in demand this might bring and the possible repercussions that any drop in standards might have on its reputation. The full-cost approach would be to calculate all costs including an allowance for fixed overheads, add to this the usual percentage profit margin and put the onus on the customer to pay the computed price or do without.

Product-analysis pricing would therefore seem to be more in line with the objective of profit through efficient resource allocation advocated in this book. However, if this method were to be used by an oligopolist it is unlikely that the price arrived at would be the same as the price under perfect competition. It is more likely to reflect the price the consumer *has* to pay given the market structure which exists in practice. Price cutting could disturb the market equilibrium and this therefore means that product-analysis pricing is not an instrument for drastic change. No firm can deviate too far from the prevailing price unless it is willing to accept the consequences of a price war and market upheaval.

7-6 The Economist Versus the Accountant

W. T. Baxter and A. R. Oxenfeldt [15] have compared and contrasted the alternative views on pricing echoing our argument that prices based on full absorption costing methods do not meet the criteria of the economist. However, it is vital to know what a product really costs to produce and sell, whatever pricing method is advocated. How, for example, can the product analyst determine the desirability of an opportunity unless he has a cost figure with which to compare his market oriented price?

First of all let us repeat that the economist's concern with marginal cost does not mean that variable costs are the only elements that he ever considers. We must dispel the myth that the economist advocates accepting any opportunity whose selling price covers variable costs. The misunderstanding arises because many businessmen and even some accountants, who should know better, remember that in their elementary course of economic theory firms were supposed to produce at that output where marginal cost equals price. This pertains to the theory of perfect competition and it can be proved that such a rule gives the profit maximising output. However, marginal cost is not to be confused with unit variable cost. Economists brought up on the law of diminishing returns believe that marginal cost rises steeply after a certain point so that it exceeds eventually both average variable cost and average total cost. Without repeating the cost curve controversy here, the economist certainly does not argue that pricing to cover short run variable costs is always adequate. In fact the only situation where the decision to produce rests on a simple consideration of variable costs against sales revenue is when there is ample spare capacity.

As we have stressed throughout this book, there are two stages to the economist's approach. The determination of avoidable costs (e.g. variable costs in the short run — see Chapter 4, Section 4-8) and the comparison of these with incremental revenue is only the first of these stages. The second is to assess the cost of using resources the company already owns. Let us examine the implications of the economist's approach in the following example.

Suppose that a factory's estimated fixed costs including administrative and selling overheads are £1,000 per week and that initially it is working at full capacity. This involves a production rate of 50 units of product A per week, each unit requiring two hours machine time in the factory. The £1,000 fixed costs are absorbed at the rate of £10 per hour or £20 per unit of A produced. Variable costs are £20 per unit so the full unit cost is £40. Product A is sold at £50 thus carrying a margin, over full cost, of £10, or 25 per cent.

The product analyst has been requested by a customer for a quotation for product B. Thirty units per week would be required and the input requirements involve one hour production time in the factory and £20 in variable costs — an apparent full cost of £30. The product analyst feels that £25 is the right price for product B after consideration of market prices quoted by competing firms. Given the profits currently made on product A he is not surprised that product B is regarded unfavourably by his firm. Times change however, and soon demand for A drops sharply so that there is adequate capacity for the manufacture of 30 units of B per week. The cost department however still recommends rejection of the opportunity even though no alternative use for the capacity has emerged. Their case is based on the full cost of £30 per unit against a selling price of £25.

Here, of course, the idea of just covering the variable cost is quite acceptable. Stage one of the economist's approach compares the variable costs of £20 with the selling price of £25 and shows that £5 contribution per unit is offered, i.e. £150 per week when 30 units are made. This would not be enjoyed otherwise since no other alternative for using the firm's capacity has emerged. Stage two is to find the opportunity cost (or shadow price) of using productive facilities already owned. No alternative use means zero opportunity cost so the argument is resolved at stage one.

To show that this is an exceptional case, let us consider now the economist's approach to a different situation this firm may encounter. The factory is working at full capacity and making only product 'A'. A new product C is being considered but its production would involve displacement of product A. Before calling in the product analyst to quote a price, the cost department is approached. Since each unit of C would require 3 hours production time and would also incur variable costs of £10, the following estimate is prepared:

Fixed costs	(3 hours @ £10 per hour)	..	£30
Variable costs	.. ..	..	£10
	Full cost	..	£40

Since product A carries a 25 per cent margin, the cost department argues that £50 would be an appropriate selling price for C (£40 + 25%). However, had an economist been approached, the following picture would have emerged:

Avoidable cost (variable cost)	..	£10
Opportunity cost of using factory	..	£45
Total cost	..	£55

The opportunity cost figure is calculated on the basis of each unit of C displacing 1½ units of A (three hours as against two hours production time). Each unit of A contributes £50 − £20 = £30. So 1½ × £30 is foregone every time one unit of C displaces 1½ units of A. The economist would then request the product analyst for a price quotation for C, or a range of quotations to cover the feasible levels of production of that product. A selling price of less than £55 would not show a profit according to the economist's calculation so that had the cost department's advice been taken and a price of £50 been set, the firm would have lost £5 for each unit of C produced instead of yielding an apparent profit of £10 over and above full cost.

7-7 Pricing in the Long Run

Suppose now that the firm is selling a new product and that existing productive facilities are unsuitable for its manufacture. The normal selling price for a new product is a complex calculation, particularly if it is unlike anything that the firm has sold before. Some guidance may be forthcoming from market research or market experiments as we illustrated in Chapter 5, but a greater understanding of the forces governing the product's demand will often only be possible over time as experience eliminates some of the uncertainty.

Of course, if a firm is committing the vast resources that are necessary to develop, produce, launch and sell a new product it requires some knowledge before the event about the likely price the product will fetch. J. K. Galbraith [43] argues that demand can be managed through appropriate marketing strategies, in particular advertising on commercial television, but there are limits to the manipulation of the consumer, so that firms in practice will only market products which have a high probability of acceptance by the consumer. Knowledge about demand is therefore still vital and certainly a price calculated entirely on the basis of cost is unlikely to be appropriate except purely by coincidence. Referring back to the price of the new Jaguar XJ 12 which was calculated on a cost-plus basis, it could be seen that a higher price was appropriate, once feedback data revealed a long waiting list. A firm can admittedly make adjustments in response to feedback, but with government control over prices it is becoming more important to anticipate demand by forecasting.

To establish a normal price for the long run, market and product analysts must try their best to plot a demand function relating expected sales to price, and the necessary promotional expenditure to maintain that volume of sales. The economist should be able to make a substantial contribution to this exercise, given his understanding of demand analysis, and in particular his knowledge of possible changes in the economic environment, including growth, inflation and the implications of fiscal, monetary, and prices and incomes policies.

The long run pricing decision cannot be divorced from the investment decision and indeed we indicated in Section 7-4 that many firms already relate their prices to target rates of return on capital employed. Here again the economist has an important part to play in determining the necessary investment expenditure to provide capacity for the range of sales levels enumerated in the demand analysis, and hence the long run incremental cost of production. Different sales levels require differing scales of plant and because these may operate with varying unit costs it is impossible to state the cost of production without first identifying the volume of sales and output. The optimum long run price is the one which will give the biggest discounted profit (or Net Present Value — see Chapter 8, Section 8-3), given the anticipated sales volume, output, necessary promotional expenditure and investment.

Some firms may find the task of obtaining accurate demand information for a new product almost impossible or too costly to be worthwhile gathering. They may therefore be tempted to revert to a cost-based method, however unsatisfactory that may be. However, if they identify the long run marginal cost* of producing and selling the assumed volume, using the most efficient production techniques, and then allow a mark-up on cost which reflects the customary target rate of return appropriate to the type of business, the resultant price may be a useful guide. This is because rival firms could only offer the same product at a similar price if they too were faced with similar cost conditions. Price based on long run marginal cost would at least be competitive but whether or not the assumed sales volume could be attained at that price would still be an imponderable for the firm making decisions without a knowledge of market demand.

If long run marginal cost serves as the basis for the pricing of existing products as well as new products it is likely to lead to better resource allocation within the economy than prices based on current or historical costs. This point was stressed by the National Board for Prices and Incomes in its recommendations for pricing policy (see A. Silbertson [131]) and this method is also frequently advocated for pricing in the public sector.

If a normal price for the long run is established, it is unlikely that this will be appropriate at all stages of the product's life cycle. Initially the firm may choose to sell at a reduced price, even below cost, if it believes that it will thereby attract sufficient consumers who will remain loyal to the product even when price reverts to the 'normal'. Again when the market has been saturated and sales cease to grow or even decline, the firm may adjust the price, typically, along with some product modification and promotional activity in order to give the product a new lease of life. Demand may also change with the level of economic activity such that price reductions may be appropriate in a depression and price rises during a boom. Also pricing to take account of peak demand for services like telephone calls can lead to a differential tariff according to the time of day and week. The latter is essentially a form of price discrimination which relies on the fact that business calls can only be made during the peak period so that the market for private calls in the evening and at weekends can be regarded as distinct (see Chapter 6, Section 6-3). Ensuring compatability between prices charged at different periods of time is certainly an important matter, but an equally vital consideration is the compatability of prices between products.

---

* Long run marginal cost includes expenditure on necessary capital equipment and a return on that capital. We are however including the latter in the mark-up on cost.

7-8 Product-Line Pricing

In Section 7-6 above it was suggested that if a firm identifies unit costs, according to avoidable and opportunity cost principles, and finds that these exceed the anticipated selling price, then it will find the venture unprofitable. It would seem too, from our discussion of long run pricing, that a firm must, over the life cycle of a product, be able to sell at a price which exceeds long run marginal cost and allows for the opportunity cost of capital, expressed as a rate of return on new investment. This however is an oversimplification, given the propensity to multiple production in the modern business enterprise. This means that the price of one product in the product line cannot be assessed in isolation if demand inter-relationships exist. We encountered, albeit briefly, both competitive and complementary relationships in Chapter 5, Section 5-11 and now we must return to this subject.

If a firm sells a line of products which are substitutes for each other, e.g. a car manufacturer offering a variety of styles, sizes and engine capacities, the appropriate price for each product can only be determined by considering the total problem. In other words, when choosing the price of one product the firm must examine the effect that this will have on the sales of competitive products and consequently the prices at which they should sell.

R. H. Coase [27] has shown how a profit maximising firm with inter-related demands would make its pricing decisions in theory. The lesson that can be learned from this analysis is that a price/output change of one product should not be appraised simply in terms of marginal cost against marginal revenue of the product itself, but also the change in net receipts from sales of the other products in the product line. This presupposes a knowledge of cross-elasticities of demand and given that firms are usually in doubt even as to the direct elasticity of demand for their products, the assumption of calculable cross-elasticities is therefore highly unrealistic. There is thus a great danger that demand may be ignored entirely in a multi-product firm because the job of acquiring the necessary information may seem insurmountable. Even cost-plus becomes difficult to apply in these circumstances because of joint costs which cannot be apportioned on an unequivocal basis. We can but urge firms to try methods like product-analysis pricing as a means of identifying the different characterisitics between one model and another that warrant price differentials, and to use such sales statistics as may be available to learn more about demand inter-relationships. In short we have no ready answer to this problem other than more research by the firm itself.

When demands are complementary, i.e. products are bought in association with each other, like instant loading cameras and the special film cartridges made by the same firm, the same kind of comments about pricing difficulties are pertinent. In addition there is the possibility of 'loss leadership'. This practice involves selling products below the price at which they would have been sold had there been no complementary relationship. The aim is to boost sales of the complementary item which may also be able to command a higher price than would have been possible without loss leadership. Some attempts at loss leadership have resulted in failure because the price cut has simply caused an increase in sales of the loss item, thereby reducing profits, and failing to make sufficient impact on sales of the complementary item. Supermarkets employ this practice to encourage customers to shop at their establishment in the hope that not only will they buy the loss items but do the rest of their week's shopping there as well. Too tempting an offer on cigarettes (one of the favourite products for loss leadership) may however make it worthwhile for the consumer to make a trip just to buy cigarettes. Sometimes, therefore, supermarkets will ration their special offers, only permitting one item per £x worth of other goods purchased. There is close similarity between this practice and that of tie-in sales which we have covered in more detail in Chapter 6, Section 6-3.

7-9 Pricing Below Cost and Basing Point Pricing

Pricing Below Cost

The successful application of loss leadership shows that pricing to cover costs is not always the best way to achieve the company's objectives. Paradoxically selling below cost is sometimes regarded as being against the public interest, despite the frequent outcries against firms which sell at prices well above cost. It seems therefore that public responsibility in pricing is almost impossible to define. The argument against selling below cost is not only that loss leadership might distort consumers' valuations of goods, but that price reductions across a wide range of merchandise might drive other firms out of business, leaving the price cutting firm in a monopoly position and therefore ultimately able to raise prices to higher levels than prevailed in the market before.

A classic case in the anti-monopoly literature is M. A. Adelman's [1] study of the A & P Company, an American grocery chain. This company was accused of unfair competition because it lowered its gross margins in order to increase business to the detriment of other retail concerns. A & P replied that, by increasing their sales volume, they would be able to reduce unit costs so that in effect the prices they were charging reflected their anticipated long run costs. However, this self-fulfilling prophecy was not allowed to bear fruit, and indeed many of the company's own managers were too conservative in outlook to engage in such an exercise, even before the company lost its case.

A variation on this theme, also regarded as being against the public interest, is the use of a 'fighting company'. Local and selective reductions in prices are achieved by setting up one of these companies under the concealed ownership of the parent. The fighting company eliminates regional competition by making it financially impossible for rival companies to exist and this is an example of the predatory tactics which dominant firms may use to preserve a monopoly position.*

Basing Point Pricing

Another perplexing issue is the devising of a pricing system to take account of transportation costs to the customer from the point of production. This element of cost may be an important consideration, particularly nowadays with recurrent increases in fuel costs. If the seller distributes to customers in different locations at *a uniform delivered price*, he is effectively accepting different *net* payments from his customers, because of the variations in freight costs. The seller is therefore discriminating between customers, some of whom are being subsidised by other customers, and this is why controversy surrounds this issue.

Basing point pricing is, if anything, an even more controversial method of allowing for freight charges. A basing point price consists of a factory price plus a transportation charge. The latter however does not necessarily correspond to the actual costs incurred, but is calculated from a designated basing point. If a single basing point is adopted, all buyers regardless of location will be charged the same price even if the production centre is nearer the customer than the basing point. The steel industry in the United States used to follow this practice, which was known as 'Pittsburgh Plus'. The US Steel Corporation was the industry leader and would always quote the Pittsburgh mill price of steel plus the rail freight from Pittsburgh to its destination, irrespective of the origin of the shipment or its actual freight cost; all firms in the industry follows a similar practice.

Multiple basing points have sometimes been adopted so that the buyer could in principle be quoted a number of different prices built up from factory price plus delivery charge from each basing point. Obviously in practice, the buyer can only be quoted a single price for a given product and this is normally the cheapest combination of basing point price plus transport cost.

The argument against the practice is that basing point pricing is a means of eliminating price competition, it can involve discrimination

---

* For an example of this practice, see the Monopolies Commission Report on Industrial Gases [96].

and if practiced throughout an industry, as it was in the US steel industry, then it is *prima facie* evidence of collusion. In its defence is the argument that the system is easier to operate than rival systems when plant locations are scattered relative to markets, and that its adoption in an industry reflects this convenience rather than collusive intentions.

Rival systems include the uniform delivered price system described above, zonal pricing and ex-works pricing. With a *zonal pricing* system there is a uniform delivered price within a zone of a country or region, but prices between zones vary. This method has been used in the pricing of oil and domestic coal and can be regarded as discriminatory, but not to the same extent as a uniform price throughout the whole country. Increasing the number of zones could reduce the degree of cross subsidisation between customers but of course it would involve higher administrative costs.

Ex-works pricing has been proposed by the severest critics of basing point pricing. Suppliers adopting this method quote a factory price, sometimes referred to as f.o.b. (free on board), and either allow the buyer to arrange his own transport or if the buyer prefers it, the supplier will quote a delivery charge which reflects the actual transport costs involved. Economists argue that greater efficiency would result from this practice as a result of the buyer being able to choose the cheapest means of transport. It would reduce the scope for collusion between firms and induce more active competition. The drawbacks are that local monopolies may arise with each producer having a competitive advantage in areas around his location. Other practical disadvantages are the administrative costs of quoting separate prices and invoicing. Further problems could occur at the despatch side of the supplying firm if customers were allowed to arrange their own transportation.

It is likely that this whole issue will remain the subject of debate in anti-monopoly policy. Fortunately for many firms the simplest method, namely the uniform delivered price, is unlikely to arouse a public outcry, if transport costs are low relative to the factory price of the product. However, where freight costs are substantial and goods are distributed nationally, zonal pricing is likely to be preferred.

7-10 Interdepartmental Transfers

Usually a parent company with subsidiaries or a company split into product divisions is so organised to facilitate decentralisation of decision making rather than to conceal ownership for nefarious purposes as with a fighting company. Quite often the divisions of a company will reflect a process of vertical integration where each division is involved in a different stage of manufacture. Automobile manufacturers may choose to manage component production and assembly in separate divisions. A chemical firm may use the basic chemicals produced in one division for the manufacture of pharmaceutical products in another division and one well-known British company takes vertical integration a step further by selling the final products in its own chemists shops. While this form of departmentalisation facilitates decentralisation, it can only be effective through proper coordination and control at head office. One big problem in control is measuring the profitability of each part of the business, and if such a measure could be found it would also be possible to relate one division's performance to the overall objectives of the company, thereby facilitating coordination.

It is in this context that the determination of prices for interdepartmental transfers comes about. If a price can be agreed for the intermediate products 'sold' by one division to another, a means of apportioning profit between these divisions is immediately established. Moreover if the price is chosen according to sound economic principles it is possible to reallocate resources in an optimal manner if one division is faced with changing circumstances. Unfortunately the apportioning of profit for prestige purposes sometimes takes priority as managers in rival divisions haggle over the issue of who is making the biggest profit. Not only will there be controversy over the transfer price but also the way in which common overheads are apportioned. The conflict over the price can be resolved if outside suppliers are able to offer the same intermediate product, in which case the prevailing market price is then appropriate and relative profitability can be readily calculated. The knowledge of a market price and profit also enables each division to make decisions which will serve the interests of the company as a whole. Let us suppose, for example, that a company has two divisions involving components and assembly. The activities of both may seem to be making a satisfactory profit when taken together but if the components division could be seen to be highly inefficient and consequently run down, the company might then achieve better profits by purchasing its components from an outside supplier. One way of proving the inefficiency of the components division is to appeal to the market price for its output and show that its profitability would be below normal if it had to sell on the open market at that price.

Even if a market price is not available it is often possible to show the minimum price a product would have to sell at in order to justify the allocation of machine time to its production. In Section 7-6 above for example, we showed that product C would have to sell at £55 or more if it was to compete with product A for production time. This figure was calculated using avoidable costs and the shadow price (opportunity cost) of machine time. Let us now imagine that product C is an intermediate product, not normally sold on the open market, which passes to another division for a further stage of manufacture. Unless the receiving division can achieve its desired profit performance on an assumption that £55 has to be 'paid' for intermediate product C, then resources should not be directed to the production of C. The factory involved in the first stage should then stick to product A and the factory involved in the next stage should manufacture something which will make a profit assuming that alternative uses are possible. Specificity of productive resources and the desire to produce a range of complementary products will complicate the picture in practice but there can be little doubt that prices for interdepartmental transfers have an important part to play in the management of complex business organisations. Once again the economist's concepts of avoidable and opportunity cost can prove invaluable.

8 THE INVESTMENT DECISION

8-1 Introduction – The Nature of the Investment Decision

Economists use the word 'investment' as a synonym for *capital formation* but in every day usage the term can be used to describe the purchase of stock exchange securities and other financial assets as well as purchases of land, machinery and buildings. To avoid such confusion, we shall use the term investment for the capital formation by a nation (including its companies, public corporations and others) which represents an increase in productive capacity in terms of its ability to supply goods and services. Capital formation can be net or gross depending on whether the depreciation of capital assets (say by obsolescence or wear and tear) is deducted and can relate not only to fixed assets such as machines, buildings and so on, but also to inventories. Because investment is undertaken in many different sectors of the economy, it is unlikely that a simple theory will explain the determinants of investment.

Perhaps the most common explanation of investment is contained in the so-called *Accelerator Principle*, which claims that companies adjust their capital stock in accordance with movements (or anticipated movements) in their output. Thus if a company has little spare capacity in a situation in which sales are expected to increase, then it will need to install new productive capacity. If we write investment (the addition to capital stock per period of time) as I and ΔS as the rate of change in sales,* then the accelerator principle may be expressed as:

$$I = f(\Delta S)$$

According to the accelerator principle, then, rising sales are a prerequisite for new investment. If sales are static, the only capital expenditure will be for replacement of existing productive capacity.

When obsolescence dictates replacement, *substitution* for labour may be involved in a world of changing technology in which, generally speaking, capital intensive methods of production have been substituted for processes requiring comparatively higher labour input proportions. Rising wages have also been responsible for this substitution of capital for labour although union resistance has often limited the degree to

---

* This refers to real changes in sales – i.e. consumption of output in physical units rather than monetary value.

which this has occurred. The financing of investment is something that we shall discuss in greater depth later in this chapter, but an important issue to raise in the present context is the balance between externally raised and internally generated funds. Although retention of earnings for reinvestment is often regarded as not being conducive to the efficient deployment of capital resources between companies, in practice firms are heavily reliant on internal sources of finance for investment purposes. Consequently the *flow of funds* may be an immediate factor influencing investment decisions, which means that a good current performance may encourage capital formation. Current performance also influences the expectations of management and often leads to optimism which in itself may be a stimulus to investment (see Chapter 2).

It is however the opportunity for *future profit* that is usually regarded as the ultimate causal factor. Merrett and Sykes [91] begin their first chapter with the words: 'The defining characteristic of an investment is the outlay of valuable resources in the expectation of future gain' (p. 3). It is on the assumption that the objective of management, in investment, is a profitability target measured over an appropriate time horizon, that our analysis is developed in the present chapter. The accelerator principle, factor substitution, and flow of funds are certainly relevant but perhaps best regarded as proximate, rather than ultimate, causes of investment.

The decision to commit resources for investment purposes is probably the most important decision of management. Indeed if we go back to the hierarchy of decisions introduced in Chapter 1 we argued (following Ansoff [6]) that the investment decision is a strategic decision and the responsibility of top management. High level decisions often involve a distant time horizon and this is certainly true of investment decisions. Resources are committed at one point in time and the benefits do not accrue until later. The forward looking nature of these decisions means that the whole issue of knowledge: certainty, risk and uncertainty, will be a very important one in the present chapter.

The basic condition on which investment proceeds is that in return for paying out, or committing a given amount of resources to a particular project, a larger amount will be received back over a period of time. This amount should not only repay the original outlay but also provide a target rate of return on the outlay. Because the outlay of resources and the benefits derived (often referred to as cash flows or income stream) do not occur simultaneously but arise in different time periods, the whole life of a capital project must be considered in its appraisal.

Once resources are committed, the decision is irreversible or only reversible at a high cost.* Industrial progress has been accompanied by

---

* The decision to cancel an investment project becomes, in itself, another investment decision weighing up the expected savings as against the expected gains of continuing.

increasing requirements for capital equipment which is not only more complex technologically but specific to the use for which it was designed. The consequences of the choice made will be felt in the future and will thus influence the firm's prospects of long run survival and growth. Moreover, aggregate investment in industry is the key to economic growth for the nation, and the emphasis placed on this national policy objective has intensified the search for techniques which will lead to optimal investment decisions. Whilst there is some evidence available now to suggest that a more rigorous analysis takes place within firms (and within the public sector)* it is less than a decade since the National Economic Development Council (NEDC) published a report on Investment Appraisal [102] in which they concluded that:

> 'investment decisions are too often reached by methods which are unlikely to produce the pattern or level of investment most profitable to firms or most favourable to economic growth. Many firms appear to apply criteria for assessing investment projects which have little relevance to the measurement of the expected profitability of the capital investment.' ([102] p. 1)

One of the reasons why this may be the case is the time period over which the investment is likely to generate returns, and the related question of uncertainty. Managers do not possess the necessary knowledge either of alternatives open to them or of the pay-offs of these various alternatives. The actions of governments and the behaviour of rival firms are difficult to predict. The longer the returns extend into the future and the greater the pace of technological change the more criticial become these imperfections in knowledge. This of course makes it all the more tempting to rely on simple rules of thumb in appraisal but unless they have a rational basis their use cannot be justified. Indeed the case is made even stronger for an analytical framework within which it is possible for management to utilise what information is available and to facilitate the testing of the sensitivity of the result to changes in key parameters.

In Chapter 4, Section 4-8, we indicated that the economist's decision rules involving avoidable cost and opportunity cost concepts were not only appropriate to short run decision making but also for long period plans when capital projects are evaluated. Avoidable cost in the long run includes all costs associated with a particular project, not just direct labour, materials and expense but capital outlays,** installation and dismantling charges, tax payments, research and development, the

---
* Some of the problems encountered in public sector investment are covered in Section 8-9.
** This includes investment in stocks and other elements of working capital such as payroll.

advertising of new products associated with the project, insurance of the buildings, machinery and stocks involved in the project and so on. The analyst must ensure that the outlays he includes are strictly incremental, i.e. they are in addition to expenditure which the company is already committed to, since commitments already entered into are non-avoidable. Similarly when the benefits of the project are brought into the calculation, these must be incremental with all profits or cash flows that would be enjoyed even in the absence of the new project, excluded from consideration.

Following this stage of analysis the economist then examines the project for requirements of factors already in existence. In the long run, the only non-specific resource that is bound to be present in a surviving company is finance. The opportunity cost of finance (henceforth cost of capital) is the rate of return which could be obtained in the best comparable use. Whether finance has been acquired through retention of profits or through new capital issues, the opportunity cost principle dictates that the company can only justify its use in financing a particular venture if the latter can earn an appropriate rate of return. This rate will reflect what shareholders could earn by placing their money in alternative investments whose business and financial risks were similar.

When a project is being appraised in these terms, it is not only necessary to calculate its profitability with a given set of estimates for costs, revenues and other appropriate parameters, but also to estimate the likelihood that these estimates will be realised. We cannot claim here that sophisticated analysis can ever completely reduce the investment decision to a routine mechanical process.* The exercising of managerial judgement will never be removed but judgement must be backed by systematic analysis of appropriate information before a decision can be made. Before showing how the economist's approach can be incorporated into such a systematic analysis it is important to look again at the objectives of management.

The usual starting point is to assume that the objective of management is to maximise profits in order to maximise the wealth of stockholders. We have already illustrated in this book that to make this an operational concept is difficult because of the presence of uncertainty and competing organisational goals which include profit but which are not exclusively concerned with profits. In consequence decisions are taken on the basis of an acceptable performance which in the context of investment is usually taken as a target rate of return. The concept of target rate of return on investment has been built into some reformula-

---

* Although in the analysis of investment projects involving small outlays, some firms have compiled a manual which sets out the procedures to be followed in evaluating the proposal. These are attempts to routinise the investment decision.

tions of the theory of business behaviour in the form of a constraint to ensure long run survival of the firm by providing sufficient funds for future investment plans. The level of this acceptable return should also be sufficiently high to maintain a stock market valuation of shares sufficient to deter take over-raiders (as in the R. Marris model [87]). This aim of achieving satisfactory returns rather than optimal does not benefit either the firm or the economy in the long run since ideally resources should be directed to their most profitable uses. In this chapter we aim to set out some of the problems and methods of securing more efficient appraisal of capital investment.

We introduce the concept of 'discounting' in Section 8-2 as a prerequisite for the discussion of modern discounted cash flow (DCF) methods of appraisal (Section 8-3) of which there are two main alternatives, namely Net Present Value (NPV) and Internal Rate of Return (IRR or what economists refer to as the marginal efficiency of capital). In Section 8-4 we look at conventional techniques of appraisal for example, pay back and average rates of return. Initially in both Sections 8-3 and 8-4 fairly restrictive assumptions are utilised in order to develop the framework. These assumptions include certainty, a perfect capital market with no borrowing restrictions (i.e. no capital rationing) but these are relaxed in the sections that follow since we believe that the investment decision is so vital to the firm that it cannot be entered into without regard for the complexities of the real world.

The versatility of DCF methods is illustrated in Section 8-3 when we discuss their application to three types of investment decision: the buying decision (accept/reject), leasing propositions and replacement decisions. In all types of investment decisions the same framework of analysis can be used whether a replacement or a new purchase is involved, the key question relates to the marginal profit contributed by the acquisition. This will of course be materially affected by investment grants and allowances and corporate tax considerations. These are also introduced and analysed in that section. In Section 8-5 we compare the two principal varieties of DCF and relax some of the restrictive assumptions we posited earlier. There we shall also look at abnormal patterns of cash flow and the problem of mutually exclusive projects. The latters leads on to capital rationing which forms Section 8-6, and we follow this with a consideration of the problems of risk and uncertainty (Section 8-7). The relaxation of the assumption of perfect capital markets introduces the question of the financing problem and the importance or otherwise of the financial structure of the firm in terms of the cost of capital and this is examined in Section 8-8. A final section (8-9) examines the rather different considerations involved in public sector investment introducing the concepts of cost-benefit and cost-effectiveness analysis.

8-2 Discounting

We have indicated earlier that in considering an investment project the initial outlay and the receipts following from this do not occur simultaneously and these receipts (net cash flows) will extend in some pattern into the future. Some technique is required for comparing cash receipts at different points in time since even with a constant price level, cash flows or costs incurred at different points of time are not worth the same so long as funds can be invested and earn a positive return. This illustrates that money has a time value.

Suppose that £100 was invested today at 10 per cent p.a. compound interest (on an annual basis); in one year it will be worth £110, in two years it will have grown to £121, in five years £161.05 and in ten years £259.37. We arrive at these figures using the standard compound interest formula which is derived as follows:

if we let A represent the capital sum, r the rate of interest as a decimal and n the appropriate period of investment in years, then we can find the resultant sum S:

$$S = A(1+r)^n$$

Compound interest tables* enable us to compute the future value of £1 at any rate of interest (r) for any length of time (n). The factor for £1 can then be applied to the sum invested, so with £100 invested at 10 per cent for one, two, five, and ten years respectively we would have:

One year $:- 100(1 + 0.10)^1$ $= 100 \times 1.1000 =$ £110
Two years $:- 100(1 + 0.10)^2$ $= 100 \times 1.2100 =$ £121
Five years $:- 100(1 + 0.10)^5$ $= 100 \times 1.6105 =$ £161.05
Ten years $:- 100(1 + 0.10)^{10}$ $= 100 \times 2.5937 =$ £259.37

$$\uparrow$$
(FACTORS)

Thus if an individual were given an option of £100 due to him now or £161.05 to be paid to him in five years time, he would be indifferent between these two alternatives provided that 10 per cent interest per annum was the best return he could enjoy in a prospect bearing similar risk. But clearly he could not be indifferent between £100 now and £100 in five years because of the interest foregone. The further in the future that benefits are likely to materialise the less and less they are worth to the investor in present terms. Equally true is that the further into the future that a firm's costs are to be incurred (say in a maintenance contract) the less they represent a burden on the firm. The

---

*   For compound interest and discount tables see G. H. Lawson and D. W. Windle [76]. Calculations in this book have been based on these tables.

procedure by which one computes the *present* value of future cash flows is *discounting* and it is in fact the opposite of compounding which is concerned with determining the *future* value of present cash flows. We can write for instance that:

The future value of £100 invested for two years is £121, compounding at 10 per cent; which is equivalent to the statement that:

The present value of £121 receivable in two years is £100 discounting at 10 per cent.

In general, the future value of A invested for n years is $A(1+r)^n$ compounding at a rate r, and

The present value of $A(1+r)^n$ receivable in n years is A discounting at a rate r.

Rewriting the latter by dividing throughout by $(1+r)^n$ we find:

The present value of A receivable in n years is

$$\frac{A}{(1+r)^n}$$ discounting at a rate r.

To emphasise this relationship between compounding and discounting let us consider an example:

Suppose a firm borrows £10,000 from a bank repaying £7,000 at the end of the first year, £5,000 at the end of year two and £201 at the end of the third year. The bank levies a 15 per cent interest charge at the end of each year based on the balance outstanding at the start of that year. We can set out the essentials of the transaction as in Table 8.1:

Table 8.1

	Balance outstanding beginning of year £	Interest at 15% £	Balance outstanding end of year £	Repayments made at end of year £
1st year	10,000	1,500	11,500	7,000
2nd year	4,500	675	5,175	5,000
3rd year	175	26.25	201.3	201.3

The firm on its borrowing of £10,000 has paid out £2,201.25 in interest charges but its repayments have not only paid this but recovered the original capital sum borrowed. The bank has earned a 15 per cent compound interest on its loan and we can set out the transactions from the point of view of the bank as in Table 8.2. In this table, year 0 refers to the start of the project, year 1 to a time one year hence, etc. When summed, the present values of the cash receipts equal the £10,000 initially lent by the bank.

Table 8.2

Year	0	1	2	3
Loan £	−10,000			
Repayments £		7,000	5,000	201.3
Discount factor @ 15%		(0.869565)	(0.756144)	(0.657516)
PV @ 15%		6086.955	3780.72	132.358

Since we have discounted at 15 per cent, we have proved that these cash receipts represent a 15 per cent return on the sum lent and complete repayment of that sum. We use the formula: Present value of $A = A/(1+r)^n$, the factors $1/(1+r)^n$ being found directly from discounting tables and applied to each cash receipt arising after time period n with the discount rate r of 0.15 (or 15 per cent). If cash receipts are irregular (as in the above example) then each year's figure has to be discounted separately and then summed. If however there is a constant or regular stream, sometimes called an annuity, then there is no need to discount individually, since tables are available to show the cumulative discount factors for £1 receivable annually for n years. Having found the factor for the appropriate period and discount rate, it is a simple matter of multiplying the cash receipt by the factor to give the present value of the stream of income. The factors are calculated according to the relationship: Present Value of £1 receivable annually for n years, discounting at a rate r

$$= £ \frac{1-(1+r)^{-n}}{r} \quad *$$

so that the value of the expression can be found for any values of r and n.

---

* If we are discounting annually for a stream of cash flows each of value A

Suppose a firm expects a five year income stream of £100 per annum (say from leasing out a piece of office equipment) and its opportunity cost of capital is 10 per cent. How do we calculate the *present value* of this annuity of £100? If we use the discount tables for an annuity with n = 5 and r = 0.1 (10 per cent) we would arrive at a discount factor of 3.3522 so that

$$PV = 100 \times 3.3522 = £335.22 \ .$$

Alternatively we could have used individual discount factors for each year and discounted each £100 separately, *viz*.

End year 1 :—	100 × 0.869565 =	£86.96
End year 2 :—	100 × 0.756144 =	£75.61
End year 3 :—	100 × 0.657516 =	£65.75
End year 4 :—	100 × 0.571753 =	£57.18
End year 5 :—	100 × 0.497177 =	£49.72
		£335.22

In this section we have attempted to illustrate the concept of the time value of money. Income receivable at some future date is worth less than a corresponding sum of money receivable now, and by the same token costs incurred at some future time period represent less of a burden than equivalent sums incurred now.*

---

then we would have:

$$PV = \frac{A}{1+r} + \frac{A}{(1+r)^2} + \frac{A}{(1+r)^3} + \ldots + \frac{A}{(1+r)^n} \quad (1)$$

Dividing each side by $(1 + r)$ we find:

$$\frac{PV}{(1+r)} = \frac{A}{(1+r)^2} + \frac{A}{(1+r)^3} + \ldots + \frac{A}{(1+r)^n} + \frac{A}{(1+r)^{n+1}} \quad (2)$$

Subtract (2) from (1):

$$PV - \frac{PV}{(1+r)} = \frac{A}{1+r} - \frac{A}{(1+r)^{n+1}}$$

Multiplying both sides by $(1 + r)$:

$$PV(1+r) - PV = A - A(1+r)^{-n}$$

$$\therefore \quad PVr = A[1 - (1+r)^{-n}] \quad \therefore \quad PV = A[1 - (1+r)^{-n}]/r \ .$$

(Hence the factors for £1 receivable annually.)

If the income stream stretches into the very distant future so that we can treat it as a 'perpetuity', then n tends to infinity and

$$A[1 - (1+r)^{-n}]/r \to A[1/r] \ .$$

* Normal practice is to forecast cash flows at constant prices and to discount at a rate appropriate to nil inflation.

8-3 DCF Methods of Appraisal

It is through the process of discounting and the calculation of present values that economists allow for the opportunity cost of capital in investment appraisal. The calculations are much facilitated by the availability of discount tables which can be incorporated into computer programmes if desired. We are now going to apply the analysis we have developed to the appraisal of various hypothetical projects, but initially it will be necessary to make a number of simplifying assumptions:

The first assumption we make is that the projects to be analysed are small scale and independent of other projects. Such projects can be analysed uniquely whereas if there is interdependence, or if the project is so large that it may cause changes in relative prices of goods and services then a wider approach is necessary. Three further assumptions are made and relaxed later. These are that knowledge is perfect; that projects are not mutually exclusive; and there are no budgetary constraints. By assuming perfect knowledge or certainty we appraise hypothetical projects with known future consequences in terms of the duration of the project and all relevant costs and revenues. On that basis we can then assess whether the capital outlays are justified by the benefits.

Net Present Value

We have demonstrated in Section 8-2 the procedure for discounting a stream of cash flows whether these be regular or irregular. Cash flows are rather different from accounting profits because they (cash flows) reflect the difference between the outgoings (negative flows) and inflows (positive flows) of money resulting from the project under consideration. They are the avoidable costs and incremental revenues anticipated at each point in time during the project's life. Depreciation (see Chapter 4, Section 4-10), a cost in accounting profit calculation, does not measure a cash outflow, it is a book-keeping device to spread capital outlays over a project's life. In appraising investments, we show capital outlays as outflows of cash *at the time they occur*, i.e. at t = 0 (but possibly extending into one or more years if a long setting up period is involved). The other main difference is that when calculating accounting profit, one deducts fixed interest commitments, and then shows any dividend payments as distributions out of profit. The discounted cash flow approach however uses the (opportunity) cost of capital concept to assess the effect of all required rates of return in one process. Consequently neither interest payments nor distributions of profit are deducted from our cash flows, rather these cash flows are discounted at an appropriate rate which reflects the opportunity cost of capital. Suppose a company has an earnings stream of $A_1 \ldots A_n$, these cash flows arising after one year ... n years. To obtain the present value of this we discount this stream at the company's cost of capital. To obtain the *net* present value the original capital outlay is subtracted and what is left represents the amount by which the share value of the company should increase. This would apply in a capital market where a company's earning power (discounted) was reflected in its share valuation. Net present value is a measure of *discounted economic profit or wealth*. Economic profit is a measure of the surplus enjoyed from a venture, allowing for all avoidable costs, incremental revenues, and the opportunity cost of productive services. Economic profit in its strict sense only exists when there is a residue even after all factor inputs have been rewarded at opportunity cost. A positive NPV therefore means that a surplus exists after paying for all capital outlays, avoidable costs and allowing for the opportunity cost of capital. Projects showing positive NPVs should therefore be accepted by a company since they will add to the wealth of its owners, or taking a rather wider view they will create resources out of which all the firm's interest groups can be satisfied. In symbols, net present value is calculated as:

$$NPV = -C + \frac{A_1}{(1+r)} + \frac{A_2}{(1+r)^2} + \ldots + \frac{A_n}{(1+r)^n}$$

where

C = capital outlay
$A_1 \ldots A_n$ = earnings stream of net cash flows
r = cost of capital or required rate of return

or $$NPV = -C + \sum_{t=0}^{n} \frac{A_t}{(1+r)^t}$$

Suppose for example that an initial outlay of £1,000 is expected to yield two net of tax inflows of £650. Assuming that the cost of capital is 10 per cent, the NPV calculations can be set out as in Table 8.3. The NPV of £128.1 shows that the project is acceptable at a discount rate of 10 per cent.

Table 8.3

Year	0	1	2	NPV
Outlay £	−1,000			
Inflows £		$\frac{650}{(1+0.10)}$	$\frac{650}{(1+0.10)^2}$	£128.1

Internal Rate of Return

In calculating NPV, the rate of discount used had to be known in advance. Internal rate of return is so-called because it is calculated without reference to an *external* discount rate. It is determined by relating the capital outlays to the net cash flows through discounting. IRR is the return that renders the discounted present value of the future net returns exactly equal to the original outlay. Alternatively:

> 'The DCF return (Internal Rate of Return) on a project is ... defined as the annual net of tax profit or return on the capital outstanding (not yet repaid) at the end of each year of the project's life: this return is the true profit over and above the full recovery of capital.' (Merrett and Sykes [90] p. 10)

This often involves an iterative procedure — or more simply, trial and error.

If we take the illustration used in the calculation of NPV of the two after tax inflows of £650 from an initial investment of £1,000, we can deduce that since a surplus was enjoyed when discounting at 10 per cent that the cash flows could have been discounted at a higher rate before the surplus vanished. We solve for IRR by finding that discount rate which reduces the cash flows arising in a project to the original capital outlay. In Table 8.4 three alternative discount rates are tried.

Table 8.4

Cash Flow £	Discount Factors		
	17%	19%	19½%
End Year 1 650	0.854701	0.840336	0.836820
End Year 2 650	0.730514	0.706165	0.700268

	Present Value of Cash Flows (£) at rates of:		
	17%	19%	19½%
End Year 1	555.6	546.2	543.933
End Year 2	474.8	459.0	455.174
	1,030.4	1,005.2	999.11

The answer is about 19.5 per cent and this is the rate of return on capital tied up in a project. This is analogous to a bank overdraft where interest is only payable on capital outstanding. Implicit in the internal rate of return calculation is the reduction of capital outstanding whenever positive cash flows arise. This can be readily appreciated by studying Table 8.5. The internal rate of return of 19.5 per cent is interpreted be referring to the cost of capital. If the latter is only 10 per cent then the project would be accepted.

Table 8.5

1st year	Opening balance Interest @ 19.5%	£1,000 £ 195	Cash Flow Balance	£650 £545
2nd year	Opening balance Interest @ 19.5%	£ 545 £ 106	Cash Flow	£650

Let us now look at three more projects in order to emphasise the link between NPV and IRR.

Table 8.6

Years	0	1	2	3	4	NPV @ 7%	IRR
A (£)	−1000	375	375	375	375	270.2	18.46
B (£)	−1000	250	325	425	500	245.9	16.25
C (£)	−1000	500	425	325	250	294.5	21.22

The ABC Company is appraising three projects, details of which are given in Table 8.6. The cost of capital to company ABC is 7 per cent and the NPV calculation shows that all three projects yield a surplus. However, if analysis in IRR terms were preferred this would equally well show that all three projects were desirable, since the IRR is greater than 7 per cent in all cases. In this problem both NPV and IRR give identical *ranking* of projects, *viz.* C, A, B. This however is not always the case, it is possible to get an inverse ranking from the two approaches (see Section 8-5 below).

For the present, however, it can be assumed that the two approaches are generally equivalent, particularly if analysis is restricted to accept/reject situations rather than ranking problems. Equivalence can be demonstrated in two ways, algebraically or graphically:

Consider the project:

```
0    1    2    3    .   .   .   n
-C   A₁   A₂   A₃   .   .   .   Aₙ
```

where C is the initial capital outlay and $A_1, A_2, A_3, \ldots A_n$ are the cash flows arising after one year, two years, three years, ... and n years.

Then (discounting at a rate of r)

$$\text{NPV} = -C + \frac{A_1}{1+r} + \frac{A_2}{(1+r)^2} + \frac{A_3}{(1+r)^3} + \ldots + \frac{A_n}{(1+r)^n} \quad (1)$$

And if i is the internal rate of return,

Then $$0 = -C + \frac{A_1}{1+i} + \frac{A_2}{(1+i)^2} + \frac{A_3}{(1+i)^3} + \ldots + \frac{A_n}{(1+i)^n} \quad (2)$$

(Since i is that discount rate which equates the present value of the cash flows $A_1 \ldots A_n$ to the original capital outlay, C.)

Suppose we find that i is greater than r, i.e. the internal rate of return is greater than the cost of capital — this would indicate acceptability. The NPV rule gives exactly the same answer since:

In formulae (1) and (2),

$-C$ is common to both.

$$\frac{A_1}{(1+r)} > \frac{A_1}{(1+i)} \qquad \text{when} \quad i > r$$

$$\frac{A_2}{(1+r)^2} > \frac{A_2}{(1+i)^2} \qquad \text{when} \quad i > r$$

. . .

$$\frac{A_n}{(1+r)^n} > \frac{A_n}{(1+i)^n} \qquad \text{when} \quad i > r$$

∴ RHS (1) > RHS (2)

∴ NPV > 0.

As we have explained, positive NPV indicates acceptability. Similarly it can be shown that whenever i is less than r, a negative value for NPV arises and the project would be rejected. Also, when i = r, NPV = 0, indicating that the project would break even by just earning the required rate of return but no surplus.* Such a project could be accepted

---

* Zero economic profit does not mean that zero return is earned on a project, but rather that all factors are paid at opportunity cost, so that all parties are just satisfied with their return.

Figure 8.1 Net Present Value and Internal Rate of Return

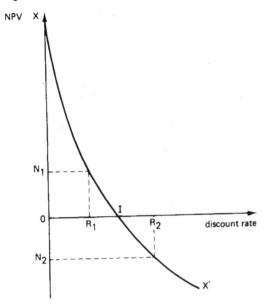

if finance were freely available but the company would be no better off by adopting it.

The graphical demonstration of equivalence relies on Figure 8.1. This shows that as the discount rate is increased, the net present value of a project similar to that described above, decreases. The curve XX' indicates the NPV for any discount rate, and it intersects the discount rate axis at point I. This intercept indicates the internal rate of return, which is represented by distance OI, since discounting at the internal rate of return reduces NPV to zero. Suppose the cost of capital is less than the IRR, for example magnitude OR_1 in the diagram; the NPV is represented by ON_1 which is positive. Taking a discount rate greater than the IRR, say OR_2 in the diagram, we find that NPV is given by ON_2 which is negative, thus confirming the equivalence of the two criteria for appraisal.

Consequently DCF (discounted cash flow) analysis can generally proceed via either route, NPV or IRR. The choice is normally a matter of administrative convenience.

Applications of the Basic Technique
Taxes, Allowances and Grants: In practice the cash flows which have

to be forecast from cost and revenue estimates will be subject to corporation tax. The method of assessing the latter depends upon government fiscal policy which may provide for various allowances to be offset against profits when taxes are computed. Offering substantial allowances at the start of the project can reduce the tax bill to an extent which may induce companies to invest more. Another inducement is a cash grant which may be offered at a number of different rates to encourage certain categories of investment in areas scheduled for development.*

In the example which follows we shall make the following assumptions:

(a) The company is already a going concern and enjoying profits so that it can take advantage of any allowances against corporation tax.
(b) Corporation tax is levied at a rate of 50 per cent.**
(c) Dividend payments necessitate an advance payment of corporation tax equal to 3/7** of the amount distributed.
(d) Investment grants are available at the rate of 22 per cent for new machinery purchased by firms in the region where this firm is located.
(e) 100 per cent of the asset's value can be depreciated in the first year of its life, for tax assessment purposes.***
(f) The following delays occur:
The grant is received between 6 and 18 months after the acquisition of the asset. We shall use a figure of 12 months in this calculation. Corporation tax is payable between 9 and 18 months after profit is reported. Again we shall use a figure of 12 months for convenience. (Advance corporation tax is however payable as soon as dividends are declared so we shall assume that this portion is payable immediately.)

Suppose that a company is contemplating an investment of £110,000 of which £100,000 is for new machinery and its installation, and £10,000 for working capital — mainly increased stocks of raw materials and finished goods. Assume that all of the fixed capital qualifies for the investment grant.

Forecasts are made as shown in Table 8.7. (It was estimated that a loss would be made in year 5 so that this investment is to be terminated after four years.) In addition to the cash flows shown in Table 8,7, the

---
* The Department of Trade and Industry can provide details of allowances and grants currently available.
** At the time of writing, the appropriate figures are 52 per cent and 33/67 for corporation tax and advance corporation tax respectively.
*** See Chapter 4, Section 4-10 on this topic of free depreciation.

Table 8.7

	1	2	Years 3	4	5
Sales Revenue less selling expenses	80,000	100,000	90,000	90,000	0
Materials	20,000	25,000	22,000	22,000	0
Wages and Salaries	25,000	28,000	26,000	25,000	0
Maintenance	3,000	6,000	10,000	15,000	0
Other Expenses	2,000	1,000	2,000	8,000	0
Cash Flow	30,000	40,000	30,000	20,000	0

(Figures are in £'s and at prices prevailing at t = 0)

company recovers its working capital of £10,000 when the project is terminated. Next we show the effect of taxes and grants which are subject to the delays described above. A company experiencing a rise in profits as a result of new capital projects might increase its dividends and this of course will influence the amount of advance corporation tax paid. In this example it will be assumed that the company increases its dividends by £7,000 per annum so that 3/7 × £7,000 = £3,000 of the tax bill must be paid in advance of the mainstream corporation tax, which follows twelve months later. Table 8.8 shows the effects of these payments.

Suppose that the company's cost of capital, for net of tax cash flows is 12 per cent. The present value of the net cash flows from year 1 to year 5 is then calculated using the appropriate factors and then the NPV:

PV @ 12%	£116,218
Less initial capital outlay	− £110,000
NPV	£ 6,218

The positive NPV shows the acceptability of the project.

Table 8.8

		Years				
	0	1	2	3	4	5
(1) Cash Flow (Table 8.7)	-	30,000	40,000	30,000	20,000	-
Depreciation (100% year 1)*	-	(−100,000)	-	-	-	-
(2) Advance Corporation Tax	-	↑ −3,000	↑ −3,000	↑ −3,000	↑ −3,000	
(3) Corporation Tax less A.C.T.	-	-	+38,000†	−17,000	−12,000	−7,000
(4) Grant (22%)	-	+22,000	-	-	-	-
(5) Fixed Capital	−100,000	-	-	-	-	-
(6) Working Capital	−10,000	-	-	-	+10,000	-
(7) = Sum (1) to (6) Net Cash Flow	−110,000	+49,000	+75,000	+10,000	+15,000	−7,000

* Depreciation is entered here to facilitate the calculation of corporation tax. It is *not* a cash flow.

† This amounts to a tax rebate brought about by the fall in *taxable* profit of £70,000 (= £30,000 − £100,000) in year 1. Provided that the company is earning taxable profits greater than £70,000, it will therefore benefit from a fall in tax payments of £35,000. If £3,000 advance corporation tax were paid after one year (on dividends of £7,000) this would bring a total reduction in mainstream corporation tax of £38,000, a year later.

(Figures are in £'s)

The Lease or Buy Decision

The ABC Company has appraised the purchase of a piece of office equipment which costs £31,400. This would bring benefits in terms of cost savings equivalent to a 10.3 per cent internal rate of return, and since the company's cost of capital is 9 per cent this appears to be a worthwhile investment. A leasing alternative has been offered involving £6,300 annual rental, payable in advance for the first five years of the contract and thereafter a rental of £1,000 p.a. for as long as the company wishes to continue the contract. If the equipment were purchased its expected life would be ten years and at the end of this period no residual value is expected.

The best method of analysing whether to purchase outright or lease is to examine the costs saved by taking the former option. If the equipment is purchased the firm saves the rental payments. If we assume that there are no investment grants or allowances or corporation tax then the calculation can be set out as in Table 8.9. Discounting the net cash advantage at 9 per cent gives a negative NPV, suggesting that the purchase is not worthwhile when compared with the leasing alternative. If IRR were a preferred method of presenting this result, we could try:

Discounting at 7%
NPV @ 7% = £24,467 − £25,100 = −£633
Discounting at 6%
NPV @ 6% = £25,167 − £25,100 = +£67 .

The IRR therefore lies somewhere between 6 per cent and 7 per cent, rather nearer to 6 per cent. Interpolation gives an answer, *viz.*

$$6\% + \frac{67}{67 + 633}(1\%) = \underline{6.1\%} .$$

Table 8.9

					Years						
0	1	2	3	4	5	6	7	8	9	10	
−31,400											(A)
	6,300	6,300	6,300	6,300	6,300	1,000	1.000	1,000	1,000	1,000	- (B)
−25,100	6,300	6,300	6,300	6,300	1,000	1,000	1,000	1,000	1,000		- (C)

(A) = Purchase price (£)
(B) = Rental saved (£)
(C) = Net Cash advantage of purchase (£) .

The advantages gained from purchasing therefore only amount to a return of 6.1 per cent compared with a cost of capital of 9 per cent. Viewed the other way, the cost of leasing is only 6.1 per cent to the ABC Company so this option should be adopted in favour of the outright purchase. (The payments to the leasing company are of course certain so this is a risk free investment.) Evaluation of this leasing decision therefore involved two appraisals. In the first instance there was the consideration of whether to acquire the asset or not irrespective of the method of payments. The second stage was to assess the relative desirability of the two alternatives — purchase or lease. Decisions of this type are common in practice as there are a large number of assets which are available on leasing terms. Normally lease payments would be made say quarterly or half yearly in advance which would involve discount factors $\simeq 1/(1 + r/4)^n$ or $1/(1 + r/2)^n$ in the nth quarter or half year. The various investment incentives would also be important considerations when comparing lease/purchase options.

The Replacement Decision

The replacement decision has received little mention so far in this chapter which has given prime consideration to the decision to expand by acquiring new plant and machinery. Yet replacement investment accounts for roughly half of the capital investment of firms[*] and analysis is necessary not only to assess whether or nor replacement is desirable but on the timing of the replacement. The DCF framework can be modified so as to compare the profitability of replacing now or at some future date. The question of postponability obviously hinges on the fact that the equipment concerned will still perform technically (though perhaps with a declining earnings profile) so that in replacement we are referring more to the optimal economic life rather than to the physical life of the equipment. Merrett and Sykes [90, 91] have been pioneers in the development of optimal replacement methods in the UK and the example that follows draws heavily on their work.

Suppose a firm has a piece of machinery that would cost £1,500 to replace now, and (assuming no inflation and no technical change) the same at any date in the future. If the machine is retained it will give a cash flow of £50 p.a. for two years before collapse whereas if it is replaced. the new machine would return a cash flow of £500 for four years before breaking down. Again we use incremental analysis to compare replacement now with replacement at some future date — say in two years time, and set out the calculation in tabular form (Table 8.10). The incremental net cash flows from year 4 to year 7 are repeated into perpetuity. The pattern of cash flows is best analysed in three parts:

---

[*] In 1972 with a Gross National Product of £48,116m, Britain invested £11,214m (23 per cent of GNP) in fixed capital but at the same time capital consumption was of the order of £5,824m or 52 per cent of gross investment.

Table 8.10 The Replacement Decision

Years		0	1	2	3	4	5	6	7	8
(1)	Replace in year 0 (£)	−1500				−1500				−1500
	Cash flows		500	500	500	500	500	500	500	500
(2)	Replace in year 2 (£)			−1500				−1500		
	Cash flows	-	50	50	500	500	500	500	500	500
	Incremental net cash flows (1)−(2) (£)	−1500	450	1950	0	−1500	0	1500	0	−1500

(i)   year | 0 | 1 | 2 |
              | −1500 | 450 | 1950 |

(ii) year | 4 ... | 8 ... | 12 ... | → ∞
              | −1500 .. | −1500 .. | −1500 ... |

(iii) year | 6 ... | 10 ... | 14 ... | → ∞
              | +1500 .. | +1500 .. | +1500 ... |

Suppose the company's cost of capital is 8 per cent, which means that in our discounting formulae, r = 0.08.

Discounting the second part of the above stream at this rate we find:

$$PV = \frac{-1500}{(1+0.08)^4} - \frac{1500}{(1+0.08)^8} - \frac{1500}{(1+0.08)^{12}} - \cdots$$

When summed to infinity this becomes: $\dfrac{-1500/(1.08)^4}{1-(1.08)^{-4}}$ * = $\underline{-4161}$.

Discounting the third part of the above stream at 8 per cent and summing to infinity gives

$$\frac{+1500/(1.08)^6}{1-(1.08)^{-4}} = \underline{+3567}.$$

* The sum to infinity of a geometric progression with constant ratio less than unity equals (First term in series)/(1 − constant ratio).

The remaining part of the calculation can be completed using the appropriate discount factors:

NPV of $\dfrac{0 \quad\quad 1 \quad\quad 2}{-1500 \quad 450 \quad 1950}$ @ 8% = 588 .

∴ For the whole series

NPV @ 8% = £(588 + 3567 − 4161)
= −£6 .

The very small negative NPV brought about as a result of immediate replacement rather than postponement is insignificant given the error in computation due to rounding off, and the total sums involved. The decision maker should therefore be indifferent between the two options, although in practice the analysis would be far more complicated than this to allow for residual values, changing capital purchase price, technical change bringing improvements in earnings, taxation and investment allowances.

8-4 Conventional Appraisal Techniques

In this section we introduce the two main conventional methods of appraising investment projects, the pay-back approach and the rate of return method.

Pay-Back Approach

This is an approach often used in practice, particularly by small firms, and a study by the British Institute of Management published in 1965 [18] reported that only about 5 per cent of the firms used DCF methods and that pay-back was far more popular, accounting for between 67-80 per cent of firms in the individual surveys within the report. For small businesses the figure was 73 per cent.

The pay-back period is the number of years it takes to recover the initial cost of a project and it is often calculated on gross cash flows before tax although it can be modified to include only net cash flows. In appraising projects two standards can be used. A firm may have a 'standard' pay-back criterion and this was well illustrated in the survey mentioned above, with 17 per cent of the firms looking for a 3-year pay-back, 17 per cent for a 4 year, 24 per cent for a 5 year, 11 per cent for a 6 year and 6 per cent for a 7 year pay-back period. Projects can then be compared with this standard period and accepted or rejected. Alternatively if different projects are being compared with a view to a choice being made, the one with the shortest pay-back period would be chosen whereas if two projects gave the same pay-back the firm presumably would be indifferent if one were to apply the strict interpretation of the pay-back approach. Despite the popularity of pay-back, it does not meet the standards of economic analysis since it imparts bias in favour of short run projects and ignores the timing of cash flows within the pay-back period as well as ignoring cash flows that follow this critical period. The omission of timing is perhaps the most apparent in the light of our discussion of DCF methods. This issue is well illustrated in the following example:

Suppose two projects A and B each have an initial outlay of £12,000 and they have a time profile as illustrated below:

	0	1	2	3	4	5
A	−12,000	8,000	2,000	1,000	1,000	1,000
B	−12,000	3,000	3,000	3,000	3,000	1,000

Both projects pay-back in four years but A is superior to B since it realises the largest cash flows in the early years when they have most impact on present value. One cannot therefore be indifferent between the two propositions.

Pay-back does not measure profitability but it may give a guide to liquidity and to risk provided the returns used are adjusted for tax payments and also for tax allowances which may be enjoyed by the projects, particularly in the early years of the life of the project. Liquidity may be particularly important to small firms because they generally rely on internally generated funds as opposed to external financing. So that although pay-back perhaps places too much emphasis on liquidity its popularity with small firms is understandable; but its chief advantage in comparison with DCF methods is ease of computation and the fact that it is widely understood. Pay-back also gives an allowance for risk but this is limited to a particular type of risk: that of sudden loss of earnings. This may be due to a number of circumstances which could include technical change making the firm's products obsolete; imposition of protective tariffs by importing nations; seizure of the firm's assets by a government; etc. Where risks of this nature are expected, it is useful to have a measure of how soon the initial capital can be recovered. But other kinds of risk, for example that of costs increasing or that of sales not reaching their anticipated level cannot be safeguarded against by the use of pay-back.

The main criticism of the pay-back approach, namely that it does not take account of the time profile of the cash inflows, can be handled in part by a method suggested by J. Hellings [57] in which a mixture of pay-back and discounting is used. Suppose that two projects have the following cash flows:

	0	1	2	3	4
Project A	−300	150	100	50	100
Project B	−300	50	100	150	50

Both projects repay after three years but project A should be preferred in that it does return an extra £100 in year 1. If we use the discounted cash flows of both projects to arrive at the pay-back period we get the following pattern of cash flows (assuming a 10 per cent discount rate):

	0	1	2	3	4
Project A	−300	136.4	82.64	37.57	68.3
Project B	−300	45.5	82.64	112.7	34.2

By summing the present values of the cash flows we observe that project A repays the original capital sum in about three and two-third years but project B does not recover the £300 invested. In essence what we have done is to calculate the gross present value of the cash flows arising from these projects. £324.91 and £275.04 respectively, and then to compare these results with the capital outlay. To that extent the modified pay-back approach is similar to the NPV method, but the pay-back period is the focus of attention here rather than the magnitude of NPV, and its application need not involve discounting the cash flows arising after the pay-back period. This modified procedure is certainly preferable to the simple pay-back method of appraisal but once a firm has accepted the principle of discounting, it hardly seems rational to adapt it to the partial project analysis which characterises pay-back. We believe that the total project should be analysed even if considerations of risk or liquidity favour projects with rapid repayment of capital. There is no substitute for DCF appraisal plus a thorough analysis of a company's financing requirements.

Average Rate of Return

This method is also known as book rate of return on capital and the accountants' rate of return. We define average rate of return as *the ratio of average profit, after depreciation allowances, to capital employed.* The calculations are usually performed before tax. This rate of return is then compared with the company's cost of capital. Variations on this theme take peak profit or initial profit rather than the average over a project's life. For the measure of capital it is usually the initial capital outlay (including working capital) which is taken or sometimes an average of the first and last years of the capital employed. The method is beset by ambiguities as the following example illustrates.

Suppose the ABC manufacturing company is intending to manufacture and market a new product. This would involve an investment of £250,000 in new plant and machinery in 1975 and an outlay of working capital in 1976 of £50,000. The company from its knowledge of the market and competitors thinks that the product is unlikely to be copied for several years and therefore in this period can fix a price that gives market penetration and substantial profit. After this period it is expected that competitors will have imitated the product so that after 1978 the expected profits will decline. The expected life of the project is ten years and because of its specificity, will have a scrap value of only £10,000. The working capital is recovered from the project at the termination of the project. We shall ignore tax at this juncture.

Table 8.11 The Calculation of Average Rate of Return

	Outlay £	Inflow £
1975	250,000	
1976	50,000	60,000
1977		70,000
1978		75,000
1979		70,000
1980		60,000
1981		50,000
1982		40,000
1983		30,000
1984		20,000
1985	(60,000)†	10,000
Totals:	240,000	485,000

† Return of working capital and scrap value.

Table 8.11 sets out the outlay and inflow data. Gross profit is £485,000 with total depreciation of £240,000 giving a net profit figure of £245,000. Average profit is therefore £24,500 per annum which when expressed as a return on the £300,000 capital employed gives

$$\frac{24,500}{300,000} \times 100\% = \underline{8.17\%}$$

If this calculation had been performed without the allowance for depreciation the rate of return would have been 16.17 per cent. If initial profits (1976) or peak profits (1978) had been taken the answer would have differed yet again. Whilst rate of return calculations are usually performed prior to tax there is nothing to stop the inclusion of investment incentives and corporation tax on profits.

The main shortcoming of the method is that it ignores the timing of cash flows, since any pattern of inflows amounting to £485,000 in total would have given the same average rate of return. Average rate of return, may however give a reasonable guide to the true (internal) rate of return in certain instances. For example, the option:

0	1	2	3	4
−10,000	1,000	2,000	3,000	10,000

has an *internal* rate of return of about 15¼ per cent and an average rate of return of 15 per cent. The former figure was calculated using the normal trial and error approach involving a number of calculations, while the latter was obtained directly by observing that:

gross profit = £16,000
net profit after allowing for £10,000 total depreciation = £6,000

or £1,500 per annum, which represents a 15 per cent return on the capital invested. However, average rate of return only gives such a good approximation when cash flows are initially small, with their bulk arriving late in the project's life, as in this example. If cash flows were more evenly distributed, e.g.

0	1	2	3	4
−10,000	4,000	4,000	4,000	4,000

the average rate of return would still be 15 per cent, yet the internal rate of return is much higher than this because one does not have to wait for the large cash flows to arrive. In fact the internal rate of return can be calculated directly in this example because of the constant stream of cash flows. It is only necessary to find a 4 year factor in the annuity discounting tables which when multiplied by £4,000 gives the original capital outlay of £10,000. This factor is 2.5 and it is the 4 year annuity factor for a discount rate of just under 22 per cent. The internal rate of return is therefore approximately 22 per cent, substantially higher than the average rate of return, which clearly cannot serve as a useful approximation in this instance.

8-5 Comparisons of NPV and IRR

When there is only one project under consideration and the decision is one of accept or reject and the cash flows follow the typical pattern of the initial outlay being followed by a series of positive cash flows then the two methods are equivalent. Problems arise when the cash flows are not normal or when one has to rank projects which have different outlays and different lives or when there is capital rationing situation with limitations on the amount of finance available. We shall examine the problems involved in coping with abnormal cash flows and mutually exclusive projects in this section, and capital rationing in Section 8.6.

Abnormal Cash Flows

If the cash flows anticipated from a project are not normal in that there are sign changes, the IRR criterion cannot be used to judge whether to accept or reject a given investment project unless it is modified. Suppose for instance that a capital project 'fades' in the middle of its life and requires further injections of capital for major replacements and maintenance of equipment. Perhaps too, major product modifications will become necessary to meet competition from other firms. Cash flows could then become negative in the middle of the project's life so that the project starts with the usual capital outlays followed by positive cash flows, as in the examples we have used so far, but then a sign change occurs with the arrival of the negative flows. Cash flows then switch to positive again but may terminate with a further negative flow to allow for tax payments due after the completion of the project or dismantling and restoration expenditures such as may be experienced in extractive industries.

Sign switching can result in multiple solutions for internal rate of return, since the curve relating net present value to the discount rate may behave as in Figure 8.2 (see also J. Hirshleifer's [58] article in which a number of graphical representations of projects can be found). Each of the intercepts I_1, I_2, I_3 and I_4 indicates a solution for IRR and the more sign changes that occur in a project's cash flows, the more scope there is for multiple solutions. Our typical well-behaved project only experiences one sign change, as positive cash flows follow the initial outlays and there is only one solution for IRR (Figure 8.1). The situation described here with abnormal flows and four sign changes, *viz*: capital outlay (−), inflows (+), outflow (−), inflows (+), outflow (−) may result in as many as four solutions for internal rate of return.

The internal rate of return criterion can no longer be used, since when comparing the multiple values with the cost of capital, no interpretation can be given unless the NPV function is known. In Figure 8.2, NPV is positive (indicating acceptability) when discounting at rates between I_1 and I_2 and between I_3 and I_4, but NPV is negative when discounting at rates less than I_1, greater than I_4 or between I_2 and I_3. Clearly a knowledge of the multiple solutions is useless on its own, and it is only through an understanding of how NPV varies with the discount rate

Figure 8.2 Multiple Solutions for Internal Rate of Return

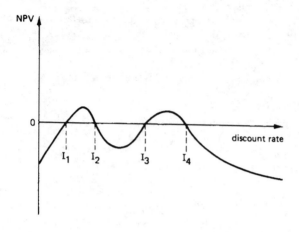

that any conclusion can be drawn.

The failure of internal rate of return can also be demonstrated algebraically. Suppose that a project is not well-behaved and that a cash outflow must be experienced at the end of the project's life before it can be terminated, such that A_n the final cash flow is negative:

```
  0      1     2     3   ...   n-1       n
 -C    +A_1  +A_2  +A_3       +A_{n-1}  -A_n
```

We can write

(1) $\text{NPV} = -C + \dfrac{A_1}{1+r} + \dfrac{A_2}{(1+r)^2} + \dfrac{A_3}{(1+r)^3} + \ldots + \dfrac{A_{n-1}}{(1+r)^{n-1}} - \dfrac{A_n}{(1+r)^n}$

(2) $0 = -C + \dfrac{A_1}{1+i} + \dfrac{A_2}{(1+i)^2} + \dfrac{A_3}{(1+i)^3} + \ldots + \dfrac{A_{n-1}}{(1+i)^{n-1}} - \dfrac{A_n}{(1+i)^n}$

where r is the cost of capital and i is the IRR. The fact that i may be greater than r no longer provides us with a guarantee that NPV is greater than zero, because although $A_1/(1+r)$ is greater than $A_1/(1+i)$ and similarly for the terms in A_2, A_3, etc., we now have a term $-A_n/(1+r)^n$ in (1) which *is less than* the corresponding term $-A_n/(1+i)^n$ in (2), so that NPV may be negative when $i > r$. Clearly our usual interpretation of internal rate of return is no longer applicable, and if multiple solutions for i are derived there is the question of which one is to be compared with r.

Remembering that our straightforward project, with a series of positive cash flows, presented no difficulty at all, is there any means of financing negative cash flows so that we are left with a series of positive cash flows? One way of achieving this *in theory* is for the company to set up a 'sinking fund' in order to provide for any anticipated cash outflows, by re-investing the positive cash flows generated by the project. *e.g.* To provide for the outflow A_n in year n we could set aside $A_n/(1+r)$ in year $n-1$ which would grow to A_n one year later after earning interest at $100r\%$. Thus an outflow of £1,100 could be provided for by putting £1,000 into a sinking fund earning 10 per cent for one year.

(N.B. r is no longer just the cost of capital or the borrowing rate, but also the lending rate for the company.)

Our new pattern of cash flows becomes:

```
       0     1     2     3   ... n-1                          n
      -C   +A₁   +A₂   +A₃  ... +A_{n-1}                    -A_n )
                                -A_n/(1+r)                  +A_n )

or    -C   +A₁   +A₂   +A₃  ... +[A_{n-1} - A_n/(1+r)]      +0
```

If $[A_{n-1} - A_n/(1+r)]$ is positive, we have obtained a normal pattern of cash flows and we need make no further provision for negative cash flows. Should we still have a net outflow at the end of the project, we would have to set up a sinking fund in year $n-2$, and so on. However, let us take the simplest case and assume that $[A_{n-1} - A_n/(1+r)]$ is positive.

The net present value of the project is the same:

$$NPV = -C + \frac{A_1}{1+r} + \frac{A_2}{(1+r)^2} + \frac{A_3}{(1+r)^3} + \ldots + \frac{A_{n-1}}{(1+r)^{n-1}} - \frac{A_n}{(1+r)^n}$$

which may be rewritten:

(1a) $$NPV = -C + \frac{A_1}{1+r} + \frac{A_2}{(1+r)^2} + \frac{A_3}{(1+r)^3} + \ldots + \frac{A_{n-1} - A_n/(1+r)}{(1+r)^{n-1}}$$

We can find a new internal rate of return i* for the hybrid project which we call the *extended yield*, such that:

(2a) $$0 = -C + \frac{A_1}{1+i^*} + \frac{A_2}{(1+i^*)^2} + \frac{A_3}{(1+i^*)^3} + \ldots + \frac{A_{n-1} - A_n/(1+r)}{(1+i^*)^{n-1}}$$

Provided that $[A_{n-1} - A_n/(1+r)]$ is positive we can see by comparing (1a) and (2a), term by term, that:

i* > r   gives a positive NPV and indicates acceptability
i* = r   gives a zero NPV and indicates acceptability (break-even situation)
i* < r   gives a negative NPV and indicates unacceptability.

We have once again, a rate of return approach entirely consistent with NPV for appraising capital projects.

Consider now a very simple example with an investment opportunity in which two sign changes occur:

0	1	2
−£5,000	+£16,000	−£12,000

The *normal* internal rate of return or yield would be found by solving for i in the expression:

$$0 = -5{,}000 + \frac{16{,}000}{(1+i)} - \frac{12{,}000}{(1+i)^2}$$

This is a quadratic equation which can be solved without recourse to discount tables.

For, by multiplying throughout by $-(1+i)^2$,

$5{,}000i^2 + 10{,}000i + 5{,}000 - 16{,}000 - 16{,}000i + 12{,}000 = 0$
∴ $5{,}000i^2 - 6{,}000i + 1{,}000 = 0$
∴ $(i - 1)(5i - 1) = 0$
∴ $i = 1$ or $i = 1/5$

meaning that *IRR is 100% or 20%.**

This result gives the intercepts on the discount rate axis of the project's graph, but no one can deduce the project's desirability at a given cost of capital without knowing the behaviour of NPV. It can be shown that discounting at 50 per cent, for example, gives a surplus, but this necessitates calculation of NPV:

$$\text{NPV (@ 50\%)} = £[-5{,}000 + \frac{16{,}000}{1.5} - \frac{12{,}000}{(1.5)^2}]$$
$$= £333 \quad \text{(acceptable)}$$

However, discounting at 300 per cent,

$$\text{NPV} = £[-5{,}000 + \frac{16{,}000}{4} - \frac{12{,}000}{(4)^2}]$$
$$= -£1{,}750 \quad \text{(unacceptable)}$$

---

* Any normal project with a two year life would yield a quadratic, but there would only be one meaningful (positive) root for i. Here we have two positive roots.

The acceptability or otherwise could not have been deduced from the information that IRR = 100 per cent or 20 per cent. However, *extended yield* could have been used as follows:

Suppose that 50 per cent is not just the cost of capital but the rate at which cash flows can be re-invested. By re-investing £8,000 at the end of the first year and using this 'sinking fund', plus 50 per cent interest for one year to finance the liability of £12,000, the pattern of cash flows would become:

	0	1	2
project	−£5,000	+£16,000	−£12,000
sinking fund		−£ 8,000	+£12,000
project plus sinking fund	−£5,000	+£ 8,000	0

We now solve for the extended yield i*:

$$-5{,}000 + \frac{8{,}000}{1+i^*} = 0$$

∴ i* = 0.6   or 60%

i* is therefore greater than r indicating acceptability (60 per cent as against 50 per cent).

At 300 per cent the sinking fund would be £12,000/(1+3) = £3,000 and the calculation would proceed thus:

	0	1	2
project	−£5,000	+£16,000	−£12,000
sinking fund		−£ 3,000	+£12,000
project plus sinking fund	−£5,000	+£13,000	0

∴ $-5{,}000 + \dfrac{13{,}000}{1+i^*} = 0$

∴ i* = 1.6   or 160%

i* is therefore less than r indicating unacceptability (160 per cent as against 300 per cent).

Mutually Exclusive Projects

If the acceptance of one project automatically leads to the rejection of other alternatives even though they are acceptable under the usual criteria (of positive NPV or IRR in excess of the cost of capital) then the investments are said to be mutually exclusive. An example of this would be choosing from a number of alternative machines for doing a particular job. The firm would typically choose just one of these, i.e. the best. In attempting to rank alternatives NPV and IRR may give different answers, so it may not be entirely clear which is the best alternative.

Consider three projects that involve outlays of £2,000 for A, £2,000 for B and £1,000 for C. As usual we shall assume there is no risk attached to these projects. The cash flows, NPVs and IRRs are set out below:

	0	1	2	NPV @ 10%	IRR
Project A	−2000	0	+2800	+314	18.3%
B	−2000	+1300	+1300	+256	19.4%
C	−1000	0	+1450	+198	20.4%

Ranking these projects with a view to accepting only one gives a contradictory recommendation. The NPV method advocates Project A and the IRR method Project C. The danger with using the IRR in this situation is that figures are not comparable unless they are returns on exactly the same amount of capital *outstanding*.* This is not the case if one compares either A with C or B with C. Neither are A and B strictly comparable since B returns £1300 at the end of year one, thus reducing the amount of capital outstanding. The NPV can rank mutually exclusive projects (taking the project with the highest NPV as the most acceptable) because NPV is an absolute measure of (discounted) profit. It is however possible to adapt the IRR criterion. In the above example, C is seen to be acceptable in its own right but for purposes of comparison it is necessary to find whether the outlay of an additional £1,000 on A or B would yield a sufficient additional return. This can be answered by employing an 'incremental yield' approach as illustrated below.

	0	1	2	IRR
A	−2000	0	+2800	18.3
C	−1000	0	+1450	20.4
A − C	−1000	0	+1350	16.2

---

* There is a danger here of assuming that differences in outlays or lives are necessary conditions for the conflict between NPV and IRR. However, J. R. Gould [45] has demonstrated that with two projects of the same life and same initial outlays IRR and NPV can conflict because of differences in capital outstanding.

This illustrates that the incremental return on the additional capital outlay of £1,000 the project A entails as against project C, gives a return of 16.2 per cent, which is above the cost of capital of 10 per cent. Projects A and B have the same initial outlay but then in selecting A the firm loses £1,300 in year 1 for the gain of £1,500 in year 2. Again this can be evaluated by calculating incremental yield:

A	−2000	0	+2800	18.3%
B	−2000	+1300	+1300	19.4%
A − B	0	−1300	+1500	15.4%

This illustrates that project A should be chosen, as it offers more than project B and more than project C which is also shown in the higher NPV figure. Clearly the incremental yield method involves extra computational time and when there are many possibilities the best method is to use NPV to screen the projects and then perhaps to utilise incremental yield if desired in the final presentation. S. M. Keane [67] does not even favour the use of yield methods in the presentation of reports to management, even though businessmen allegedly comprehend rates of return rather more easily than net present value. He points out that in practice managers do have to rank projects in some priority ordering and that attempts to use IRR or incremental yield are proving an obstacle to the wider acceptance of the net present value concept. It is our view too, that internal rate of return is seldom appropriate since it may give misleading results despite the lengthy computations typically involved. Of the two criteria, we would therefore prefer NPV to IRR, but our choice is restricted to these. We would never entertain the use of the traditional methods of pay-back or average rate of return beyond an initial rough and ready 'guesstimate' of a project's viability.

8-6 Capital Rationing

If investments can be financed, we conclude that any project with a positive NPV should be accepted except when mutually exclusive projects are being ranked when the one with the highest NPV should be selected. In practice, however, not all investments can be financed and it is therefore time to relax this restrictive assumption.

Firms can draw on a variety of sources of long term capital, e.g. the retention of earnings (including depreciation provisions) and the raising of external finance by the issue of securities (equity or debenture). These are the broad categories of sources for long term capital though sometimes specialist agencies such as the Industrial and Commercial Finance Corporation (ICFC) may assist in giving finance. The past profitability of the firm will determine the availability of capital funds both from the point of view of providing retained earnings and also by giving it credit worthiness when competing in the capital market for funds. The importance of having a ready supply of capital is demonstrated by the part that the profit constraint can play in managerial models of the firm (e.g. Baumol [14], Williamson [157] and Marris [87]). Without an infinite supply of funds, projects will compete for the funds available and the constraints on finance may be not only for a short period but perhaps for an indefinite period of time. The short period restrictions may be due to an unexpected fluctuation in net cash flow or an acceleration of technological development which increases the supply of investment opportunities. In the long term, rationing may exist because the available and acceptable projects are greater than the expected means of finance, particularly if the firm is unwilling to resort to the capital market for funds. The problem is to determine an 'efficient set' of projects out of the total set available, to maximise the firm's net present worth.

Suppose a firm has a set of investment projects, A to J, which under the normal accept/reject criterion would all be accepted if the firm had the available resources. Table 8.12 sets out the outlays, inflows, NPVs (at 10 per cent) and IRRs for all projects. There are two approaches to this problem of selecting the optimal portfolio of investments. The first involves the use of *ranking* and the second mathematical programming.

Table 8.12 Capital Rationing

	Outlay £	Inflows £			NPV @ 10%	IRR %	NPV per £1 invested
	0	1	2	3			
A	20,000	10,000	10,000	10,000	4,869	23.38	0.2435
B	30,000	15,000	11,000	10,000	240	10.49	0.0080
C	20,000	12,000	10,000	8,000	5,184	25.35	0.2592
D	20,000	10,000	8,000	6,000	210	10.66	0.0105
E	40,000	16,000	24,000	16,000	6,401	18.83	0.1600
F	100,000	50,000	50,000	40,000	16,829	19.70	0.1683
G	10,000	3,000	6,000	4,000	691	13.71	0.0691
H	35,000	17,000	20,000	10,000	4,497	17.73	0.1285
I	30,000	12,000	14,000	11,000	744	11.42	0.0248
J	40,000	25,000	14,000	16,000	6,319	19.68	0.1580

Under the ranking approach there are three methods:

(a) ranking by NPVs,
(b) ranking by NPVs per £1 invested,
(c) ranking by IRRs.

Under any of these three methods projects are ranked in decreasing order and accepted up to the point when the capital of the firm is exhausted. But two problems arise here. In the first place ranking by these three methods can give contradictory recommendations — as has already been demonstrated for (a) and (c). Secondly projects may not be divisible. The existence of indivisibilities is unlikely to be serious when the majority of investment projects are a small proportion of the total capital budget but where there are large projects, indivisibility can be a problem although this can be handled by integer programming. The point is developed later in this section.

Suppose the firm has a budget of £255,000 and the total demands on the funds are £345,000 as in Table 8.12. Ranking the 10 projects by NPV (@10%) gives F, E, J, C, A, H, I, G, B, and D, thus leading to F, E, J, C, A and H being accepted. The drawback to this approach, when finance is scarce, is that each pound invested in a project has an opportunity cost in terms of present value foregone as a result of having a pound less to invest elsewhere. What we should do therefore is to calculate NPV per £1 invested. These figures are also given in Table 8.12 and on this ranking the firm would choose C, A, F, E, J, H. Both methods produce the same group of projects (and therefore the same total NPV of £44,099) but a different ranking. If we utilised the third variant, ranking by IRRs we would have C, A, F, J, E and H; again the same group but in a different order to the other two methods. It should be clear by now that the ordering on the basis of IRR is irrelevant.

Suppose the budget were only £100,000, the NPV ranking would select project F giving a total NPV of £16,829. NPV per £1 invested would select projects C and A initially and would then advocate project F which would not be possible with the limitation of funds. Next in line would be project E and then there would be just £20,000 left to commit which rules out projects J and H so that G would be selected using £10,000 uncommitted; this selection would give a total NPV of £17,145. On the basis of an IRR ranking C, A, J and G would be chosen, again leaving £10,000 uncommitted and giving a lower total NPV of £17,063. In this simple example therefore all three give different recommendations and if the objective is to maximise the total net present value, experimentation with various project combinations shows that none of these are optimal but that E, J and C should be selected as together they give £17,904. The present of indivisibilities means that ranking may leave funds uncommitted and result in a less than optimal portfolio of investments. However, if the highest ranking projects can absorb all the available funds, the NPV per pound criterion will give an optimal portfolio. For instance a budget of £180,000 enables

(1) F, E and J to be adopted, using the NPV criterion giving a total NPV of £29,549.
or (2) C, A, F and E to be adopted, using the NPV *per pound* invested criterion giving a total NPV of £33,283.
or (3) C, A, F and J to be adopted, using the IRR criterion giving a total NPV of £33,201.

In all three instances, the budget of £180,000 is fully utilised and no combination other than C, A, F, and E, as advocated by the NPV per pound invested criterion, will give as large a total NPV. Note however that the NPV criterion is useless in the capital rationing situation, until it is expressed as a proportion of the sum invested; in fact IRR, though still inappropriate, gives a portfolio closer to the optimal one than does the simple NPV.

The other techniques available to solve the rationing problem are programming techniques. Linear programming can be used where there are no indivisibilities and integer programming where there are indivisibilities. We can illustrate the former with an example. Suppose a firm has three projects, A, B and C, which absorb capital for the first three years and then give rise to positive cash flows for a number of years. Standard DCF analysis has revealed that the gross present value of the projects cash flows at 10 per cent are £10,000, £12,000 and £8,000 respectively but the firm has limited financial resources available of £6,000 in year 1, £4,000 in year 2 and £3,000 in year 3. (These figures being expressed in present value equivalents.) The capital requirements, also in present values, are set out in Table 8.13.

Table 8.13 Capital Rationing and Linear Programming Method

Project	A	B	C	Available capital (discounted)
Gross Present Value @ 10%	10,000	12,000	8,000	
Capital requirements (discounted)				
Year 1	2,000	3,000	3,000	6,000
Year 2	2,000	4,000	1,000	4,000
Year 3	2,000	1,000	1,000	3,000

The objective function can now be set out as:

Maximise $10a + 12b + 8c$ *   (where a, b and c are the proportions of each project adopted, assuming divisibility.)

Subject to $2a + 3b + 3c \leq 6$
               $2a + 4b + c \leq 4$
               $2a + b + c \leq 3$ where $a, b, c \geq 0$.

The solution of this problem follows the approach set out in Chapter 3 and the solution can be reached after four iterations when the values of a, b and c are respectively 0.75, 0.33 and 1.17 with a value of £20,833 in the objective function representing GPV. The capital outlays in present terms amount to £6,000 in year 1, £3,990 in year 2 and £3,000 in year 3, i.e. a total capital outlay of £12,990 so that the NPV of the programme is £20,833 − £12,990 = £7,843.

With indivisibility of investment projects our programming problem is an integer-programming model where the optimum values of the decision variables are integers.

Whilst capital rationing is seen by many as an important problem in capital budgeting, perhaps too much is made of it in that firms have the ability to raise funds for investment by cutting working capital or selling assets or reducing the amount of trade credit extended so that internally at least the capital constraint may not be as rigid as some commentators may suggest.

8-7 Investment Decisions and Risk and Uncertainty

Although it is apparent that risk and uncertainty are fundamental issues in the subject of investment, we have yet to show how they can be accommodated in our analysis. This is the subject we now tackle.

We have already discussed this subject in a general way in Chapter 2 where we explained that while some writers attempt to draw a strict demarcation line between risk and uncertainty, there is no clear cut division in practice. F. H. Knight's [70] distinction is probably the most useful. To refresh our memories Knight defined risk as being a situation where there is no certainty with regard to the outcome but where there exists a range of possible outcomes and where there are known probabilities (objective rather than subjective) which can be applied to these outcomes. Uncertainty exists when it is not possible to determine either the outcome or the probability of any outcome occurr-

---

*   By maximising gross present value, we automatically maximise NPV because the capital outlays will be constant if the constraints are fully operative. The small proportion of year 2's budget which remains uncommitted makes no difference to the answer.

ing by objective standards. In practice the two concepts merge although it is possible to recognise situations of *pure risk* which can be protected against by insurance.

The handling of decision making under risk and uncertainty is a difficult exercise as we illustrated in Chapter 2, particularly as this is an area where informed judgement plays a key role with objectivity often replaced by subjectivity. However, this does not justify the abandonment of formal analysis under such circumstances. In practice these are to a greater or lesser extent the conditions which will prevail and as the investment decision will often determine the destiny of the firm, this is a particularly fertile area for the consideration of decision making under conditions of imperfect knowledge.

The investment decision has two necessary first steps. The first relates to the work of evaluating the returns expected to arise from the decision to invest. The second step which has occupied us for most of this chapter so far has been that of actually calculating the return earned on the investment or the net present value. With the assumption of certainty, NPV is a single figure but as soon as we allow for imperfect information in evaluation, additional work is necessary before the available information can be presented for decision purposes. There are various approaches which can be used in this context, *sensitivity analysis*, perhaps being the most usual.

Sensitivity Analysis

This method is a convenient way of screening investment projects which proceeds by selecting key parameters in the project which are uncertain, and then assessing how sensitive the return is to likely changes in this or that key variable. It should then be possible to identify what Merrett and Sykes [90] refer to as 'fail safe' category of investment projects. So that, if management is convinced that changes in the parameters will not cause the return to enter that range which would make the project inviable (i.e. a return below the acceptable level) then the project becomes a 'fail-safe' proposition. Of course in this instance we are not invoking a probability measure as such, rather a subjective assessment or judgement that some event, e.g. a change in costs, relative prices, interest rates, etc., might or might not occur.

Sensitivity analysis is not just to be regarded as post-optimality testing because where the investment plan under consideration is of a magnitude that could make or break the company then all likely outcomes need to be evaluated and alternative calculations made so that the decision makers are fully aware of the financial implications and consequences of the project.

Let us analyse a project where an initial outlay of £1,000 yields returns of £500 at the end of year 1, and £400 at the end of years 2 and 3.

	0	1	2	3	NPV @ 10%	IRR%
Outlay £	−1000				85.7	15.02
Inflows £		500	400	400		
Sensitivity Test (1)		400	400	400	− 5.2	9.70
Sensitivity Test (2)		500	400	300	10.5	10.66

This project has a higher inflow in year 1 than the other two years and if this were to fall to £400 as in sensitivity test (1) then the NPV would be negative. If however, the figure returned in the last year is the one most subject to uncertainty, sensitivity test (2) shows that it could fall to £300 and still result in a positive NPV. If the whole project was subject to uncertainty there is a strong margin by which the discount rate could be raised before a negative NPV would result, since the internal rate of return is 15.02 per cent, against a discount rate reflecting a cost of capital of 10 per cent. This latter point is suggestive of an alternative method of allowing for uncertainty or risk, namely to discount risky returns more heavily than certain ones so as to give the former a lower present value.

Discounting for Risk

In Section 8-2 we illustrated that the rationale behind the process of discounting is to take account of the timing of cash flows and that as we raised the discount rate the net present values fell. The cash flows were assumed to be known, but one can take account of risk directly by loading the normal discount rate with a margin to take account of risk. Suppose, for example, that in a riskless project the rate of discount used is 14 per cent, then a risk factor of say 2 per cent may be added to take account of a moderately risky outcome and a higher factor, say 5 per cent for one which was viewed with extreme caution.

The way in which risk might be measured is to take the variance or standard deviation of the project's cash flows, or if the latter are irregular, the variance of the project's NPV or IRR. The calculation of variance implies a knowledge of probability (see below), but as was explained in Chapter 2, it can be used as a proxy for risk if interpreted correctly.

If one were measuring risk in terms of the variance in cash flows or NPV, one would have to relate it to the magnitude of the cash sums involved. Coefficient of variation which takes the standard deviation as a proportion of *expected value* (again see below) would then be the measure of risk. If however variance in internal rate of return were to be taken as a proxy for risk, this measure would serve as it stood, since rates of return are already expressed as a proportion of capital invested.

The loading factor on the discount rate would therefore be proportional to some function of either the coefficient of variation or of the variance itself when the latter relates to the internal rate of return. The amount by which the discount rate should be loaded per unit of variance cannot be determined by analysis. It will be subjective and reflect the degree of risk avoidance exhibited by the decision maker. It will also depend upon the measure of variance or variation used. Therefore, loading the discount rate is an imprecise method of allowing for risk, but once a formula has been established it has the virtue of simplicity in application. Its use is open to dispute, since it is not always appropriate to discount risky projects more heavily if there are a large number of small independent projects, where individual project risks would tend to be offset elsewhere. The approach is less contentious when appraising major projects likely to change the nature of the whole business.

Probability in Investment

As the investment decision is usually unique with past experience generally in appropriate, objective probability can play little part in an analysis of risky situation in this context. However, in Chapter 2 we introduced the Bayesian approach, using subjective probability, to calculate expected value which takes the *average* view.

Suppose that a firm is considering an investment outlay of £1,000 which has three possible outcomes over a period of three years (as set out in Table 8.14) with the probabilities in parentheses.

Table 8.14

		Years		
	0	1	2	3
Outlay £s	−1000			
Cash Flows £s I		600 (0.3)	400 (0.3)	300 (0.3)
Cash Flows £s II		700 (0.5)	650 (0.5)	550 (0.5)
Cash Flows £s III		450 (0.2)	350 (0.2)	350 (0.2)
Expected Cash Flows £s	−1000	620	515	435

The three forecasts of likely returns, I, II, and III, relate to the outcomes which management feel are in the bounds of probability. If the *most probable* outcome were to be taken, then return II, which has a 0.5 probability throughout, would be adopted in the calculation and assuming that the firm's cost of capital is 14 per cent then this project would lead to a NPV of £485.4. If the *expected* cash flow were taken, the NPV would be £233.8 illustrating that taking the expected outcome rather than the most likely makes a substantial difference to the calculation in this instance.

A major problem is the placing of the probability estimates, and with major decisions informed judgement plays an important part. We therefore recognise that it is not possible to reduce the investment decision to a mechanistic model. Informed judgement will always play its part but it is important to apply this within a sound framework, namely discounted cash flow analysis.

8-8 The Cost of Capital

So far this concept has been described as an opportunity cost, i.e. one which reflects the rate of return shareholders could enjoy in the best strictly comparable investment. So presumably the analyst should try to assess the expectations of returns of shareholders from the company in question and from other companies subject to the same kind of business risks, or earnings fluctuations. Expected income could then be compared with the market value of stock to indicate the discount rate investors are applying to future income. This is not practicable since the future earnings of companies can seldom be predicted by investors beyond a few years ahead, even if a company's management has a slightly clearer picture. Consequently, historical data are frequently used, which is justifiable only if existing shareholders' requirements in terms of return and degree of risk are similar to those of previous investors and if the nature of the company's business has not changed significantly.

Merrett and Sykes ([191] p. 73) calculated the cost of capital to the average British corporation in manufacturing industry lies in the range 7½ per cent to 8½ per cent after all taxes, measured in real terms (i.e. after allowing for inflation). Some companies may find this a satisfactory basis for calculating their own cost of capital, but others may feel that their own situations are not typical and prefer to undertake an individual assessment. This would require a comparison of share prices at two points in time for the company itself or for a comparable company, taking care that those years were not at extremes of share price movements. One should compare peak with peak, trough with trough or some intermediate position. The net of tax dividends paid per share should then be plotted year by year between the two points in time chosen, and to the last of these should be added the closing value of the share less any capital gains tax payable. This series can then be treated as if it were a capital project with initial outlay, cash flows and terminal asset value. The yield thus calculated should then be adjusted for inflation by subtracting the annual rate of increase in the price index* and this then gives an estimate of the company's cost of capital.

A company using retained earnings is in fact using money withheld from its shareholders and can only justify this policy if the money can be re-invested at the cost of capital or a better return. Such re-investment effectively increases the company's equity base and should be reflected in the market valuation of its shares. There is thus little difference in principle between a new issue of shares or a retention of earnings and the latter should properly be regarded as having the same cost as the former.**

Of course, equity capital whether in the form of new shares or retained earnings is not the only source of capital although undoubtedly the most important, in recent years accounting for over 50 per cent of new money raised by industry. By far the greatest proportion of this is from retentions. Other sources include bank borrowing, though normally this relates to working capital needs rather than investment in fixed assets; then there are other fixed interest loans on a long term basis including debentures and mortgages. Preference shares, which used to be a significant form of financing are less so nowadays, since they demand a fixed commitment from the company and attract no tax advantages, unlike debt finance. Capital transfers which include investment grants are also important in investment appraisal but account for less than 10 per cent of new money.

The presence of non-equity sources complicates the cost of capital issue. For the moment let us think of all non-equity finance as being fixed interest debt on which there is a contractual requirement to pay a given sum of interest each year, regardless of profits, and a commitment to repay the investor his full capital sum at a given maturity date. The required rate of return on long term debt should be lower than the expected return from equity and approximate to the interest rate on long term government securities because it is risk free (not subject to fluctuation). Equity holders are the risk bearers of the enterprise; their earnings are subject to fluctuations in business profits which are rendered greater proportionately when fixed interest commitments on debt are incurred. Shareholders risks therefore consist of both business risk and financial risk and in the event of the company winding up they cannot receive any compensation until the obligations to debt holders

---

*   This is an approximate allowance for inflation but valid when both inflation rates and yields are small.

**   In practice tax differentials may favour one or the other such as was the case under the 1965 Finance Act where retained earnings attracted less tax. The present imputation system does not discriminate in terms of total tax paid although dividends necessitate an advance payment. A further practical difference is that new issues involve flotation costs whereas retention is free of these. On the other hand retention leading to capital gains involves a tax payment when the latter are realised.

are discharged.

A certain amount of controversy exists over the question of how debt finance influences the cost of capital. The traditional view is that the cost of capital is a function of the capital structure such that the cost of capital can be reduced by a judicious use of debt finance. However, the use of debt (often referred to as gearing or leverage) will tend to magnify fluctuations in the earnings of equity so that there is a trade-off between debt finance with its lower cost, and risk (in terms of variations in company earnings). A further aspect of the traditional view is that there exists some optimal level of gearing which will minimise the cost of capital. Any increase in gearing beyond this point would cause the average cost of capital to rise because of increasing risk giving rise to the 'U-shaped' cost of capital function illustrated in Figure 8.3.

Figure 8.3 The Traditional View of Leverage

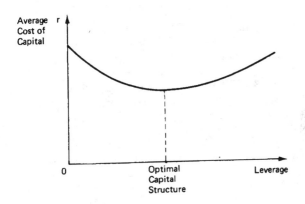

The Modigliani-Miller (MM) viewpoint (proposition I) [94] is that the cost of capital to a firm is independent of its gearing so that the cost of capital is a horizontal straight line as in Figure 8.4. Their argument is that although debt finance is a cheaper source than equity, its intro-

Figure 8.4 The Modigliani-Miller Theorem

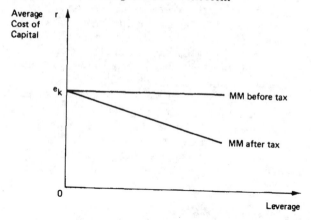

duction into a company's financial structure immediately increases financial risk to shareholders who require a premium to compensate them for this risk (MM proposition II). This premium offsets the apparently lower cost of debt and leaves the overall cost of capital to the company unaltered. Their basic propositions change when corporation tax is brought into the picture [95] because interest payments on debt qualify as an expense when corporation tax is being assessed. In other words, the greater the proportion of debt finance the smaller the tax bill. Distributions to equity holders do not bring any tax relief, indeed they accelerate the payment of corporation tax under the imputation system. At a 50 per cent tax rate the real cost of debt is only half of the coupon rate (i.e. the annual interest payable to debt holders), because of the effect on the company's tax bill. This influences both propositions of the MM theorem in that equity holders no longer require such a large premium for a given degree of leverage (proposition II) and that the reduction in the tax bill does effectively lower the cost of capital so that the latter is no longer independent of leverage (proposition I).

The MM after tax view (also illustrated in Figure 8.4) is thus similar to the traditional view in that the cost of capital declines with leverage. MM do not recognise an optimal point as such, but stress that companies should increase debt as far as possible subject to the constraints of the financial world. Crude rules of thumb are found in such guidelines as 'The proportion of debt must nor exceed one fifth of total financial assets' (measured either at par or current market value) or 'interest payments on debt must be covered four or five times by earnings'. Each case should, of course, be treated on its merits. Companies with stable profits, those who own highly marketable assets, and those with sales covered by contractual agreements, can reach higher gearing levels than their counterparts operating in unstable markets or involved in lease obligations. For example, companies in the multiple retail business, breweries and restaurant chains, often have substantial freehold properties which can be used as collateral for debt finance (mortgage debentures). On the other hand, oil companies typically have substantial lease obligations which impair their credit status and reduce debt raising capability. The traditional point of view is perhaps still worth heeding in that if the use of debt finance by a company is not judicious, but is carried to excess, its whole livelihood can be threatened and this will be reflected in its market valuation as investors discount its earnings more heavily.

To find the average cost of capital to a company one must weight the costs of the different sources by the appropriate proportions of assets in the capital structure. Some theorists favour the measurement of asset proportions in terms of book values but market values* are finding increasing favour. The formula for the average cost of capital which then serves as the company's discount rate, r, is as follows:

$$r = W_1 \rho + W_2 m .$$

Where W_1 and W_2 are the values of debt and equity respectively as a proportion of total financial asset values. ρ is the cost of capital for equity and m is the effective interest payment on debt after allowing for tax savings. Preference shares could be incorporated with an additional term consisting of the proportion of these assets multiplied by the appropriate interest (dividend) rate. If ρ, the cost of equity capital, is calculated on an historical basis as described earlier, it may need adjustment if the company has changed its gearing level since the years of the study. MM proposition II suggests that a premium would be necessary if geating had increased.** Otherwise the cost of capital is a simple matter of substituting in the above formula and making some adjustment for inflation. As an example suppose that the cost of equity is found to be 12 per cent when the inflation rate is 4 per cent and the coupon rate on debt is 10 per cent.

---

* Book values of equity would not reflect the typically large component of reinvested earnings within a company's assets. Thus market values are the only valid basis of computation for firms with large retention ratios.

** If ρ_k is the cost of capital to an ungeared company (pure equity) and ρ_j is the cost of equity to an equivalent company which is geared with D_j debt and E_j equity, then ρ_j exceeds ρ_k by an amount = $D_j/E_j \times (\rho_k -$ gross interest rate on debt$)(1 -$ corporation tax rate$)$.

The company is valued at £10,000,000 on the stock market consisting of £8,000,000 equity and £2,000,000 debt. Thus

W_1 = 8/10
W_2 = 2/10
ρ = 12%
m = 5% (if corporation tax is levied at 50%).

Therefore the average cost of capital,

$$r = \left(\frac{8}{10} \times 12\%\right) + \left(\frac{2}{10} \times 5\%\right)$$
$$= \underline{10.6\%}.$$

To use this for discounting cash flows in the analysis of capital projects one must adjust for inflation if the cash flows have been expressed in constant prices as is customary. An approximate adjustment for the 4 per cent rate of inflation reduces the average cost of capital to 6.6 per cent which then serves as the discount rate for investment appraisal.

This very briefly then is the method of deriving the cost of capital. A more sophisticated analysis would involve a breakdown of assets into subcategories of debt and include preference shares. Allowances would also be made for the costs of issuing securities, including the expenses of preparing a prospectus, publicity and all charges of the issuing agency. The basic principles we have used here involving weighted averages are however fairly widely accepted.

8-9 Public Sector Investment

In this book we have been developing a framework of analysis for decision making primarily for private enterprise. Investment appraisal in the nationalised industries can proceed along similar lines since they are in the main supposed to operate as commercial organisations with target rates of return except where there is a clear case for social considerations. In this section it is our purpose to analyse the rather different considerations that apply in appraising investment undertaken by public authorities other than nationalised industries. The significance of this category of investment can be gauged from the fact that on current account alone (excluding transfer payments) the central government and local authorities spend 12.7 per cent and 8.5 per cent of the nation's income (GNP, based on 1973 figures) respectively and their capital expenditure accounts for a further 5.5 per cent (and 9.3 per cent if public corporations are added). We cannot at this stage discuss the rights and wrongs of more or less public expenditure. What concerns us here is that any commitment of funds by the public sector deprives other potential users of the resources those funds command and consequently will have an impact on the direction of the economic growth of the nation. It is therefore important that an efficient system of appraisal takes place within the public sector so that the signals and controls of the market system which are absent in the public sector are replaced by some alternative check or control to ensure long run efficiency.

Commercial and Social Investment

We can distinguish between two types of investment decision within the public sector. On the one hand there are *commercial* investments and on the other *social* investments. Commercial types of investment decisions are of similar form to those undertaken within firms, i.e. where costs and revenues can be satisfactorily measured in terms of outflows and inflows of funds (or net savings on costs) to the sponsoring organisation. For instance, suppose that a local authority were assessing the most economical way of providing for refuse disposal within its boundaries and that it is considering a capital investment plan which will save labour. The costs of this project are represented by the initial cash outlay on the equipment and any cash outlays required over its life such as maintenance. The benefits can be represented by the savings in payroll which are equivalent to cash inflows. Assuming that the level of service is unaffected so that the community enjoys no additional benefits nor suffers any detriments from pollution, etc. the decision can be taken solely on the financial returns. Similarly decisions on whether to lease or buy equipment or to expand the stock of equipment or to replace it, are all of a commercial nature. Therefore the DCF framework advocated in Section 8-3 can be adopted, though there is debate over the appropriate discount rate to be used.*

However in many instances the costs and benefits cannot be satisfactorily (or at least directly) measured in terms of cash. Such projects may have implications for the community that are not reflected in cash receipts and payments of the organisation, either because some (or all) of those benefiting from the project are not required to make payments for those benefits, or cash receipts do not adequately represent the benefits derived. Suppose a local authority provided free parking for cars; there is no monetary measure of benefits since the car parking is not sold. If they did levy a charge, this would typically be nominal and fail to measure the value of benefits to users, or of course to other parties (e.g. shopkeepers). Such indirect benefits and any social costs that might arise are called *externalities* and these are very much a

---

* Nationalised industries appeal to a target rate of return on new investment of a commercial nature, and this practice has been adopted by local authorities to a certain extent.

feature of social investment and often extremely difficult to identify let alone measure in terms suitable for quantitative analysis. This is not to say that these are absent from the investment of firms since both beneficial and harmful externalities often exist in the shape of improved amenities and employment opportunities on the one hand and pollution on the other, but the decision rules that firms apply normally relate to private costs and benefits. Government intervention can then be aimed at directing the beneficial externalities (for instance by means of a regional policy)* and reducing the social costs (by means of statutory controls). The very nature of many social investment programmes leads to a wide dispersion of benefits throughout the community and there is no coincidence of private and social costs/benefits and no direct cash measure, although monetary measures can often be determined indirectly through cost-benefit analysis.

Cost-Benefit Analysis

Cost-benefit analysis (CBA) is one of a body of analytical techniques aimed at introducing economic analysis into public expenditure decisions and is advocated where the effects may be long lived and delayed (e.g. education) and spread throughout the community. It aims to do for public investment what DCF analysis has done for commercial investment decisions, i.e. to facilitate choice between alternative ways of using scarce resources. Cost-benefit analysis has become very fashionable and high fashion invariably involves controversy. To some writers CBA is attempting to quantify the unquantifiable, yet to others who have seized on the analysis it is seen as a panacea and a means of removing the political lobbying bound up with many public sector investment decisions. It is our purpose here to examine the methodology of CBA and to expose the problems that exist in applying the technique.

There is no agreed definition of cost-benefit analysis but the following is fairly typical: 'CBA purports to describe and quantify the social advantages and disadvantages of a policy in terms of a common monetary unit' (D. W. Pearce [107] p. 8). Whilst the underlying theory of cost-benefit analysis can be traced back to the welfare economics of the nineteenth century (for example, J. Dupuit's [37] classic paper on the utility of public works) in the present century it first came into prominence in the USA, particularly in the 1930s with the New Deal where a broader social justification was allowed for projects. Since then there have been developments in the theory with the formalising of public investment criteria so that CBA now has sound theoretical underpinnings. On the practical side CBA now has extensive applications and in many instances, e.g. in transport studies, it is a standard tool of analysis.

---

* For instance, offering investment incentives and other assistance to encourage firms to locate in areas of high, persistent unemployment.

CBA also has applications to land use and town planning problems; expenditure on education, health, recreation, research and development, military defence; in other words the whole area of public expenditure (see G. M. Peters [110]. R. Layard [77] and E. J. Mishan [92]). CBA can only be successfully applied to projects which are sufficiently small so that their introduction does not disturb the structure of relative price/quantities in the economy. Additionally all projects considered should be independent of one another.

There are several necessary stages in a cost-benefit study. The first stage is the same as with any formal decision analysis, namely that of identifying the problem(s) to be tackled. This requires a clear statement of the objectives to be pursued and an assessment of the current situation. Following this is the consideration of possible alternative courses of action (including doing nothing) and at this stage of the analysis it is important to identify which sections of the community are expected to be affected by the project; the time period over which the project offers its benefits and incurs costs, and also the constraints on the decision. There may be a considerable number of the latter including physical limitations, legal impediments or administrative and financial constraints upon the range of alternatives (and active search for them) and of course there may be political constraints which should be clearly stipulated. The third stage involves the identification of all costs and benefits on whomsoever they fall for the time period taken. This is essentially a survey exercise in that the costs and benefits will be felt by both the providing organisation and external parties. This requires the preparation of forecasts but the difficulty here is how far to go. In a sense it is like the ripples in a pond after a stone has disturbed the calm of the water. As one proceeds to go wider in one's coverage of incidence of costs and benefits the return for each use of resources in the study will decrease. Inevitably therefore it will not be possible to give full coverage to every conceivable repercussion, but this does not render the analysis invalid so long as all the major differences between the effects of alternative proposals are isolated so that it is possible to identify costs that are particularly those of committing resources to one use rather than another and benefits that are derived from one pattern of resource usage rather than another.

Once the costs and benefits have been enumerated, and it must be stressed that in practice, this is no easy matter, then these costs and benefits have to be valued in monetary terms over the relevant time period. On the cost side this is likely to be fairly straightforward in that the cost to society of using resources in a project is represented by the market prices at which these resources are bought.* Even so there are

---
* Economic theory shows that in competitive markets, price equals marginal cost. See Chapter 7, Section 7-3.

many resources to which it is almost impossible to ascribe a market price, e.g. resources on which there are no property rights but whose use in a project cannot be regarded as costless, especially if environmental damage occurs. The disturbance and destruction of wild life, frequently cited in the appraisal of the Foulness proposal cannot readily be valued, neither can the destruction of historic buildings which was a consideration in some of the other possible sites for the third London airport. Sometimes it is argued that such assets are priceless, although in the case of buildings it is possible to impute a kind of 'shadow price'* by estimating the cost of rebuilding an ancient monument on another site.

The benefit side of the evaluation usually poses the most difficulties since there is normally no existing measure of social benefit. Here again shadow prices are used to estimate the price (at the margin) the community would be willing to pay for benefits *as if* they were distributed through the market system. In other words the analyst is attempting to simulate the working of the market system. These shadow prices may be estimated directly or indirectly. For instance it is possible to conduct a survey of travellers and ask what they would be willing to pay to save an extra thirty minutes travel time by virtue of, say, a road improvement. An alternative approach is to value benefits in terms of the savings induced, e.g. the savings in time from a road improvement can be valued in terms of the output or earnings people would achieve in that time; the benefit of reduced accidents on motorways, as a result of the placing of crash barriers in the central reservations, can be valued in terms of reduced damage to vehicles, lower hospital costs, savings in police time and a reduction in the loss of output to the community and even the savings of having to provide for fewer orphaned children. Benefits from a given health programme can be valued in terms of output or earnings otherwise lost through premature death or sickness, and savings in treatment and rehabilitation costs. A third approach to assessing benefits which can be used where the analyst is confronted with intangibles is to use a 'contingency' approach. This has a possible application in the evaluation of programmes for the mentally handicapped where the costs are identifiable and calculable but positive benefits are not immediately translatable into monetary terms. Decision makers would then be asked to put a figure on the maximum amount they would be prepared to spend on these patients if the worst came to the worst and this would give the analyst a measure, however rough and ready, of the 'intangible' benefits.

There is always the temptation to come up with quantitative results which give the impression of precision when the truth of the matter is

---

* Not used here in the precise linear programming sense adopted in Chapter 4. In the present context it has the same general meaning as 'surrogate'.

that they are only estimates. At times great ingenuity has been shown in the calculation of apparently intangible costs and benefits, but it is important to stipulate the assumptions made in these calculations, and a range of estimates should be given so as to provide all the relevant information to the decision makers. The actual statement of costs and benefits to the community is normally presented in terms of amounts per annum with a clear statement of where there are intangibles. Net present value or internal rate of return is then derived with appropriate allowance for risk and uncertainty as described in Section 8-7. Either type of DCF approach requires a suitable discount rate at one stage or another and this in itself is a complex issue.

Choice of Discount Rate

The problem that follows the evaluation of costs and benefits is that of the choice of discount rate. There is a wealth of literature and considerable disagreement over the measurement of a social discount rate. One suggestion is the use of a social time preference rate which reflects society's preference for present benefits as against future benefits, but recognising the need to provide for unborn generations.* This rate has to be chosen by the government on behalf of the community but its determination is speculative and it is likely to be lower than that in the private sector. Another view is that the social discount rate should reflect the rate of return foregone on the project it displaces — in other words an opportunity cost rate. The displaced project is usually assumed to be in the private sector so the appropriate rate of discount is the rate of return on marginal projects in the private sector. This involves further computation but results in a standard less subjective than a social time preference rate. However, while it is part of the logic of CBA to stress the displacement of alternatives there may well be some projects where a private sector rate would not truly reflect the way society ought to value social benefits, e.g. where most of the benefits accrue to future generations. A third alternative is to use the long term borrowing rate proxied by the rate on long term gilt-edged securities. However, there are many borrowing rates in the public sector and the use of an overall proxy clearly has disadvantages. Additionally market rates are affected by many other influences (e.g. monetary policy) that are not strictly relevant to the choice of a social discount rate.

In conclusion, cost-benefit analysis is a systematic method of assessing the desirability of projects where it is vital to take both a wide and long view. It imposes discipline by demanding the evaluation of all relevant costs and benefits but at the same time it exposes the assump-

---
* A. C. Pigou [111] suggested that individuals have 'defective telescopic faculty' so that governments need to intervene in the long run interests of society.

tions underlying forecasts. It is not a substitute for decision making but a systematic analysis which facilitates choice from among alternatives.

Cost-Effectiveness Analysis

Cost-effectiveness analysis is a special, narrower form of the cost-benefit approach. We have seen that the cost-benefit approach represents an attempt to apply systematic measurement to projects or programmes in the public sector, where market prices are often lacking and external effects in production or consumption are important. CBA is characterised by:

(1) complete enumeration as far as is possible, of all costs and benefits expected;
(2) the recognition that costs and benefits tend to accrue over time.

In principle, cost-effectiveness analysis possesses both of these characteristics as it requires a complete listing of inputs and outputs, and the recognition of time through the use of a discount rate, in order to convert future sums into present value terms. Cost-effectiveness is employed when the various benefits are difficult to measure or when the several benefits that are measured cannot be reduced to a single dimension. Under cost-effectiveness analysis (discounted) costs are calculated and compared for alternative ways of achieving a specific set of results. It is assumed that the results sought can be afforded.

For example, although health programmes can be appraised using CBA, there are many benefits that cannot be valued in monetary terms. While reduction in treatment costs, and increases in the nation's output can be incorporated into a cost-benefit appraisal, this is not true of some of the most important results such as the alleviation of pain and increased joy from living. H. E. Klarman, *et al* [69]* preferred to use the cost effectiveness approach to compare the alternative methods of treating chronic renal disease. The three alternatives in this study were, kidney transplantation, dialysis at home, or dialysis at a centre. For each of these, it was possible to find present cost and an estimate of expectancy of life, the latter being the measure of effectiveness. The trading off between increased effectiveness and the higher cost of achieving it inevitably involves judgement as does the assessment of greater freedom enjoyed by recipients of a transplant compared with their counterparts on dialysis. Ethical issues surrounding transplantation also complicate the evaluation which would otherwise point to this alternative as being superior to the others on cost effectiveness grounds. Even if transplantation were adopted as the best course of action its

---

* See M. H. Cooper and A. J. Culyer's book of readings on Health Economics [30].

success in implementation would be constrained by the availability of donated organs and progress in tissue-typing.

This brief resume of applications in the public sector hopefully communicates to the reader the versatility of the economist's approach to decision making. Indeed wherever major projects are concerned economic appraisal is not just an aid to decision making but absolutely essential to it.

BIBLIOGRAPHY

1. Adelman, M. A. 'The A and P Case: A Study in Applied Economic Theory', *Quarterly Journal of Economics*, 1949, pp. 238-57.
2. Alchian, A. A. 'Costs and Outputs' in M. Abramovitz (Ed.) *The Allocation of Economic Resources*, California, Stanford University Press, 1959. Reprinted in Townsend, H. (Ed.) *Price Theory*, Selected Readings, Harmondsworth, Penguin, 1971, pp. 228-49.
3. — 'Uncertainty, Evolution and Economic Theory', *Journal of Political Economy*, June 1950, pp. 211-21.
4. Alfred, A. M. 'Company Pricing Policy', *Journal of Industrial Economics*, Nov. 1972, pp. 1-16.
5. Allen, C. M. 'The Demand for Herring — A Single Equation Model', *Scottish Journal of Political Economy*, Feb. 1972, pp. 91-8. Reprinted in Wagner, L. and Baltazzis, N. [151].
6. Ansoff, H. I, *Corporate Strategy*, McGraw Hill, 1965, Penguin, 1968.
7. Archibald, G. C. (Ed.) *The Theory of the Firm*, Selected Readings, Harmondsworth, Penguin, 1971.
8. Bach, G. L. *Economics*, New Jersey, Prentice Hall, 1954.
9. Bain, J. S. 'Economies of Scale, Concentration, and the Condition of Entry in Twenty Manufacturing Industries', *American Economic Review*, Vol. 64, 1954, pp. 15-39.
10. Barback, R. M. *The Pricing of Manufactures*, London, Macmillan, 1964.
11. Battersby, A. *Sales Forecasting*, Harmondsworth, Pelican, 1970.
12. Baumol, W. J. *Economic Theory and Operations Analysis*, 3rd Ed., New Jersey, Prentice Hall, 1972.
13. — 'On a Theory of Expansion of the Firm', *American Economic Review*, 1962, pp. 1078-87.
14. — 'On the Theory of Oligopoly', *Economica*, Vol. XXV, 1958, pp. 187-98.
15. Baxter, W. T. and Oxenfeldt, A. R. 'Approaches to Pricing: Economist Versus Accountant', *Business Horizons*, 1961. Reprinted in Carsberg, B. V. and Edey, H. C. [23], pp. 184-208.
16. Berle, A. A. and Means, G. C. *The Modern Corporation and Private Property*, New York, Harcourt, Brace and World. Revised Edition 1967.
17. Bernoulli, D. 'Specimen theorae novae de mensura sortis', 1738,

translated by L. Sommer, *Econometrica*, 1954, pp. 23-6.
18. BIM Information Note 42, *Capital Investment Projects — Methods of Evaluation*, 1965.
19. Bodenhorn, D. 'A Note on the Theory of the Firm', *Journal of Business*, April 1959, pp. 164-75.
20. Boulding, K. E. 'General Systems Theory: The Skeleton of a Science', *Management Science*, April 1956, pp. 197-208.
21. Brown, W. and Jaques, E. *Product Analysis Pricing*, London, Heinemann, 1964.
22. Buxton, M. J. and Rhys, D. G. 'The Demand for Car Ownership', *Scottish Journal of Political Economy*, June 1972, pp. 175-81. Reprinted in Wagner, L. and Baltazzis, N. [151].
23. Carsberg, B. V. and Edey, H. C. (Eds.) *Modern Financial Management*, Selected Readings, Harmondsworth, Penguin, 1969.
24. Caves, R. E. and Associates *Britain's Economic Prospects*, London, George Allen and Unwin, 1968.
25. Chamberlin, E. H. *The Theory of Monopolistic Competition. Reorientation of the Theory of Value*, Cambridge, Harvard University Press, 1956.
26. Clayton, G. and Osborn, W. T. *Insurance Company Investment. Principles and Policy*, London, George Allen and Unwin, 1965.
27. Coase, R. H. 'Monopoly Pricing with inter-related costs and demands', *Economica*, New Series, Vol. XIII, Nov. 1946, pp. 278-94.
28. Cohen, K. J. and Cyert, R. M. *Theory of the Firm. Resource Allocation in a Market Economy*, New York, Prentice-Hall, 1965.
29. Consumer Credit. Report of the Crowther Committee, Cmnd. 4596, HMSO 1971.
30. Cooper, M. H. and Culyer, A. J. (Eds.) *Health Economics*, Harmondsworth, Penguin, 1973.
31. Cyert, R. M. and Grunberg, E. *Assumption, Prediction and Explanation in Economics*, Appendix of Cyert, R. M. and March, J. G. [32].
32. Cyert, R. M. and March J. G. *A Behavioural Theory of the Firm*, New Jersey, Prentice-Hall, 1963.
33. Davies, J. R. 'On the Sales Maximisation Hypothesis. A Comment', *Journal of Industrial Economics*, April 1973, pp. 200-02.
34. Dorfman, R. 'Mathematical or "Linear" Programming: A Non-Mathematical Exposition', *American Economic Review*, Vol. 43, 1953, pp. 797-825.
35. Drakatos, C. 'Leading Indicators of the British Economy', *National Institute Economic Review*, No. 24, May 1963, pp. 42-9.
36. Drucker, P. F. *The Practice of Management*, London, Pan Books

1968. (First published by Heinemann, 1955.)
37. Dupuit, J. 'On the Measurement of Utility of Public Works', *International Economic Papers*, Vol. 2.
38. Earley, J. S. 'Marginal Policies of "Excellently Managed" Companies', *American Economic Review*, March 1956, pp. 40-70.
39. Elliott, D. 'Concentration in UK manaufacturing industry', *Trade and Industry*, August 1974, pp. 240-1, HMSO.
40. Friedman, M. *Essays in Positive Economics*, University of Chicago Press, 1953.
41. — 'Theory and Measurement of Long-Run costs in *Business Concentration and Price Policy*', National Bureau Committee of Economic Research, Princeton University Press, 1955, pp. 230-7.
42. Gabor, A., Granger, C. W. J. and Sowter, A. P. 'Real and Hypothetical Shop Situations in Market Research — A Study in Method', *Journal of Marketing Research*, 1970.
43. Galbraith, J. K. *The New Industrial State*, London, Hamish Hamilton, 1967 and Harmondsworth, Pelican, 1969.
44. Glicksman, A. M. *Linear Programming and the Theory of Games*, New York, J. Wiley, 1963.
45. Gould, J. R. 'On Investment Criteria for Mutually Exclusive Projects', *Economica*, February 1972, pp. 70-7.
46. Hague, D. C. 'Economic Theory and Business Behaviour', *Review of Economic Studies*, No. 3, 1949, pp. 144-57.
47. — *The Economics of Man-made Fibres*, London, Duckworth, 1957.
48. — 'The Economist in a Business School', *Journal of Management Studies*, October 1965, pp. 303-18.
49. — *Pricing in Business*, The Centre for Business Research, University of Manchester, London, George Allen and Unwin, 1971.
50. Haldi, J. and Whitcomb, D. 'Economics of Scale in Industrial Plants', *Journal of Political Economy*, August 1967, pp. 373-85. Reprinted in B. S. Yamey (Ed.) *Economics of Industrial Structure* [160].
51. Hall, M. 'Sales Revenue Maximisation: An Empirical Examination', *Journal of Industrial Economics*, April 1967, pp. 143-56.
52. Hall, R. L. and Hitch, C. J. 'Price Theory and Business Behaviour', *Oxford Economic Papers*, May 1939, pp. 12-45.
53. Harrison, R. and Wilkes, F. M. 'A Note on Jaguar's Pricing Policy', *European Journal of Marketing*, Vol. 3, 1973, pp. 242-6.
54. Hart, P. E., Utton, M. A. and Walshe, G. *Mergers and Concentration in British Industry*, Cambridge University Press, 1973.
55. Hawkins, C. J. 'On the Sales Revenue Maximisation Hypothesis', *Journal of Industrial Economics*, April 1970, pp. 129-40.

56. Hawkins, E. C. 'Methods of Estimating Demand', *Journal of Marketing*, April 1957, pp. 428-38.
57. Hellings, J. 'Technical Note: The Case for Pay-back re-examined', *Journal of Business Finance*, Vol. 4, No. 1, 1972, pp. 99-102.
58. Hirshleifer, J. 'On the Theory of Optimal Investment', *Journal of Political Economy*, Vol. 66, 1958, pp. 329-72. Reprinted in Carsberg, B. V. and Edey, H. C. [23], pp. 73-112.
59. Horngren, C. T. *Cost Accounting – A Managerial Emphasis*, 3rd Ed., New Jersey, Prentice-Hall Inc., 1972.
60. Howe, M. 'Marginal Analysis in Accounting', *Yorkshire Bulletin of Economics and Social Research*, Nov. 1962, pp. 81-9.
61. – 'A Study of Trade Association Price Fixing', *Journal of Industrial Economics*, July 1973, pp. 236-56.
62. Hunter, A. *Competition and the Law*, London, George Allen and Unwin, 1966.
63. Hurwicz, L. 'Optimality Criteria for Decision Making under Ignorance', Cowles Commission Discussion Paper. *Statistics*, No. 370, 1951.
64. ICI Monograph No. 2, *Short Term Forecasting*, 1964.
65. Johnson, R. A., Kast, F. E. and Rosenzweig, J. E. 'Systems Theory and Management', *Management Science*, Vol. 10, 1964, pp. 367-84 and reprinted in Carsberg, B. V. and Edey, H. C. [23], pp. 279-302.
66. Johnston, J. *Statistical Cost Analysis*, New York, McGraw Hill, 1960.
67. Keane, S. M. 'Let's Scrap IRR, once and for all!', *Accountancy*, February 1974, pp. 78-82.
68. Kirkman, P. R. A. *Accounting Under Inflationary Conditions*, London, George Allen and Unwin, 1974.
69. Klarman, H. E., Francis, J. O's and Rosenthal, G. D. *Efficient Treatment of Patients with Kidney Failure* in Cooper, M. H. and Culyer, A. J. [30].
70. Knight, F. H. *Risk Uncertainty and Profit*, Boston, Houghton Mifflin, 1921.
71. Knox, A. D. 'The Acceleration Principle and the Theory of Investment: A Survey', *Economica*, August 1952, pp. 269-97.
72. Koutsoyiannis, A. P. 'Demand Function for Tobacco', *Manchester School*, Jan. 1963, pp. 1-20. Reprinted in Wagner, L. and Baltazzis, N. [151].
73. Labini, S. *Oligopoly and Technical Progress*, Guiffre, Milan, 1957.
74. Lanzillotti, R. F. 'Pricing Objectives in Large Companies', *American Economic Review*, Dec. 1958, pp. 921-40.
75. Lawrence, R. J. 'Market Forces and Business Success' in *On the Nature of Business Success*. Edited by G. L. S. Shackle, Liver-

pool, the University Press, 1968.
76. Lawson, G. M. and Windle, D. W. *Tables for Discounted Cash Flow, Annuity Sinking Fund, Compound Interest and Annual Capital Charge Calculation*, Edinburgh and London, Oliver and Boyd, 1965.
77. Layard, R. (Ed.) *Cost Benefit Analysis*, Harmondsworth, Penguin, 1972.
78. Leibenstein, H. 'Allocative Efficiency versus X-Efficiency', *American Economic Review*, June 1966, pp. 392-415.
79. Leser, C. E. V. 'The Measurement of Elasticities of Demand', *Applied Statistics*, June 1954, pp. 74-84.
80. Lewellen, W. G. 'Management and Ownership in the Large Firm', *Journal of Finance*, May 1969, pp. 299-322.
81. Lloyd, B. 'Economies of Scale', *Moorgate and Wall Street*, Autumn 1970, pp. 22-47.
82. McGuire, J. W., Chiu, J. S. Y. and Elbing, A. O. 'Executive Incomes, Sales and Profits', *American Economic Review*, September 1962, pp. 753-61.
83. Machlup, F. *The Political Economy of Monopoly*, Baltimore, John Hopkins Press, 1952.
84. — 'Theories of the Firm, Marginalist, Behavioural, Managerial', *American Economic Review*, March 1967, pp. 1-33.
85. Margolis, J. 'The Analysis of the Firm, Rationalism, Conventionalism and Behaviourism', *Journal of Business*, July 1958, pp. 187-99.
86. — Sequential Decision Making in the Firm', *American Economic Review*, Papers and Proceedings, May 1960, pp. 526-59.
87. Marris, R. *The Economic Theory of Managerial Capitalism*, London, Macmillan, 1967.
88. Massie, J. L. *Essentials of Management*, 2nd Ed., New Jersey, Prentice-Hall, 1971.
89. Masson, R. T. 'Executive Motivations and Earnings and Consequent Equity Performance', *Journal of Political Economy*, December 1971, pp. 1278-92.
90. Merrett, A. J. and Sykes, A. *Capital Budgeting and Company Finance*, 2nd Ed., London, Longmans, 1973.
91. — *The Finance and Analysis of Capital Projects*, London, Longmans, 1963.
92. Mishan, E. J. *Cost Benefit Analysis*, London, George Allen and Unwin, 1971.
93. Modigliani, F. 'New Developments on the Oligopoly Front', *Journal of Political Economy*, June 1958, pp. 215-32.
94. Modigliani, F. and Miller, M. H. 'The Cost of Capital, Corporation Finance and the Theory of Investment', *American Economic*

95. — 'Corporate Income Taxes and the Cost of Capital: A Correction', *American Economic Review*, 1963, pp. 433-43.
96. Monopolies Commission. *Report on the Supply of Certain Industrial and Medical Gases*, HC 13, HMSO, December 1956.
97. — *Report on the supply of Electrical Equipment for Mechanically Propelled Land Vehicles*, HMSO, December 1963.
98. — *Report on the Supply of Household Detergents*, HC 105, London, HMSO, 1966.
99. — *Report on Man-made Celluloic Fibres*, HC 130, London, HMSO, 1968.
100. Moore, F. T. 'Economies of Scale: Some Statistical Evidence', *Quarterly Journal of Economics*, May 1959, pp. 232-45.
101. Moore, H. K. *Economic Cycles: Their Law and Cause*, New York, Macmillan, 1914.
102. National Economic Development Council. *Investment Appraisal*, Second Edition, HMSO, 1967.
103. *National Institute Economic Review*. 'The Demand for Domestic Appliances', November 1960.
104. — 'Long Term Forecasts of Demand for Cars, Selected Consumer Durables and Energy', May 1967.
105. Neumann, Von J. and Morgenstern, O. *Theory of Games and Economic Behaviour*, Princeton, Princeton University Press, 1947.
106. Patton, P. 'Top Executives Pay: New Facts and Figures', *Harvard Business Review*, 44, September 1966.
107. Pearce, D. W. *Cost Benefit Analysis*, London, Macmillan, 1971.
108. Pearce, I. C. 'A Study in Price Policy', *Economica*, May 1956, pp. 114-27.
109. Pessemier, A. 'An Experimental Method for Estimating Demand', *Journal of Business*, October 1960, pp. 373-83.
110. Peters, G. M. *Cost Benefit Analysis and Public Expenditure*, Eaton Paper 8, 3rd Ed., I.E.A., 1973.
111. Pigou, A. C. *The Economics of Welfare*, 4th Ed., London, Macmillan, 1950.
112. Prais, J. T. 'A New Look at Concentration', *Oxford Economic Papers*, July 1974, pp. 273-88.
113. Pratten, C. F. *Economies of Scale in Manufacturing Industries*, Occasional Papers No. 28, University of Cambridge, Department of Applied Economics, Cambridge University Press, 1971.
114. Pratten, C. F. and Dean, R. M. *The Economies of Large-Scale Production in British Industry*, Cambridge University Press, 1965.
115. Quade, E. S. 'System Analysis Technique for Planning — Pro-

gramming – Budgeting', Chap. 12 in Lyden, F. J. and Miller, E. G. (eds.) *Planning – Programming – Budgeting a System Approach to Management*, 2nd Ed., Chicago, Markham Publishing Co., 1972.
116. Rees, R. D. 'Optimum Plant Size in United Kingdom Industries, Some Survivor Estimates', *Economica*, Nov. 1973, pp. 394-401.
117. Roberts, D. R. *Executive Compensation*, Glencoe, Free Press, 1959.
118. Robinson, E. A. G. 'The Pricing of Manufactured Products', *Economic Journal*, Vol. LX, December 1950, pp. 771-80.
119. Robinson, J. *The Economics of Imperfect Competition*, London, Macmillan, 1933.
120. – 'The Industry and the Market', *Economic Journal*, Vol. LCVI, 1956, pp. 360-1.
121. Rowley, C. K. 'The Monopolies Commission and the Rate of Return on Capital', *Economic Journal*, March 1969, pp. 42-65.
122. Samuelson, P. A. *Economics*, 7th Ed., Tokyo, McGraw Hill, 1967.
123. Savage, L. J. 'The Theory of Statistical Decision', *Journal of the American Statistical Association*, Vol. 46, 1951, pp. 55-67.
124. Saving, T. R. 'Estimates of Optimum Plant Size by the Survivor Technique', *Quarterly Journal of Economics*, No. 1961, pp. 569-607.
125. Shackle, G. L. S. *Uncertainty in Economics and Other Reflections*, Cambridge, Cambridge University Press, 1955.
126. – *Expectations, Enterprise and Profit. The Theory of the Firm*, London, George Allen and Unwin, 1970.
127. Shepherd, W. G. 'On Sales Maximising and Oligopoly Behaviour', *Economica*, November 1962, pp. 420-4.
128. – 'What does the Survivor Technique show about Economies of Scale?', *Southern Economic Journal*, July 1967, pp. 113-22.
129. Shupack, M. B. 'The Predictive Accuracy of Empirical Demand Analysis', *Economic Journal*, Vol. XXII, September 1962, pp. 550-75.
130. Silbertson, A. 'Economies of Scale in Theory and Practice', *Economic Journal*, March 1972 Supplement, pp. 369-91.
131. – 'Price Behaviour of Firms', *Economic Journal*, Vol. LXXX, September 1970, pp. 511-82.
132. Simon, H. A. *Administrative Behaviour*, 2nd Ed., New York, Macmillan, 1957.
133. – *The New Science of Management Decision*, New York, Harper Row, 1960.
134. Skinner, R. C. 'The Determination of Selling Prices', *Journal of Industrial Economics*, July 1970, pp. 201-77 and reprinted in

Wagner, L. and Baltazzis, N. [151].
135. Smith, C. A. 'Empirical Evidence on Economies of Scale', in Archibald, G. C. [7], Harmondsworth, Penguin, 1971, abridged from 'Survey of the Empirical Evidence on Economies of Scale' in *Business Concentration and Price Policy*, Princeton University Press, 1955, pp. 213-30.
136. — 'The Cost-Output Relations for the United States Steel Corporation', *Review of Economics and Statistics*, 1942, pp. 166-176.
137. Sowter, A. P., Gabor, A. and Granger, C. W. J. 'The Effect of Price on Choice — A Theoretical and Empirical Investigation', *Applied Economics*, 1971, pp. 167-81.
138. Stewart, M. *Keynes and After*, Harmondsworth, Pelican, 1967.
139. Stigler, G. J. 'The Kinky Oligopoly Demand Curve and Rigid Prices', *Journal of Political Economy*, October 1947, pp. 432-449.
140. — 'The Limitations of Statistical Demand Curves', *Journal of the American Statistical Association*, Vol. XXXIV, September 1939.
141. — 'The Economies of Scale', *Journal of Law and Economics*, Vol. 1, 1958, pp. 54-71.
142. — 'A Theory of Oligopoly', *Journal of Political Economy*, February 1964, pp. 44-61.
143. Stone, R. 'The Analysis of Market Demand', *Journal of the Royal Statistical Society*, Series A, Part 3, 1945, pp. 286-382.
144. Sutherland, A. 'The Monopolies Commission: A Critique of Dr Rowley', *Economic Journal*, June 1971, pp. 264-72.
145. Sweezy, P. M. 'Demand Under Conditions of Oligopoly', *Journal of Political Economy*, 1939, pp. 568-73.
146. Tangri, Om. P. 'Omissions in the Treatment of the Law of Variable Proportions', *American Economic Review*, Vol. 56, 1966, pp. 484-93.
147. Udell, J. G. 'How Important is Pricing in Competitive Strategy', *Journal of Marketing*, January 1964, pp. 44-8.
148. Utton, M. A. *Industrial Concentration*, Harmondsworth, Penguin, 1970.
149. Vickers, Sir G. *Towards a Sociology of Management*, London, Chapman and Hall, 1967.
150. Wagner, H. M. *Principles of Operations Research: with Application to Managerial Decisions*, New Jersey, Prentice Hall, 1969.
151. Wagner, L. and Baltazzis, H. (Eds.) *Readings in Applied Microeconomics*, Clarendon Press and Open University Press, Oxford, 1973.
152. Wald, A. *Statistical Decision Functions*, New York, J. Wiley and

Son, 1954.
153. Watson, D. S. (Ed.) *Price Theory in Action*, 2nd Ed., Boston, Houghton Mifflin, 1969.
154. Weiss, L. W., 'The Survival Technique and the Extent of Suboptimal Capacity', *Journal of Political Economy*, June 1964, pp. 246-61.
155. Wenders, J. T. 'Excess Capacity as a Barrier to Entry', *Journal of Industrial Economics*, April 1972, pp. 14-19.
156. Weston, J. F. 'Pricing Behaviour of Large Firms', *Western Economic Journal*, Vol. 10, No. 1, 1972, pp. 1-18.
157. Williamson, O. E. *The Economics of Discretionary Behaviour: Managerial Objectives in a Theory of the Firm*, New Jersey, Prentice Hall, 1964.
158. — 'Managerial Discretion and Business Behaviour', *American Economic Review*, 1963, pp. 1032-57.
159. Working, E. J. 'What do Statistical "Demand Curves" Show?', *Quarterly Journal of Economics*, Vol. 41, 1927, pp. 212-25.
160. Yamey, B. S. (Ed.) *Economics of Industrial Structure*, Harmondsworth, Penguin, 1973.
161. Yntema, T. O. 'Steel Prices, Volume and Costs', *Temporary National Economic Committee Papers*, Vol. 1, 1944, pp. 223-323.

INDEX

abnormal cash flows 245, 267-71
absorption costing 108, 230
accelerator principle 241
accounting
    cost 91-3, 108
    inflation 112
    profit 112-3, 250
Adelman, M.A. 236
advertising expenditure 191, 202-3, 206
    change in 136
    self cancelling 190
Alchian, A. A., 55n, 104-6, 119, 129, 222n
Alfred, A. M. 216
Allen, C. 171
allocative inefficiency 214-5
Ansoff, H. I. 10-13, 190n, 216, 242

Bach, G. L. 62
Bain, J. S. 127, 141n, 192
Barback, R. M. 218n
barometric firm 195
barriers to entry 141n, 186, 190-3
Battersby, A. 164
Baumol, W. J. 2n, 19-20, 23, 66, 161n, 200, 204-6, 217, 226, 274
Baxter, W. T. and Oxenfeldt, A. R. 171, 230
Bayes-Laplace 37-9
behavioural theory 14, 20-1
Berle, A. A. and Means, G. C. 9
Bernoulli, D. 46
black box 3-6, 7, 9
blending 82-5
Bodenhorn, D. 8
Boulding, K. E. 2
Brookings Report 165
Brown, W. and Jacques, E. 227
budget constraint 134, 138
    line 138
Buxton, M. J., Rhys, D. G. 171n

cardinal utility 134, 137
cartel 193-4
Caves, R.E. and Associates 165

Chamberlin, E. H. 9n, 186
Coase, R. H. 235
Clayton, G. and Osborn, W. T. 34
Cohen, K. J. and Cyert, R. M. 7, 55n, 199
collusion 193-6, 217
    tacit 190, 195-6, 200, 206n, 212
    formal 190, 193-5
competition
    and market structures 8-9
    see also market structures
    imperfect 9
    perfect 8, 178-81, 186
    monopolistic 175, 186
computerisation
    and economies of scale 100
    of linear programming 75
concentration
    industry 187
    overall 188
    ratios 187-9
conjectural variation 199
consumer
    and the theory of the firm 6-8
    consumer credit 140
contingency analysis 50
contribution 17-18, 68, 106
    costing 109-10
control
    as a function of management 1, 17
    loop 5
    cost information for 91, 109
controllable variables
    price 140
    promotional expenditure 141
constant returns to scale
    see scale
Cooper, M. H. and Culyer, A. J. 292n
Corporation Tax 112-3, 140n, 245, 256n, 285n
cost
    accounting classification of 92-3
cost analysis 91-132
    empirical 118-32

303

cost,
  actual 221
  advantage, absolute 192-3,
  product differentiation 191-2
  average fixed 97
  average variable 96-7
  average total 97, 119-20, 124, 181-2, 187
  average total, for long run 102-4
  avoidable 106-10, 115, 231, 240, 243
  expected 221
  fixed 93-4, 107, 123, 204, 232
  incremental 17-18, 104, 106-7
  see also cost, marginal
  long run 99-104, 110, 124-31
  marginal 18, 94-5, 123, 124, 179
  long run marginal cost 103-4, 234n
  see also marginal analysis
  opportunity 17-18, 106-10, 232, 240, 243, 254n
  in simplex method 73, 115-8
  overhead 92-3
  apportionment of overhead 109
  prime 92
  short run 95-9, 119-24
  standard 110, 221
  variable 93-4, 213, 230-2
  total 94
cost-benefit analysis 245, 288-92
cost-benefit approach to monopoly policy 215
cost effectiveness 15, 245, 292-94
cost of capital 110, 244-5, 250
  average cost of capital 285
criteria for decision making 15-16
  under uncertainty 37-45
cross elasticity 159-60, 176
Crowther Report 140n
cross section data 121, 126
Cyert, R. M. and Grunberg, E. 8
Cyert, R. M. and March, J. G. 14, 16, 20, 53, 213n, 218-9, 223n, 226

Davies, J. R. 203
the decision making process 13-17, 24
decision theory 24-53
decreasing returns to scale — see scale
demand,
  aggregate 141
  competitive 159
  complementary 159
  export 142

  forecasting 162-74
  multivariate functions 154, 157
demand curve, derivation of
  individual 136
  market 190
demand schedule 135
depreciation 112-4
diminishing marginal utility 45-8, 135
diminishing returns
  law of 63-6, 97
discounted cash flow techniques
  applications — lease/buy decision 259-60
  replacement 260-2
  tax allowance, grants, 255-8, 266-73
  comparison of NPV and IRR 266-77
  NPV 233, 245, 250-1, 253-5, 257, 259, 261-2, 266-77, 279, 281
  IRR 245, 252-5, 259, 266-8, 270-6, 279
discounting 113, 245-9
  for risk 279-80
  choice of rate 291
diversification 49, 100, 133n
division of labour 61
dominance 28, 208-10
Dorfman, R. 65
Drakatos, C. 165n
Drucker, P. 21
dual — see primal and dual
duopoly 188, 206-7
Dupuit, J. 288

Earley, J. S. 224
econometrics 122, 169
Economic Development Committees 226
economic laws 135
economic systems 6
economies of scale — see scale
elasticity
  definition of 143-4
  of demand 144-51
  arc 144-6
  cross 159-60, 176
  for automobiles 166
  income 144, 157
  point 146-8
  and multivariate demand functions 154-7
  and logarithmic demand functions 158-9

Elliott, D. 188-9
engineering approach to cost analysis 122, 124, 126-8
entrepreneur 6
entry conditions – see barriers to entry
executive polling 171
expectation
    mathematical – and expected value 29
expense preference 19-20, 101, 214
exponential weighting 163-4
extended yield 269
external economies and diseconomies 99
externalities 287-8

Fair Trading Act 1973 177
feasible solutions 70, 78, 84, 87
feedback 4-5, 13, 54
Finance Act
    1965, 282n
    1972, 113n
firm, the 1-23
    as a system 54
    the theory of 6-10, 19
fixed
    costs – see costs, fixed
    factor inputs – see short run
    technological coefficients 65-6, 97
forecasting demand – mechanical methods 162-5
    indicators 165
    statistical methods 165-71
    alternative methods 171-4
Fortune's Top 500 187, 204
Friedman, M. 127
full cost pricing – see pricing, full cost

Gabor, A. et al. 173
Galbraith, J. K. 1, 19, 22, 128, 141, 233
Game theory
    dominance 28, 208-10
    maximim 40, 199n, 207-8
    minimax 207-8
    mixed strategies 42, 209-11
    non-zero sum games 211-12
    pure strategy 207-8
    saddle point 208
    two-person zero sum games 206-11

gearing 283
General Agreement on Tariffs and Trade (GATT) 185n
general systems theory 1, 2-6
Giffen goods 135n
Glicksman, A. M. 85
goals, see objectives
Gould, J. R. 272n
growth 1, 19, 100
growth models 206

Hague, D. C. 10n, 218, 224, 226-7
Haldi, J. and Whitcomb, D. 127
Hall, M. 205
Hall, R. L. and Hitch, C. J. 9n, 196, 199n, 218
Harrison, R. and Wilkes, F. M. 219
Hart, P. E. et al. 188
Hawkins, C. J. 204
Hawkins, E. C. 166n, 174
Hirshleifer, J. 267
Horngren, C. T. 109
Howe, M. 194, 224
Hunter, A. 176
Hurwicz, L. 41
Hurwicz α criterion 41

ICI Monograph 164
identification problem 160-1, 161n
income
    consumption curve 139
    elasticity 144, 157
    household 141
    national 142, 156
increasing returns to scale – see scale
incremental analysis – see marginal analysis
incremental cost – see cost, incremental
incremental yield 272
indicators 165, 165n
indifference curves 134, 137, 141,
    map 137, 141
indivisibilities,
    of machinery and of human inputs 61, 106
Industrial and Commerical Finance Corporation (ICFC) 273
inferior goods 138, 144n
information 8, 21, 38, 51-2
input-output 3-5, 15
    the firm as an - - system 54
insurance 34-6

305

integer programming – see programming, integer
interdepartmental transfers 238-40
internal rate of return (IRR) 245, 252-5, 259, 266-8, 270-6, 279
inventory,
 control 14
 valuation 110-12
Isocost lines 57-8, 84
Isoprofit lines 70, 80-1
Isoquants 55-7, 78-80
investment decisions
 appraisal – conventional methods (payback and average R of R) 262-6
 – DCF methods (IRR and NPV) 250-5
 capital rationing in 273-7
 commercial 287-8
 cost of capital 281-6
 examples (purchase, leasing, replacement) 255-62
 problem of abnormal cash flows 267-71
 problem of mutually exclusive projects 271-3
 public sector 243n, 286-8
 risk and uncertainty in 277-81

Johnson, R. A., Kast, F. E. and Rosenzweig, J. E. 21, 54
Johnston, J. 122-3, 126, 131-2
joint products
 problems of costing - - 109, 121
Joint Stock Company 1, 9
judgement
 action 14
 reality 13
 value 16

Keane, S. M. 273
Kirkham, P. R. A. 112n
kinked demand curve 175, 196-200, 203
Klarman, H. E. 292
Knight, F. H. 26, 277
Knox, A. D. 120
Koutsoyiannis, A. P. 171

Labini, S. 192
Lanzillotti, R. F. 219, 222n, 226-7
Laplace criterion – see Bayes-Laplace
Lawson, G. M. and Windle, D. W. 246n

Leibenstein 20, 183, 213-4
Leser, C. E. V. 165
Lewellen, W. G. 205
limit pricing 191
linear programming – see programming, linear
Lloyd, B. 99, 101
long run 59-63
 cost analysis 124-31
 cost behaviour 99-104

macroeconomics 6
Machlup, F. 7, 176
management
 functions of 1-2
 process 4
 and systems theory 2-6, 21
managerial discretion 19, 175, 200
marginal analysis 17-18, 106-7
Margolis, J. 38, 52, 100, 133n, 141
market
 dimensions of 176-7
 structure – classification 8-9, 175-8
marketing, economies in 101
Marris, R. 19, 100, 128, 206, 226, 245, 274
Massie, J. L. 1
maximax 40-1
maximin 40, 199n, 207-8
maximisation and minimisation in linear programming 67-8, 82
maximisation of profit – see profit maximisation
McGuire, J. W. et al. 204-5
Merrett, A. J. and Sykes, A. 242, 260, 278, 281
microeconomics 6-8
minimax 207-8
 regret 41
Mishan, E. J. 289
mixed strategy 42, 209-11
model-building 7-10
 definition of 7
models in the structure of analysis 15
Modigliani, F. 192
Modigliani, F. and Miller, M. J. (MM) 283-5
 Proposition I 283, II 284-5
monopolistic competition 175, 186
monopoly 8, 175, 191
 assumptions of 181
 control of 213
Monopoly and Restrictive Trade

Practice Act (1948) 177
Monopoly and Mergers Act (1965) 214n
Monopolies Commission 183-5, 214-5
   Report on Detergents 191n
   Report on Electrical Equipment 185
   Report on Industrial Gases 183, 185, 237n
Moore, H. K. 127, 160
multiple discount rates 267, 271
multiple products 109, 121, 235-6

National Institute for Economics and Social Research (NIESR) 142
NIESR Review 171
Net Present Value (NPV) 233, 245, 250-1, 253-5, 257, 259, 261-2, 266-77, 279, 281
Neumann, von J. and Morgenstern, O. 20, 46, 206
New Deal 288
normative and positive 21, 53

objective – function in linear programming 67
objectives 4-5, 19-23
   in pricing, 223-7
   profit maximisation 6, 19-23. 54, 178-82, 186, 190, 200, 202-4
   sales revenue maximisation 175-90
   satisficing 226
offer curve (price consumption curve) 139
oligopoly 159, 175, 187-90, 199, 200-03, 206
   – see also market structures
open price agreements 195
opinion polling 172
optimal solutions 70-1, 72, 75, 81, 84, 88-9, 115, 118
optimising and satisficing 16, 44, 51-3, 226
ordinal utility 137
Organisation for European Cooperation and Development (OECD) 142
organisational slack 20, 213
organisation theory 51-3

Patton, P. 204
pay-off matrix 24-6
Pearce, D. W. 288

perfect competition – see competition, perfect
Pessemier, A. 173
Peters, G. M. 289
Pigou, A. C. 291n
positive – see normative and positive
potential surprise 38-9
Prais, J. T. 187
Pratten, C. F. 123, 127
Pratten, C. F. and Dean, R. M. 124
price
   consumption curve (offer curve) 139
   discrimination 184-6, 237
   leadership 196-8
   limit (price) 191
   non-discriminatory 186
   penetration 226
   shadow 229, 290
   taker 178, 196, 217
pricing
   basing point 185, 237-8
   ex works 238
   full cost 199n, 212, 220-3, 228
   long run marginal cost 232-4
   objectives in 223-6
   product analysis 227-30
   product line 235-6
   uniform delivered 185, 238
   zonal 238
prices code 217
primal and dual 117-8
probability 27-31, 280-1
   a priori and a posteriori 31-3
   subjective 36-8
problem solving 4-5
process
   the choice of 77-82
   meaning in programming 65
   multiple(es) 98-9
   in systems theory 3-5
product mix 67-75
production 54-85, 89-90
   factors of 57-9
   neoclassical view 55-64, 95-7
   see also programming
production function 54-66
profit
   accounting 112-3
   constraint 200-03
   maximisation 6, 19-23, 54, 178-82, 186, 198, 200, 202-4, 217, 224-6, 235, 244
   monopoly 193

normal 180-1
satisfactory 222
supernormal 181, 190-1
taxes on 112
profitability 15, 21-3
programming
integer 217
linear 65-90, 114-8, 211, 219
linear graphical method 69-71, 77-82, 83-4
linear simplex method 71-7, 84-5, 114-7
linear simplex method, basic solutions 71-5, 87
linear simplex method, pivoting operations 73-4
view on the nature of production 65-7, 97-9, 106
see also — blending, primal and dual, process, product mix, sensitivity analysis, shadow prices, transportation
public responsibility 91
sector 243n
see also — social

Quade, E. S. 15, 49

rationality 7-8, 54
bounded 52
Rees, R. D. 129
regression analysis
estimation 121-2, 166-9
identification problem 160
multiple regression 170
problems of estimation 169-71
regret — see minimax regret
replacement
cost 111-2
in investment 260-2
representative firms 180
Resale Prices Act (1964) 213
resource allocation 6-8, 54
internal 20
Restrictive Trade Practice Act (1956) 213
Restrictive Trade Practices Court 194
revenue
average 151-4, 179-81
incremental 106
marginal 106, 179, 181-2, 186-7
marginal — discontinuity of, 197, 203-4

total 201-2
risk
discounting for 279-80
economic and business 26-36
and insurance 34-6
spreading of — through diversification 100, 102
see also — decision theory
Robinson, E. A. G. 9
Robinson, J. 9n, 176
Rowley, C. K. 22n, 214n, 225

saddle point 208
sales 2, 405, 19-20, 23
sales revenue maximising 2n, 175, 190, 200-06
Samuelson, P. A. 63
Savage, L. J. 41
Saving, T. R. 129
scale
changes in 60-1
constant returns to 63, 99
curve 124, 132
decreasing returns to 62, 64, 99, 183, 192
economies and diseconomies of 99-104, 126-132
increasing returns to 61-2, 99
scale of preferences 137
search 14, 51-2
sensitivity analysis 49-50, 75-7, 85, 278-9
Shackle, G. L. S. 38-9, 49
shadow prices 115-8, 290
see also — cost, opportunity
Shepherd, W. G. 129, 203-4
short run 59-60, 63-4
cost analysis 119-24
cost behaviour 95-9
Shupack, M. B. 166n
Simon, H. A. 16, 44, 51-3, 88
simplex method — see programming
Silbertson, A. 127
Skinner, R. C. 218
Smith, A. 61
Smith, C. A. 123, 127
social costs 22, 91, 287-8
Sowter, A. P. et al. 173
standard costing 110
states of nature 24-6
statistical cost analysis 121-4, 126, 131
statistical decision theory — see decision theory

Stigler, G. J. 122, 129-31, 166n, 190, 200, 218
Stone, R. 158, 165
strategic, administrative and operating decisions 10-13, 38, 49
strategies 14, 24-6
sub-optimisation 52
substitution effects 138
supply – market curve 180
survivor method 128-31
Sutherland, A. 214n
Sweezy, P. M. 196
Sylos postulate 192
systems
    analysis 3-5, 14-5, 49
    see also – general systems theory

Tangri, Om. P. 95n
target-for-sales 227
target rate of return 16, 225, 242, 244
technology
    effect of changing – on scale 101-2
    see also – fixed technological coefficients
tie in sales 183, 236
time series data 121, 126
transitivity 137
transportation problem 85-9
    north-west corner solution 87

Udell, J. G. 216
uncertainty 36-43
    see also – decision theory, game theory

United Nations Association (UNO) 142
user cost 113-4
utility
    cardinal 134, 137
    conditions for maximisation 135
    consumer 7, 20
    diminishing marginal 45-8, 135
    managerial 19-20, 101n
    ordinal 137
    and risk 20
    see also – Von Neumann and Morgenstern

variance
    as measure of risk 47, 279-80
    cost variances 91, 110
variation, coefficient of 47-8
vertical integration 192
Vickers, Sir G. 13-6
Von Neumann and Morgenstern
    cardinal utility index 134

Wagner, H. M. 73, 77
Wald, A. 40
Watson, D. S. 171
weak ordering 137
Weiss, L. W. 129
Wenders, J. T. 193
Williamson, O. E. 19, 101n, 213-4, 226, 274
Wire Ropes Manufacturers Association 194-5

x-inefficiency 20, 183, 213-5

Yntema, T..O. 122-3